multithreaded programming with

JAVA™

Technology

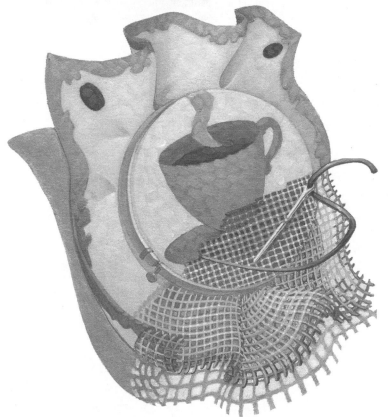

BIL LEWIS · DANIEL J. BERG

THE SUN MICROSYSTEMS PRESS
A PRENTICE HALL TITLE

The publisher offers discounts on this book when ordered in bulk quantities.
For more information, contact: Corporate Sales Department, Phone: 800-382-3419;
Fax: 201-236-7141; E-mail: corpsales@prenhall.com; or write: Prentice Hall PTR,
Corp. Sales Dept., One Lake Street, Upper Saddle River, NJ 07458.

Editorial/production supervisor: *Faye Gemmellaro*
Acquisitions editor: *Gregory G. Doench*
Editorial assistant: *Mary Treacy*
Manufacturing manager: *Alexis R. Heydt*
Cover design director: *Jerry Votta*
Cover designer: *Anthony Gemmellaro*
Cover illustrator: *Karen Strelecki*
Marketing manager: *Bryan Gambrel*
Interior designer: *Gail Cocker-Bogusz*
Sun Microsystems Press:
Marketing manager: *Michael Llwyd Alread*
Publisher: *Rachel Borden*

10 9 8 7 6 5 4 3 2

ISBN 0-13-017007-0

Sun Microsystems Press
A Prentice Hall Title

To Elaine, my wife and best friend, for her encouragement and understanding during all the late nights and weekends when I should have been spending time with her. Thank You!

— Dan

И, мочи нет, сказать желаю,
Мой анел, как я вас люблю!

— Bil

Contents

Preface

Today, there are three primary sets of multithreading (MT) libraries: the POSIX threads library, the Win32 threads library (both native), and Java. Although the APIs[1] and implementations differ significantly, the fundamental concepts are the same. The *ideas* in this book are valid for all three; the details of the APIs differ.

All the specific discussion in this book focuses on the Java multithreading model, with comparisons to POSIX and Win32 throughout. Java threads are always implemented upon a low-level library which does the real work. Hence Java on UNIX is generally based on POSIX, while Java on NT will be based on Win32 threads.

Because these lower-level libraries have so much impact on the actual performance of a Java program, we will devote significant attention to the native libraries. Because POSIX threads are

---

[1]"Applications Programming Interface." This is the set of standard library calls that an operating system makes available to applications programmers. For POSIX, this means all the threads library function calls. For Java, it's one keyword, three classes, and a few methods.

more primitive than Win32 threads, they will be our basis of comparison and explanation. This allows us to explain the inner workings of threads before jumping to the more intricate workings of Java.

A frank note about our motivation is in order here. We have slaved away for countless hours on this book because we're propeller-heads who honestly believe that this technology is a superb thing and that the widespread use of it will make the world a better place for hackers like ourselves.

Your motivations for writing MT programs? You can write your programs better and more easily, they'll run faster, you'll get them to market more quickly, they'll have fewer bugs, and you'll have happier programmers, customers, and higher sales. The only losers in this game are the competitors, who will lag behind you in application speed and quality.

MT is here today. It is now ubiquitous. As a professional programmer, you have an obligation to understand this technology. It may or may not be appropriate for your current project, but you must be able to make that conclusion yourself. This book will give you what you need to make that decision.

Welcome to the world of the future!

Who Should Use This Book

This book aims to give the programmer or technical manager a solid understanding of threads—what they are, how they work, why they are useful, and some of the programming issues surrounding their use. As an introductory text, it does not attempt a deep, detailed analysis of the most current research, but it does come close. After reading this book the reader should have a solid understanding of the fundamentals, be able to write credible, modestly complex, threaded programs, and have the understanding necessary to analyze their own programs and determine the viability of threading them.

This book has been written with the experienced Java programmer in mind. There is a definite UNIX bias, but none of that is essential to understanding. A Java programmer who does not know C will find the POSIX code fragments mildly challenging, although possible to decipher. The concepts should be clear. A technically minded nonprogrammer should be able to follow most of the concepts and understand the value of threads. A nontechnical person will not get much from this book.

This book does not attempt to explain the use of Win32 or POSIX APIs. It does contrast them to Java APIs to explain some of the higher-level Java behavior in lower-level terms.

How This Book Is Organized

Chapter 1, *Introduction*—In which we discuss the motivation for creating thread libraries, the advent of shared memory multiprocessors, and the interactions between threads and SMP machines.

Chapter 2, *Concepts*—In which the reader is introduced to the basic concepts of multitasking operating systems and of multithreading as it compares to other programming paradigms. The reader is shown reasons why multithreading is a valuable addition to programming paradigms, and a number of examples of successful deployment are presented.

Chapter 3, *Foundations*—In which we introduce the reader to the underlying structures upon which threads are built, the construction of the thread itself, and the operating system support that allows efficient implementation.

Chapter 4, *Lifecycle*—In which the reader is treated to a comprehensive explanation of the intricacies in the life of a thread—birth, life, and death—even death by vile cancellation. A small program that illustrates all these stages concludes the chapter.

Chapter 5, *Scheduling*—In which we explain the myriad details of various scheduling models and alternative choices that could be made, describe context switching in detail, and delve into gruesome detail on various design options. There is light at the end of the tunnel, however.

Chapter 6, *Synchronization*—In which the reader is led on a hunt for the intimidating synchronization variable and discovers that it is not actually as frightening as had been thought. Programs illustrating the basic use of the POSIX and Java primitives are shown.

Chapter 7, *Complexities*—In which a series of more complex synchronization variables and options are presented and the trade-off between them and the simpler ones are discussed. Synchronization problems and techniques for dealing with them conclude the chapter.

Chapter 8, *TSD*—In which explanations of thread-specific data, their use, and some implementation details are provided.

Chapter 9, *Cancellation*—In which we describe the acrimonious nature of some programs and how unwanted threads may be disposed of. The highly complex issues surrounding bounded time termination and program correctness are also covered. A simple conclusion is drawn.

Chapter 10, *Details*—In which a number of minor details are covered.

Chapter 11, *Libraries*—In which we explore a variety of operating systems issues that bear heavily upon the usability of threads in actual programs. We examine the status of library functions and the programming issues facing them. We look at some design alternatives for library functions.

Chapter 12, *Design*—In which we explore some designs for programs and library functions. Making both programs and individual functions more concurrent is a major issue in the design of these functions. We look at a variety of code examples and the trade-offs between them.

Chapter 13, *RMI*—In which we examine RMI and see what it provides in terms of a distributed object programming model. We look at how threading interacts with it and how it uses threads.

Chapter 14, *Tools*—In which we consider the kinds of new tools that a reader would want when writing a threaded program. An overview of the Solaris tool set is given, as representative of what should be looked for.

Chapter 15, *Performance*—In which we make things faster, look at general performance issues, political performance issues, and thread specific performance issues. We conclude with a discussion of the actual performance of multithreaded NFS.

Chapter 16, *Hardware*—In which we look at the various designs for SMP machines (cache architectures, interconnect topologies, atomic instructions, invalidation techniques) and consider how those designs affect our programming decisions. Some optimization possibilities are looked at.

Chapter 17, *Examples*—In which several complete programs are presented. The details and issues surrounding the way they use threads are discussed, and references to other programs on the Net are made.

Acknowledgments

Sometimes I really do think it's funny that Bil and Dan have managed to get three books out of what's basically one book of material with "a bunch of words changed."—Dave Butenhof

We didn't intend to write this book. It just sort of happened. Bil discovered that there were a lot more people interested in Java threads than in POSIX, and Dan made himself a Java Guru for Sun. There weren't any books on Java threads that covered the topic in the way we wanted, so we started by discussing the various issues with the principals. The next thing we knew, we had the makings of a book.

We owe debts of gratitude to all of the above and:

- The reviewers:

    * Dave Butenhof (Digital Classic)

    * David Holmes (Macquarie University, NSW)

    * Douglas Lea (SUNY, Oswego)

    * Tim Lindholm (Sun)

- The folks who helped us get information, fix mistakes, test programs, and avoid confusion: Ole Agesen, Alan Armstrong, Timothy Bell, Martin Bertolino, Sean Bowes, David Chase, Adrian Colley, Raj Datta, Laird Dornin, Quentin Fennessy, Linda Haight, Jarek Knap, Sheng Liang, Thomas Maslen, Himagiri Mukkamala, Hans Muller, John Murayama, Scott Oaks, Bob O'Brien, Jochen Schlick, Jan Springer, Jim Waldo, and Bob Withers.
- The editors and staff: Rachel Borden, Gregory G. Doench, Craig Little, Mary Treacy.
- The authors of all the other books that we perused so carefully.
- And: Mom.

—Dan Berg   *— Bil Lewis*

Acknowledgments to the Threads Primer

Thanks to Matt Delcambre for his support of the book and his assistance in the review process. Thanks also to John Bost and James Hollingshead for their support and funding of the trips to California. Thanks also go to Mary Himelfarb for putting up with all the paper and time I consumed on her printer.

Special thanks to Ty "Tyrone" McKercher, for all the time in the review process and for always taking the time to listen to my wild new ideas; also for his keen insight during the many late-night and weekend programming sessions where many of the examples in the book were born.

Many thanks to Tim Hayes, Richard Robison, and Jim Thompson for providing their customer testimonials and for their early adoption of threading technology in their production applications. Thanks also go to all the people who make up the POSIX committee for all their work on the Pthreads draft and the threads documentation team for all their work on the quality documentation.

We owe an enormous debt to Devang Shah and Dan Stein for their constant support, answering innumerable questions, and debating issues of presentation and concept. In spite of numerous barriers, we always managed to come to a consensus on the major issues—which speaks well for the true nature of science.

Many thanks to Charles Fineman, Eric Jaeger, Adrienne Jardetzky, Richard Marejka, and Richard Schaefer for their assistance in the review process and their numerous accurate and insightful comments and suggestions; to Ron Winacott for coming all the way to Sweden to introduce me to the subject; to Chris Crenshaw for his comments and discussion; to Karin Ellison for starting us on this book and for her enormous energy in dealing with all those little problems that always seem to crawl out of the woodwork at 2 a.m. Roses to Marianne Muller, who made the Web work for us and was always there with reassurance and support when things got rough.

Thanks to Ben Catanzaro, Larry Gee, Mukul Goyal, Morgan Herrington, Brian Kinnard, Bill Lindeman, Paul Lorence, Shaun Peterson, and Leif Samuelson for their help, comments, and guidance in the numerous fine points of writing, formatting, and interpretation; to my peers in Developer Engineering and the Shaysa council; to RMS, who did more to shape my writing abilities than he realizes; to Manoj Goyal, who was so pivotal in making the personal interactions at Sun work as they should.

Appreciation for reviewing and discussing numerous points to Tom Doeppner, Carl Hauser, Barry Medoff, and Bart Smaalders.

For assistance on numerous points, large and small, thanks to Kim Albright, Burke Anderson, Susan Austin, David Boreham, Mike Boucher, Susan Bryant, Ben Catanzaro, Don Charles, Dave Crowley, Robert Demb, Jeff Denham, Greg G. Doench, William E. Hannon Jr., Larry Kilgallen, Timo Kunnas, Greg Nakhimovsky, Christopher Nicholas, Bill Paulsen, Rob Rimbold, Bob Rushby, Michael Sebree, Tarmo Talts, and Steve Vinoski.

A special thanks to two computer scientists who I have always held in awe and whose writing abilities and finely tuned senses of humor I admire more than I can express, Peter van der Linden and the great Quux. How two people can have such depth of understanding and also be such amazing copyeditors, I don't know!

Tusan tack till alla på Sun Sverige, och kram till dej, Madelene.

Ja Tarvi, Kati, Lõvi, Tiia, Epp, Mari ja Kaur, kuna mõnikord vajab inimene sõpru rohkem kui midagi muud.

Acknowledgments to the Pthreads Primer

The first edition of this book was a rush job—we completed the manuscript in four months. After work hours. Four very *long* months. By the end of the year we could see the copious flaws and egregious omissions. "Let's just take a couple of months, change the focus to POSIX, and fix a couple of those problems," we said.

Two years later, we have this book, which we think is finally a reasonable introduction to the subject. (But not great, that's for the third edition.) This book is the product of an enormous amount of thought, discussion, and experimentation. A book, even a bad book, requires an amazing amount of effort. And to compare the fruit of our labors to a truly excellent text—it's humbling.

We didn't even do all the work on this book! The people who helped are legion. We owe debts of gratitude to:

- The roughly 3000 people who took our classes and presentations on threads, in the United States, Sweden, India, Finland, and Estonia, plus those who helped organize them.
- The hundreds of people who have asked questions, given answers, or just plain argued issues on the newsgroup.
- Everyone who brought issues to our attention that forced us to think deeper.
- The reviewers:
  * Mike Boucher (Dakota Scientific Software)
  * Gregory Bumgardner (Rogue Wave)
  * Dave Butenhof (Digital)
  * Dave Cortesi (SGI)
  * William E. Hannon, Jr. (IBM)
  * Shin Iwamoto (who both reviewed and translated!)
  * Richard Marejka (Sun, Canada)
  * Richard Schaefer (Sun)
  * Chary G. Tamirisa (IBM)

- The folks who helped us get information, fix mistakes, test programs, and avoid confusion: Glenn J. Allin, Jeremy Allison, Rolf Andersson, Tom Barton, Keith Bierman, John Bossom, Stacey Carroll, Matt Dillon, Tom Doeppner, Ian Emmon, Charlie Fineman, Pankaj Garg, Brian Hall, Asad Hanif, Pekka Hedqvist, David Holmes, Peter Jeffcock, Tarik Kerroum, Sanjay Kini, Dan Lenoski, Xavier Leroy, Toshihiro Matsu, Bertrand Meyer, Imhof Michael, Frank Mueller, Prakash Narayan, Dr. Douglas Niehaus, Scott Norton, Bryan O'Sullivan, Matthew Peters, Michael T. Peterson, James Pitcairn-Hill, Christopher Provenzano, Jacqueline Proulx Farrell, Doug Schmidt, Ted Selker, Bart Smaalders, Ivan Soleimanipour, Richard Marlon Stein, Bo Sundmark, Chris Thomas, Steve Vinoski, and Wolf-Dietrich Weber.

- The editors and staff: Rachel Borden, John Bortner, Gwen Burns, Gregory G. Doench and Mary Treacy.

- The authors of all the other books that we perused so carefully.

- All the folks on 1003.1c, who did such an excellent job.

- Bil's PacAir Formula, which never lost a thermal, or bonked a landing, which kept him both alive and sane.

- And: Mom.

       — Dan Berg   *— Bil Lewis*

Chapter 1

Introduction

In which we discuss the motivation for creating thread libraries, the advent of shared memory multiprocessors, and the interactions between threads and SMP machines.

Multithreading (MT) is a technique that allows one program to do multiple tasks concurrently. The basic concept of multithreaded programming has existed in research and development labs for several decades. Co-routine systems such as Concurrent Pascal and InterLisp's Spaghetti stacks were in use in the mid-70s and dealt with many of the same issues. Ada's tasks are a language-based construct that maps directly onto threads (so directly, in fact, that current Ada compilers implement tasks with threads). Burroughs shipped a commercial mainframe OS with co-routine-style threads as early as 1960.

The emergence of this concept in industry as an accepted, standardized programming paradigm is a phenomenon of the 1990s. As with many other concepts, the research and experimental use of threads have been widespread in specific industries, universities, and research institutes and are entering industry as a relatively well-formed whole on all fronts almost simultaneously. In 1991, no major commercial operating systems contained a robust user-level threads library. In 1999, every major player in the computer industry has one.

Some of the motivation for this emergence can be ascribed to general good sense and the recognition of a technology whose time has come. Some can be related to the unification efforts surrounding UNIX. Probably the greatest push, especially when viewed from the point of view of the independent software vendor (ISV) and the end user, is the emergence of shared memory symmetric multiprocessors (SMPs). MT provides exactly the right programming paradigm to make maximum use of these new machines.

Java was designed from the very beginning with threads in mind, and some of its functionality is based very directly on having threads. The ability to have applets is based in allowing them to run in different threads in a browser. Because of Java's high-level approach to programming, it is much easier to build a threaded program in Java than in POSIX or Win32. At the same time, the fundamental issues do not change. This may well lure many programmers into writing threaded programs before they truly understand all of the intricacies. Oh, well.

The threading models we describe are strictly software models that can be implemented on any general-purpose hardware. Much research is directed toward creating better hardware that would be uniquely suited for threaded programming. We do not address that aspect in this book.

To those of us concerned with the theoretical underpinnings of programming paradigms and language design, the true value of multithreading is significant and obvious. It provides a far superior paradigm for constructing programs. For those concerned with the practical details of getting real tasks done using computers, the value is significant and obvious as well. Multithreading makes it possible to obtain vastly greater performance than was ever before possible by taking advantage of multiprocessor machines.

At whatever price point, the purchasers of workstations want maximum performance from their machines. The demands of computationally intensive users are always growing, and they invariably exceed the provisions of their wallets. They might want a "personal Cray," but they can't afford one.

One of the solutions to this demand lies in the ever-increasing performance of CPUs. Along with the obvious technique of increasing the clock speed, a wide range of other methods is used to increase the performance of individual CPUs. The use of long instruction pipelines or superscalar techniques has allowed us to produce multiple-instruction-issue machines that can do a lot more in a single clock tick. Finer compiler optimization techniques, out-of-order execution, predictive branching, VLIW, etc., allow us to obtain better and better performance from processors. However good these methods are, they still have their limits.

One of the major limiting factors is the problem of limited bus, memory, and peripheral speeds. We can build CPUs today that operate at 600 MHz, but we can't build communications buses that operate at the same speed. RAM speeds are also falling further behind the demands of the CPUs. It is expensive to build 600-MHz CPUs, but as there are only a few in a system, it is affordable. To build memory that can keep up with these speeds would be prohibitively expensive. A great many machines today implement two- and even three-level caches to deal with this problem (single-level caches weren't enough!). Multilevel caches work effectively with well-behaved programs, where sequential data and instruction references are likely to be physically adjacent in memory. But truly random-access programs wreak havoc on this scheme, and we can point to any number of programs that run faster on slower machines that lack that second-level cache.

None of the issues addressed above play favorites with any manufacturers. Sun, Intel, HP, IBM, SGI, DEC, etc., have come up with techniques for dealing with them. Some techniques have proven to be more effective than others, but none of them avoids the fundamental limitations of physics. Nature is a harsh mistress.

This is where SMP comes into play. It is one more weapon in our arsenal for performance. Just as the foregoing techniques have allowed us to increase our single-CPU performance, SMP allows us to increase our overall system performance. And that's what we really care about—overall system performance. As one customer put it, "SMP, superscalar—buzzwords! I don't care if you have little green men inside the box! I want my program to run faster!"

We can build 64-processor machines today (e.g., the Cray CS6400) that will yield 64 times the performance of a single-processor machine (on some problems). The cost of that 64-CPU machine is a fraction of the cost of 64 single-processor machines. In a 64-way SMP machine, all 64 processors share the system costs: chassis, main memory, disks, software, etc. With 64 uniprocessors, each processor must have its own chassis, memory, etc. This fact makes SMP highly attractive for its price/performance ratio. An additional attraction of SMP is that it is also possible to purchase a machine with a small number of CPUs and add more CPUs as demands (and budgets) increase. In Figure 1–1, these advantages of SMP are clear.

The economics of purchasing an SMP machine are pretty much the same as the economics of purchasing any machine. There are some extra unknowns ("I have 600 different applications that I run from time to time; how much faster will they all run? How much time will I save in a day?"), but if we focus on the primary applications in use, we can get reasonable data upon which to make our decisions. The basic question is, "If my applications run an average of *N*% faster on a dual-CPU machine that costs *M*% more, is it worth it?"

Only you (or your customers) can answer this question, but we can give you some generalities. Here is a typical situation: The customer's major application is MARC Analysis's MARC Solver (for circuit simulation). The MARC Solver runs about 80% faster on a dual-processor SPARCstation™ 20 than it does on a single-processor SPARCstation 20. The single-processor machine costs $16,000; the dual-processor unit costs $18,000 (about 12% more).

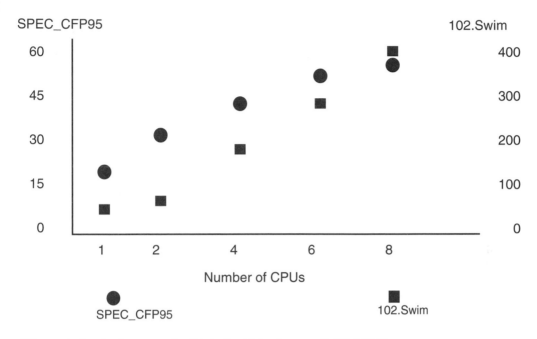

Figure 1–1 *Performance for Digital's Alpha Servers (8400 5/625)*

If the designers (who cost at least $100,000/year) are constantly waiting for the solver to complete its runs, is it worth it? Obviously, yes. You will save a lot of money on a minor investment. Indeed, MARC sells very well on SMP machines.

If you are a program developer (either in-house or an ISV), your question is going to be, "Should I spend the time to write my program so that it will take advantage of SMP machines?" (This probably means threading, although there are other possibilities.) Your answer will be related to your anticipated sales. If your program runs 50% faster on a dual-processor machine, will your customers buy SMP machines and more of your software? Or, to pose the question differently, if you don't do it, will some competitor do it instead and steal your customers?

The answer depends upon your program. If you write a simple text editor that is never CPU-bound, the answer is a clear "no." If you write a database that is always CPU-bound, it's "yes." If you write a page-layout program that is sometimes CPU-bound, the answer is "maybe." In general, if users ever have to wait for your program, you should be looking at threading and SMP.

But there is more value to threading than just SMP performance. In many instances, uniprocessors will also experience a significant performance improvement. And that bit about programming paradigms? It really does count. Being able to write simpler, more readable code helps you in almost all aspects of development. Your code can be less buggy, get out there faster, and be easier to maintain.

Multithreading is not a magic bullet for all your ills,[1] and it does introduce a new set of programming issues that must be mastered, but it goes a long way toward making your work easier and your programs more efficient.

---

[1] If you have ever spent days debugging complex signal handling code, you may disagree. For asynchronous code, it *is* a magic bullet!

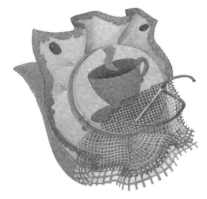

Chapter **2**

Concepts

▼ BACKGROUND: TRADITIONAL OPERATING SYSTEMS
▼ WHAT IS A THREAD?
▼ KERNEL INTERACTION
▼ THE VALUE OF USING THREADS
▼ WHAT KINDS OF PROGRAMS TO THREAD
▼ WHAT ABOUT SHARED MEMORY?
▼ THREADS STANDARDS
▼ PERFORMANCE

In which the reader is introduced to the basic concepts of multitasking operating systems and of multithreading as it compares to other programming paradigms. The reader is shown reasons why multithreading is a valuable addition to programming paradigms, and a number of examples of successful deployment are presented.

Background: Traditional Operating Systems

Before we get into the details of threads, it will be useful for us to have some clear understanding of how operating systems without threads work. In the simplest operating system world of single-user, single-tasking operating systems such as DOS, everything is quite easy to understand and to use, although the functionality offered is minimal.

DOS divides the memory of a computer into two sections: the portion where the operating system itself resides (*kernel space*[1]) and the portion where the programs reside (*user space*). The division into these two spaces is done strictly by the implicit agreement of the programmers involved—meaning that nothing stops a user program from accessing data in kernel space. This lack of hardware enforcement is good, because it is simple and works well when people write perfect programs. When a user program needs some function performed for it by kernel code (such as reading a file from a disk), the program can call the DOS function directly to read that file.

Each program has some code that it runs (which is just a series of instructions, where the *program counter* points to the current instruction), some data (global and local) that it uses, and a stack where local data and return addresses are stored (the *stack pointer* designates the current active location on the stack).

Figure 2–1 illustrates the traditional DOS operating system memory layout. Thus, as shown in Figure 2–1, the division between user space and kernel space is a division by agreement of the programmers; there is no hardware enforcement of the policy at all. The drawbacks to this technique are significant, however. Not all programs are written flawlessly, and a programming mistake (or virus!) here can bring down the entire machine or, worse, destroy valued data. Neither can a machine run more than one program at a time, nor can more than one user log in to the machine at a time. Dealing with networks from DOS machines is somewhat awkward and limited.

---

[1]*Kernel space* is UNIX lingo for this concept, but the concept is valid for all operating systems.

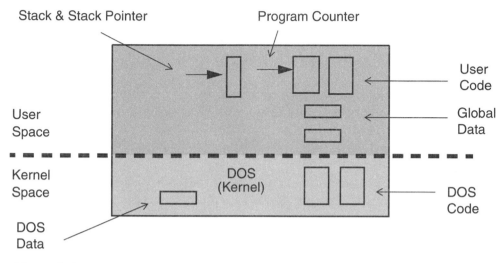

Figure 2–1 *Memory Layout for DOS-Style Operating Systems*

In a typical multitasking operating system such as VMS, UNIX, Windows NT, etc., this dividing line between the user space and the kernel space is solid (Figure 2–2); it's enforced by the hardware. There are actually two different modes of operation for the CPUs: *user mode*, which allows normal user programs to run, and *kernel mode*, which also allows some special instructions to run that only the kernel can execute. These kernel-mode instructions include I/O instructions, processor interrupt instructions, instructions that control the state of the virtual memory subsystem, and, of course, the *change mode* instruction.

So a user program can execute only user-mode instructions, and it can execute them only in user space. The data it can access and change directly is also limited to data in user space. When it needs something from the kernel (say, it wants to read a file or find out the current time), the user program must make a *system call*. This is a library function that sets up some arguments, then executes a special *trap* instruction. This instruction causes the hardware to trap into the kernel, which then takes control of the machine. The kernel figures out what the user wants (based upon the data that the system call set up) and whether the user has permission to do so. Finally, the kernel performs the desired task, returning any information to the user process.

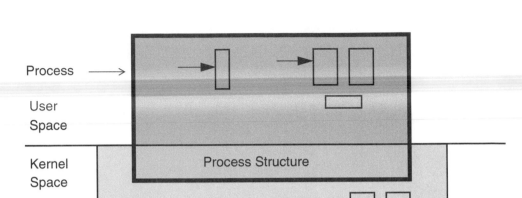

Figure 2–2 *Memory Layout for Multitasking Systems*

Because the operating system has complete control over I/O, memory, processors, etc., it needs to maintain data for each process it's running. The data tells the operating system what the state of that process is—what files are open, which user is running it, etc. So, the concept of *process* in the multitasking world extends into the kernel (see Figure 2–2), where this information is maintained in a *process structure*. In addition, as this is a multitasking world, more than one process can be active at the same time, and for most of these operating systems (notably, neither Windows NT nor OS/2), more than one user can log in to the machine independently and run programs simultaneously.

Thus, in Figure 2–3, process P1 can be run by user Kim while P2 and P3 are being run by user Dan, and P4 by user Bil. There is also no particular restriction on the amount of memory that a process can have. P2 might use twice as much memory as P1, for example. It is also true that no two processes can see or change each other's memory unless they have set up a special *shared memory* segment.

For all the user programs in all the operating systems mentioned so far, each has one stack, one program counter, and one set of CPU registers per process. So each of these programs can do only one thing at a time. They are *single threaded*.

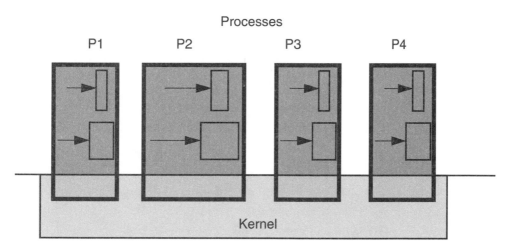

Figure 2–3 *Processes on a Multitasking System*

What Is a Thread?

Just as multitasking operating systems can do more than one thing concurrently by running more than a single process, a process can do the same by running more than a single *thread*. Each thread is a different stream of control that can execute its instructions independently, allowing a multithreaded process to perform numerous tasks concurrently. One thread can run the GUI while a second thread does some I/O and a third performs calculations.

A thread is an abstract concept that comprises everything a computer does in executing a traditional program. It is the program state that gets scheduled on a CPU; it is the "thing" that does the work. If a process comprises data, code, kernel state, and a set of CPU registers, then a thread is embodied in the contents of those registers—the program counter, the general registers, the stack pointer, etc., and the stack. A thread, viewed at an instant of time, is the state of the computation.

"Gee," you say, "That sounds like a process!" It should. They are conceptually related. But a process is a heavyweight, kernel-level entity and includes such things as a virtual memory map, file descriptors, user ID, etc., and each process has its own

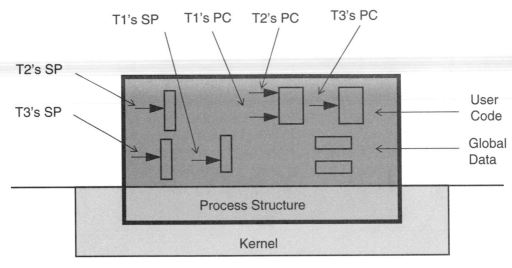

Figure 2–4 *Relationship between a Process and Threads*

collection of these. The only way for your program to access data in the process structure, to query or change its state, is via a system call.

All parts of the process structure are in kernel space (Figure 2–4). A user program cannot touch any of that data directly. By contrast, all of the user code (functions, procedures, etc.), along with the data, is in user space and can be accessed directly.

A thread is a lightweight entity, comprising the registers, stack, and some other data. The rest of the process structure is shared by all threads: the address space, file descriptors, etc. Much (and sometimes all) of the thread structure is in user space, allowing for very fast access.

The actual code (functions, routines, signal handlers, etc.) is global, and it can be executed on any thread. In Figure 2–4 we show three threads (T1, T2, and T3), along with their stacks, stack pointers (SP), and program counters (PC). T1 and T2 are executing the same function. This is a normal situation, just as two different people can read the same road sign at the same time.

13

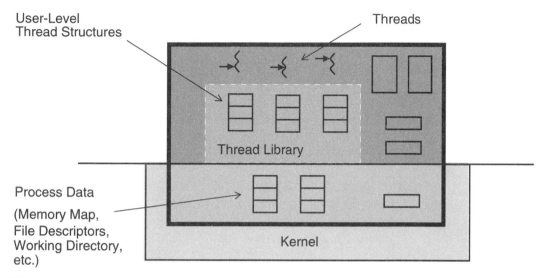

User-Level
Thread Structures

Threads

Thread Library

Process Data

(Memory Map,
File Descriptors,
Working Directory,
etc.)

Kernel

Figure 2–5 *Process Structure and Thread Structures*

All threads in a process share the state of that process (Figure 2–5[2]). They reside in exactly the same memory space, see the same functions, and see the same data. When one thread alters a process variable (say, the working directory), all the others will see the change when they next access it. If one thread opens a file to read it, all the other threads can also read from it.

Let's consider a human analogy: a bank. A bank with one person working in it (traditional process) has lots of "bank stuff," such as desks and chairs, a vault, and teller stations (process tables and variables). There are lots of services that a bank provides: checking accounts, loans, savings accounts, etc. (the functions). With one person to do all the work, that person would have to know how to do everything, and could do so, but it might take a bit of extra time to switch among the various tasks. With two or more people (threads), they would share all the same "bank stuff," but they could specialize in their different functions. And if they all came in and worked on the same day, lots of customers could get serviced quickly.

---

[2]From here on, we will use the squiggle shown in the figure to represent the entire thread—stack, stack pointer, program counter, thread structure, etc.

To change the number of banks in town would be a big effort (creating new processes), but to hire one new employee (creating a new thread) would be very simple. Everything that happened inside the bank, including interactions among the employees there, would be fairly simple (user space operations among threads), whereas anything that involved the bank down the road would be much more involved (kernel space operations between processes).

When you write a multithreaded program, 99% of your programming is identical to what it was before—you spend your efforts in getting the program to do its real work. The other 1% is spent in creating threads, arranging for different threads to coordinate their activities, dealing with thread-specific data, etc. Perhaps 0.1% of your code consists of calls to thread functions.

Kernel Interaction

We've now covered the basic concept of threads at the user level. As noted, the concepts and most of the implementational aspects are valid for all thread models. What's missing is the definition of the relationship between threads and the operating systems. How do system calls work? How are threads scheduled on CPUs?

It is at this level that the various implementations differ significantly. The operating systems provide different system calls, and even identical system calls can differ widely in efficiency and robustness. The kernels are constructed differently and provide different resources and services.

Keep in mind as we go through this implementation aspect that 99% of your threads programming will be done above this level, and the major distinctions will be in the area of efficiency.

Concurrency vs. Parallelism

Concurrency means that two or more threads (or traditional processes) can be in the middle of executing code at the same time; it could be the same code or it could be different code (see Figure 2–6). The threads may or may not actually be executing at the same time, but rather, in the middle of it (i.e., one started executing, it was interrupted, and the other one started). Every

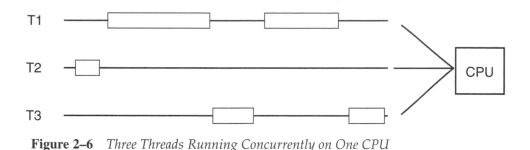

Figure 2–6 *Three Threads Running Concurrently on One CPU*

multitasking operating system has always had numerous concurrent processes, even though only one could be on the CPU at any given time.

Parallelism means that two or more threads actually run at the same time on different CPUs (see Figure 2–7). On a multiprocessor machine, many different threads can run in parallel. They are, of course, also running concurrently.

The vast majority of timing and synchronization issues in multithreading (MT) are those of concurrency, not parallelism. Indeed, the threads model was designed to avoid your ever having to be concerned with the details of parallelism. Running an MT program on a uniprocessor (UP) does not simplify your programming problems at all. Running on a multiprocessor (MP) doesn't complicate them. This is a good thing.

Let us repeat this point. If your program is written correctly on a uniprocessor, it will run correctly on a multiprocessor. The probability of running into a race condition is the same on both a UP and an MP. If it deadlocks on one, it will deadlock on the other. (There are lots of weird little exceptions to the probability part, but you'd have to try hard to make them appear.) There is a small set of bugs, however, which may cause a program to run as (naively) expected on a UP, and show its problems only on an MP (see *Bus Architectures* on page 346).

System Calls

A system call is basically a function that ends up trapping to routines in the kernel. These routines may do things as simple as looking up the user ID for the owner of the current process, or as

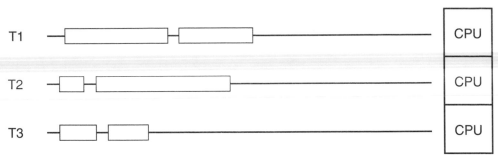

Figure 2–7   *Three Threads Running in Parallel on Three CPUs*

complex as redefining the system's scheduling algorithm. For multithreaded programs, there is a serious issue surrounding how many threads can make system calls concurrently. For some operating systems, the answer is "one"; for others, it's "many." The most important point is that system calls run exactly as they did before, so all your old programs continue to run as they did before, with (almost) no degradation.

Signals

Signals are the UNIX kernel's way of interrupting a running process and letting it know that something of interest has happened. (NT has something similar but doesn't expose it in the Win32 interface.) It could be that a timer has expired, or that some I/O has completed, or that some other process wants to communicate something.

Happily, Java does not use UNIX signals, so we may conveniently ignore them entirely! The role that signals play in UNIX programs is handled in Java either by having a thread respond to a synchronous request or by the use of exceptions.

Synchronization

Synchronization is the method of ensuring that multiple threads coordinate their activities so that one thread doesn't accidentally change data that another thread is working on. This is done by providing function calls that can limit the number of threads that can access some data concurrently.

In the simplest case (a *mutual exclusion lock*—a *mutex*), only one thread at a time can execute a given piece of code. This code presumably alters some global data or performs reads or writes to a device. For example, thread T1 obtains a lock and starts to work on some global data. Thread T2 must now wait (typically, it goes to sleep) until thread T1 is done before T2 can execute the same code. By using the same lock around all code that changes the data, we can ensure that the data remains consistent.

Scheduling

Scheduling is the act of placing threads onto CPUs so that they can execute, and of taking them off those CPUs so that others can run instead. In practice, scheduling is not generally an issue because "it all works" just about the way you'd expect.

The Value of Using Threads

There is really only one reason for writing MT programs—to get better programs more quickly. If you're an Independent Software Vendor (ISV), you sell more software. If you're developing software for your own in-house use, you simply have better programs to use. The reason you can write better programs is that MT gives your programs and your programmers a number of significant advantages over nonthreaded programs and programming paradigms.

A point to keep in mind here is that you are not replacing simple, nonthreaded programs with fancy, complex, threaded programs. You are using threads only when you need them to replace complex or slow nonthreaded programs. Threads are just one more way to make your programming tasks easier.

The main benefits of writing multithreaded programs are:

- Performance gains from multiprocessing hardware (parallelism)
- Increased application throughput
- Increased application responsiveness

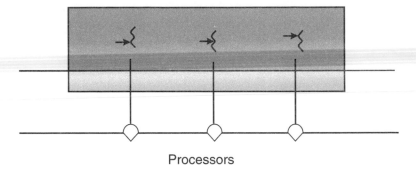

Processors

Figure 2–8 *Different Threads Running on Different Processors*

- Replacing process-to-process communications
- Efficient use of system resources
- One binary that runs well on both uniprocessors and multiprocessors
- The ability to create well-structured programs

The following sections elaborate further on these benefits.

Parallelism

Computers with more than one processor offer the potential for enormous application speedups (Figure 2–8). MT is an efficient way for application developers to exploit the parallelism of the hardware. Different threads can run on different processors simultaneously with no special input from the user and no effort on the part of the programmer.

A good example is a process that does matrix multiplication. A thread can be created for each available processor, allowing the program to use the entire machine. The threads can then compute distinct elements of the resulting matrix by performing the appropriate vector multiplication.

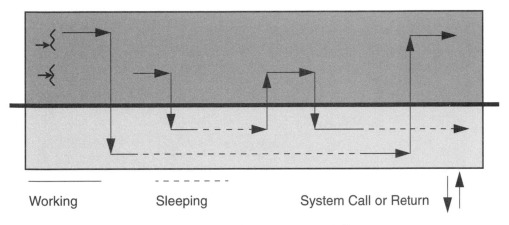

| Working | Sleeping | System Call or Return |

Figure 2–9 *Two Threads Making Overlapping System Calls*

Throughput

When a traditional, single-threaded program requests a service from the operating system, it must wait for that service to complete, often leaving the CPU idle. Even on a uniprocessor, multithreading allows a process to overlap computation with one or more blocking system calls (Figure 2–9). Threads provide this overlap even though each request is coded in the usual synchronous style. The thread making the request must wait, but another thread in the process can continue. Thus, a process can have numerous blocking requests outstanding, giving you the beneficial effects of doing asynchronous I/O while still writing code in the simpler synchronous fashion.

Responsiveness

Blocking one part of a process need not block the entire process. Single-threaded applications that do something lengthy when a button is pressed typically display a "please wait" cursor and freeze while the operation is in progress. If such applications were multithreaded, long operations could be done by independent threads, allowing the application to remain active and making the application more responsive to the user. In

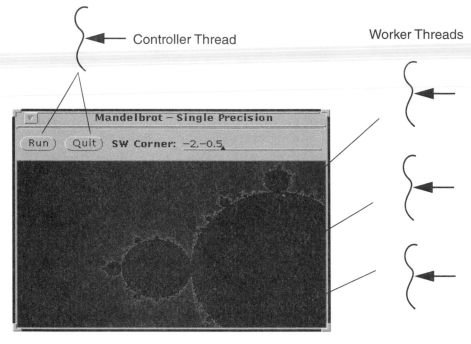

Figure 2–10   *Threads Overlapping Calculation and I/O*

Figure 2–10, one thread is waiting for I/O from the buttons, and several threads are working on the calculations.

Communications

An application that uses multiple processes to accomplish its tasks can be replaced by an application that uses multiple threads to accomplish those same tasks. Where the old program communicated among its processes through traditional interprocess communications facilities (e.g., pipes or sockets), the threaded application can communicate via the inherently shared memory of the process. The threads in the MT process can maintain separate connections while sharing data in the same address space. A classic example is a server program, which can maintain one thread for each client connection, such as in Figure 2–11. This program

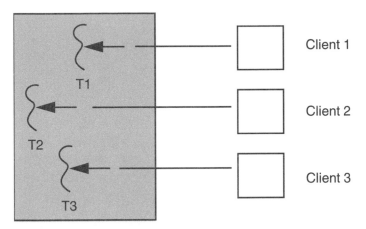

Figure 2–11   *Different Clients Being Handled by Different Threads*

provides excellent performance, simpler programming, and effortless scalability.

System Resources

Programs that use two or more processes to access common data through shared memory are effectively applying more than one thread of control. However, each such process must maintain a complete process structure, including a full virtual memory space and kernel state. The cost of creating and maintaining this large amount of state makes each process much more expensive, in both time and space, than a thread. In addition, the inherent separation between processes may require a major effort by the programmer to communicate among the different processes or to synchronize their actions. By using threads for this communication instead of processes, the program will be easier to debug and can run much faster.

An application can create hundreds or even thousands of threads, one for each synchronous task, with only minor impact on system resources. Threads use a fraction of the system resources needed by processes.

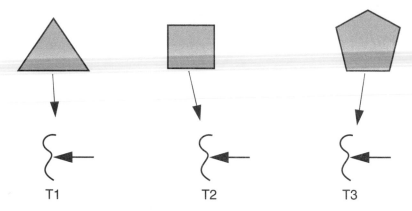

Figure 2–12   *Distributed Objects Running on Distinct Threads*

Distributed Objects

With the first releases of standardized distributed objects and object request brokers, your ability to make use of these will become increasingly important. Distributed objects are inherently multithreaded. Each time you request an object to perform some action, it executes that action in a separate thread (Figure 2–12). Object servers are an absolutely fundamental element in distributed object paradigm, and those servers are inherently multithreaded.

Although you can make a great deal of use of distributed objects without doing any MT programming, knowing what they are doing and being able to create objects that are threaded will increase the usefulness of the objects you do write.

Same Binary for Uniprocessors and Multiprocessors

In most older parallel processing schemes, it was necessary to tailor a program for the individual hardware configuration. With threads, this customization isn't required because the MT paradigm works well irrespective of the number of CPUs. A

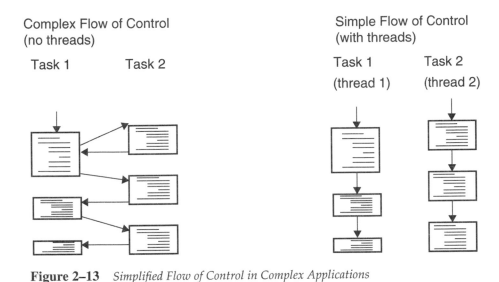

Figure 2–13 *Simplified Flow of Control in Complex Applications*

program can be compiled once, and it will run acceptably on a uniprocessor, whereas on a multiprocessor it will just run faster.

Program Structure

Many programs are structured more efficiently with threads because they are inherently concurrent. A traditional program that tries to do many different tasks is crowded with lots of complicated code to coordinate these tasks. A threaded program can do the same tasks with much less, far simpler code, as in Figure 2–13. Multithreaded programs can be more adaptive to variations in user demands than single-threaded programs can.

This is quite some set of claims, and a bit of healthy skepticism is called for. Sure, it sounds good when we say it, but what about when you try to use it? We cannot guarantee that you will experience the same wonderful results, but we can point out a number of cases where other folks have found MT programming to be of great advantage (see *Performance* on page 28).

What Kinds of Programs to Thread

There is a spectrum of programs that one might wish to thread. On one end, there are those that are inherently "MT-ish"—you look at the work to be done, and you think of it as several independent tasks. In the middle, there are programs where the division of work isn't obvious, but possible. On the far other end, there are those that cannot reasonably be threaded at all.

Inherently MT Programs

Inherently MT programs are those that are easily expressed as numerous threads doing numerous things. Such programs are easier to write using threads, because they are doing different things concurrently anyway. They are generally simpler to write and understand when threaded, easier to maintain, and more robust. The fact that they may run faster is a mere pleasant side effect. For these programs, the general rule is that the more complex the application, the greater the value of threading.

Typical programs that are inherently MT include:

Independent tasks   A debugger needs to run and monitor a program, keep its GUI active, and display an interactive data inspector, dynamic call grapher, and performance monitor—all in the same address space, all at the same time.

Servers   A server needs to handle numerous overlapping requests simultaneously. NFS®, NIS, DBMSs, stock quotation servers, etc., all receive large numbers of requests that require the server to do some I/O, then process the results and return answers. Completing one request at a time would be very slow.

Repetitive tasks   A simulator needs to simulate the interactions of numerous different elements that operate simultaneously. CAD, structural analysis, weather prediction, etc., all model tiny pieces first, then combine the results to produce an overall picture.

Not Obviously MT Programs

Not obviously MT programs are those not inherently MT but for which threading is reasonable. Here you impose threads upon an algorithm that does not have an obvious decomposition, in order to achieve a speedup on an MP machine. Such a program is somewhat harder to write, a bit more difficult to maintain, etc., than its nonthreaded counterpart, but it runs faster. Because of these drawbacks, the (portions of) programs chosen are generally quite simple.

Typical programs in this class include:

Numerical programs   Many numerical programs (e.g., matrix operations) are made up of huge numbers of tiny, identical, and independent operations. They are most easily (well, most commonly) expressed as loops inside loops. Slicing these loops into appropriate-sized chunks for threads is slightly more complicated, and there would be no reason to do so, save for the order-N speedup that can be obtained on an N-way SMP machine.

Old code   These are the "slightly modified existing systems." This is existing code that makes you think to yourself: "If I just change a few bits here and there, add a few locks, then I can thread it and double my performance."

It's true, it is possible to do this, and there are lots of examples. However, this is a tough situation because you will constantly be finding new interactions that you didn't realize existed before. In such cases (which, due to the nature of the modern software industry, are far too common), you should concentrate on the bottlenecks and look for absolutely minimal submodules that can be rewritten. It's *always* best to take the time to do it right: re-architect and write the program correctly from the beginning.

Automatic Threading

In a subset of cases, it is possible for a compiler to do the threading for you. If you have a program written in such a way that a compiler can analyze its structure, analyze the interdependencies of the data, and determine that parts of your program can run simultaneously without data conflicts, then the compiler can build the threads.

With current technology, the capabilities above are limited largely to Fortran programs that have time-consuming loops in which the individual computations in those loops are obviously independent. The primary reason for this limitation is that Fortran programs tend to have very simple structuring, both for code and data, making the analysis viable. Languages like C, which have constructs such as pointers, make the analysis enormously more difficult. There are MP compilers for C, but far fewer programs can take advantage of such compiling techniques.

With the different Fortran MP compilers,[3] it is possible to take vanilla Fortran 77 or 90 code, make no changes to it whatsoever, and have the compiler turn out threaded code. In some cases it works very well; in others, not. The cost of trying it out is very small, of course. A number of Ada compilers will map Ada tasks directly on top of threads, allowing existing Ada programs to take advantage of parallel machines with no changes to the code.

Programs Not to Thread

Then there is a large set of programs that it doesn't make any sense to thread. Probably 99% of all programs either do not lend themselves easily to threading or run just fine the way they are. Some programs simply require separate processes in which to run. Perhaps they need to execute one task as root but need to avoid having any other code running as root. Perhaps the program needs to be able to control its global environment closely, changing working directories, etc. Most programs run quite fast enough as they are and don't have any inherent multitasking, such as an icon editor or a calculator application.

In all truth, multithreaded programming is more difficult than regular programming. There are a host of new problems that must be dealt with, many of which are difficult. Threads are of value primarily when the task at hand is complex.

---

[3]Digital's Fortran compiler, Sun® Fortran MP, Kuck and Associates' Fortran compiler, EPC's Fortran compiler, SGI's MP Fortran compiler, probably more.

What About Shared Memory?

At this time, you may be asking yourself, "What can threads do that can't be done by processes sharing memory?" The first answer is, "nothing." Most anything that you can do with threads, you can do with processes sharing memory. Indeed, a number of vendors implement a significant portion of their threads library in roughly this fashion. There are a few details, such as managing shared file descriptors, which are not supported on all systems. Nonetheless, the additional expense and complication of using multiple processes restricts the usefulness of this method. Java is defined in such a way that sharing memory between processes is not an option, so we will skip over this technique, which is sometimes interesting to C/C++ programmers.

Threads Standards

There are three different definitions for native thread libraries competing for attention today: Win32, OS/2, and POSIX. The first two are proprietary and limited to their individual platforms (Win32 threads run only under NT and Win95, OS/2 threads only on OS/2). The POSIX specification (IEEE 1003.1c, a.k.a. *Pthreads*) is intended for all computing platforms, and implementations are available or in development for almost all major UNIX systems (including Linux), along with VMS and AS/400—not to mention a freeware library for Win32.

By contrast, Java threads are implemented in the JVM, which in turn is built on top of the native threads library for the specific platform.[4] Java does not expose the native threads' APIs, only its own, very small set of functions. This allows Java threads to be easier to use than the native libraries and more portable, but there are still some significant issues in making programs run uniformly across all platforms.

---

[4]Actually, the JVM is allowed to implement threads any way it feels like. Indeed, the first implementations of Java used *green threads,* which were not native. Today, most JVMs are built on native threads.

POSIX Threads

The POSIX standard defines the API and behavior that all Pthreads libraries must meet. It is part of the extended portion of POSIX, so it is not a requirement for meeting XPG4, but it is required for X/Open UNIX 98, and all major UNIX vendors have implemented this standard. In addition, UNIX98 includes a small set of extensions to Pthreads.

Win32 and OS/2 Threads

Both the NT and OS/2 implementations contain some fairly radical differences from the POSIX standard—to the degree that even porting from one or the other to POSIX will prove moderately challenging. Microsoft has not announced any plans to adopt POSIX. There are freeware POSIX libraries for Win32, and OS/2 also has an optional POSIX library.

DCE Threads

Before POSIX completed work on the standard, it produced a number of drafts that it published for comment. Draft 4 was used as the basis for the threads library in DCE. It is similar to the final spec, but it does contain a number of significant differences. Presumably, no one is writing any new threaded DCE code.

Solaris Threads

Also known as *UI threads,* this is the library that SunSoft used in developing Solaris 2 before the POSIX committee completed its work. It will be available on Solaris 2 for the foreseeable future, although we expect most applications writers will opt for Pthreads. The vast majority of the two libraries are virtually identical.

Performance

Even after reading all these wonderful things about threads, there's always someone who insists on asking that ever-so-bothersome question: "Does it work?" For an answer, we turn to

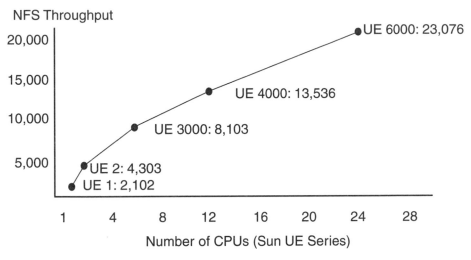

Figure 2–14 *NFS Performance on MP Machines (SPEC '96)*

some real, live shipping programs. Some of these are described in greater detail in the MT "Case Studies" (see *Threads Newsgroup* on page 410).

Operating Systems

OSs are large, complex, yet still highly efficient and robust programs. The various OSs have been in daily use by millions of users over the past couple of years and have endured the stress put on them by hundreds of thousands of programmers who are not known for their generosity toward operating system quirks. Mach, Windows NT, Windows 95, Solaris, IRIX, AIX, OS/2, and Digital UNIX are all threaded, and many of the other UNIX vendors are also moving toward a threaded kernel.

NFS

Under most UNIX systems, both the NFS client and server are threaded (Figure 2–14). There aren't any standardized benchmarks for the client side, so you'll have to take our word for it that it's faster. On the server side, however, there is the LADDIS benchmark from SPEC. A great deal of time has been spent optimizing NFS for multiple CPUs, quite successfully.

SPECfp 95

The rule for the SPECfp benchmark is that a compiler is allowed to do pretty much anything it wants to, as long as that compiler is available to customers and nobody changes the source code at all. The various Fortran 77/90 MP compilers automatically multi-thread a program with no user intervention, so they are legal. You give the compiler the code, completely unchanged, and it looks to see if there is any possibility of threading it. It is possible to thread 6 of the 14 SPECfp programs automatically. The results are *very* impressive (Table 2–1).

Table 2–1   *SPECfp95 Results for Alpha 4100 5/466 (SPEC '97)*

Number of CPUs	Tomcatv	Swim	Su2cor	Hydro2d	Mgrid	Turb3d
1	23.8	25.4	10.1	10.0	17.5	19.1
2	33.1	46.2	18.0	15.4	24.5	33.4
4	40.3	83.8	30.3	21.3	34.6	54.9

SPECint_rate95

SPECfp 95 is a reasonable set of benchmarks for single-CPU machines, but it does not give a good picture of the overall performance potential of multiprocessor machines (Figure 2–15). The SPECrate is intended to demonstrate this potential by allowing the vendor to run as many copies of the program as desired (e.g., in one test with 30 CPUs, Sun ran 37 copies of each program). This benchmark does not use the MP compiler.

Java Benchmarks

There are currently no Java benchmarks of interest to parallel processing.

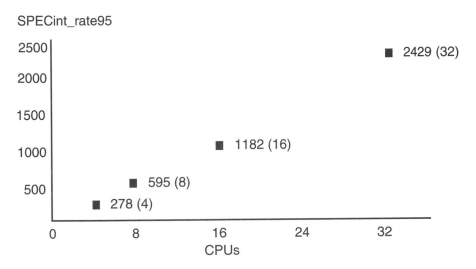

SPECint_rate95

Figure 2–15   *Running SPECrate_fp95 on an SGI Origin/200, 2000 (SPEC '96)*

Summary

Threads allow both concurrent execution in a single address space and parallel execution on multiple-processor machines, and they also make many complex programs easier to write. Most programs are simple and fast enough that they don't need threads, but for those programs that do need them, threads are wonderful.

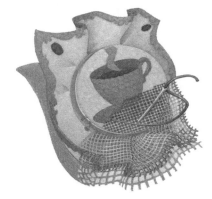

Foundations

In which we introduce the reader to the underlying structures upon which threads are built, the construction of the thread itself, and the operating system support that allows efficient implementation.

Implementation vs. Specification

When writing a book of this nature, the authors are often faced with a difficult decision: How much should they restrict themselves to the pure specifications, and how much in the way of implementation should they allow to show through? By talking only about the specifications, the reader is given a pure rendition of what the library should do and is not misled into thinking that because a particular implementation did things one way, they all have to be like that.[1]

Unfortunately, describing only the specification is rather akin to teaching the concepts of mathematics without ever mentioning the existence of numbers.[2] It's clean and pure, but terribly difficult to comprehend fully. So we have chosen to bring in implementation details when we think they will aid in comprehension. The implementation we refer to most is the Solaris implementation, largely because we know it best.

Please keep in mind that these implementation details are included for your edification, but you should never write programs that depend upon them. They can change at any time, with no notification. Learn from the implementation; write to the specification.

Thread Libraries

There are two fundamentally different ways of implementing threads. The first is to write a user-level library that is substantially self-contained. It will make calls to system routines, and it may depend upon the existence of certain kernel features, but it is fundamentally a user-level library and contains no "magic" hooks into secret kernel routines. All of the defining structures and code for the library will be in user space. The vast majority

---

[1]A specification is a description of what a program is supposed to do. An implementation is an actual program, which hopefully does what the spec says it should. The U.S. Constitution is a specification for a country. The United States is an implementation.

[2]Yes, we are members of the "New Math" generation.

of the library calls will execute entirely in user space and make no more use of system routines than does any other user-level library.

The second way is to write a library that is inherently a kernel-level implementation. It may define all the same functions as in the first case, but these functions will be completely dependent upon the existence of kernel routines to support them and may well be almost entirely in kernel space. The user-level portion of the library will be relatively small compared to the amount of kernel-level support it requires. The majority of library calls will require system calls.

Both of these methods can be used to implement exactly the same API, and they overlap in the kinds of kernel support they require. Some implementations of the POSIX standard are of the first kind, while both OS/2 and Win32 threads are of the second type. When Java is implemented on these OSs it inherits the underlying behavior.

In either case, the programmer will use an API that is implemented by a threads library. That library will provide a set of function calls (POSIX has about 50 calls, while Java has a dozen) that is the programmer's sole interface to threads. Everything not provided by those calls must come from the system's other libraries, meaning that 99% of writing a multithreaded program consists of writing regular, old-fashioned code almost the same way as before.

As you read the descriptions of the APIs, you may be struck by the lack of fancy features. This is intentional. These libraries provide a foundation for writing MT programs, but not every detail you might like. They provide you the resources with which to build more elaborate functions. Spin locks, priority-inheriting mutexes, deadlock-recovery features, etc., can be built out of these primitives with relative ease. Thus, if you want very fast, minimal functionality constructs, they are provided. If you want the slower, more complex constructs, you can build them.

We begin by talking about the parts of the system that are not inherently related to threads, but that do define a great deal about how threads must work. We use the specific example of how Solaris deals with the issues involved in building a viable interface between kernel-provided functionality and the user-level threads requirements. Other operating systems and other libraries have chosen different ways of providing this interface, and we do discuss them in general terms. We believe that by understanding one implementation in detail, you will acquire the background needed to fill in the gaps for the other implementations.

The Process Structure

The only thing the kernel knows about is the process structure. And the process structure has changed (slightly) since you last looked at it in traditional multitasking operating systems such as SunOS 4.x (see Figure 3–1).

It used to contain the memory map, the signal dispatch table, signal mask, user ID, group ID, working directory, etc., along with runtime statistics, CPU state (registers, etc.), and a kernel stack (for executing system calls). In Solaris 2, the last couple bits have been abstracted out and placed into a new structure called a *lightweight process* (LWP).[3] So a process contains all of the above, except for the runtime statistics, CPU state, and kernel stack, which are now part of the LWP structure. A process thus contains some number of LWPs (one for a "traditional" process, more for a multithreaded process). Just as the threads all share the process variables and state, the LWPs do the same.

The process structure shown in Figure 3–1 is in kernel space—below the solid line in the figures. It is not directly accessible by any user code. User code can access it only via a system call. That restriction allows the kernel to check the legality of the call and prevent user code from doing things it shouldn't, either by intention or mistake. Because a system call is required to access the process structure information, it is a more costly operation than a function call.

---

[3]The other operating systems that support user-level threads have different ways of dealing with the same issue. Some of them copy the entire process structure for each thread, some of them don't do anything. The concept of a separate, schedulable entity, such as the LWP, proves to be an excellent pedagogical concept, and the other designs can easily be described in terms of LWPs. LWP is, of course, a Solaris term.

Traditional UNIX Process Structure   Solaris 2 Process Structure

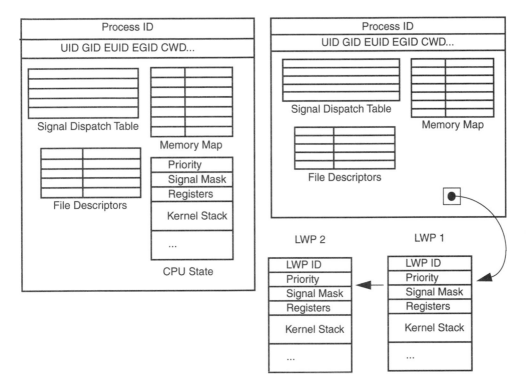

Figure 3–1   *Process Structure in Traditional UNIX and in Solaris 2*

Lightweight Processes

A lightweight process[4] can be thought of as a virtual CPU that is available for executing code. Each LWP is separately scheduled by the kernel. It can perform independent system calls and incur independent page faults, and multiple LWPs in the same process can run in parallel on multiple processors.

LWPs are scheduled onto the available CPU resources according to their scheduling class and priority, as illustrated in

---

[4]SunOS 4.x had a library known as the LWP library. There is no relationship between Solaris 2 LWPs and SunOS 4.x LWPs.

Figure 3–6 on page 44. Because scheduling is done on a per-LWP basis, each LWP collects its own kernel statistics—user time, system time, page faults, etc. This also implies that a process with two LWPs will generally get twice as much CPU time as a process with only one LWP. (This is a wild generalization, but you get the idea—the kernel is scheduling *LWPs*, not processes.)

An LWP also has some capabilities that are not exported directly to threads, such as kernel scheduling classes. A programmer can take advantage of these capabilities while retaining use of all the thread interfaces and capabilities by specifying that the thread is to remain permanently bound to an LWP (known as *system contention scope scheduling* and discussed further in *Realtime LWPs* on page 89).

LWPs are an implementation technique for providing kernel-level concurrency and parallelism to support the threads interface. There is never a reason for you to use the LWP interface directly. Indeed, you should specifically avoid it. It gains you nothing but costs you your portability.

Digital UNIX

An interesting contrast to LWPs are the techniques that DEC takes. Digital UNIX has two kinds of "LWPs," one that is an *execution engine* (the thing that runs on the CPU) and the other is an *I/O wait engine* (which contains just enough state to move its thread back onto an execution engine). This is nice because it minimizes the impact on the kernel of expensive programs which would otherwise demand numerous LWPs.

Linux

In Linux, a low-level call to `clone()` creates a new kernel thread in the same fashion as `fork()` creates a process. It also allows kernel threads of varying functionality. They can share the address space but not file descriptors, they can share both of those but not signal handlers, etc. The one noticeable distinction is that these kernel threads will never share a process ID in the way that UNIX and Win32 threads will. This is not a disaster, but it does make extra work for the library designer.

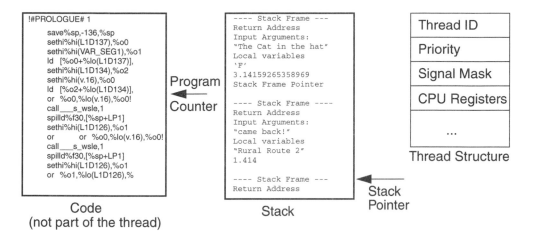

Figure 3–2 *Contents of a Thread*

Threads and LWPs

In a typical, traditional, multitasking operating system, a process comprises memory, the CPU register state, and some system state (file descriptors, user ID, working directory, etc., all stored in the *process structure*). When it's time to context-switch two processes, the kernel saves the registers in the process structure, changes some virtual memory pointers, loads the CPU registers with data from the other process structure, and continues.

When context-switching two threads, the registers are saved as before, but the memory map and the "current process" pointer remain the same. The idea is that you have a single program, in one memory space, with many virtual CPUs running different parts of the program concurrently.

What actually makes up a thread are (see Figure 3–2) its own stack and stack pointer; a program counter; some thread information, such as scheduling priority, and signal mask, stored in the thread structure; and the CPU registers (the stack pointer and program counter are actually just registers).

Everything else comes from either the process or (in a few cases) the LWP. The stack is just memory drawn from the program's heap. A POSIX thread *could* look into and even alter the

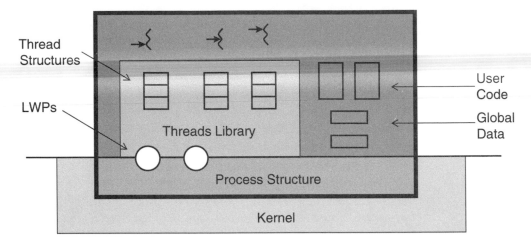

Figure 3–3   *How the Threads Library Fits into a Process*

contents of another thread's stack if it so desired. (Although you, being a good programmer, would never do this, your bugs might.)

Putting all this together, we end up with a picture such as Figure 3–3. The threads, their stacks, the code they run, and the global data that they share are all in user space, directly under user control. The thread structures are also in user space, but completely under the control of the threads library. There is no legal way for a user program to access those structures directly. The library itself, like every other system library, is just regular user code that you could have written yourself.

The LWPs are part of the process structure, but we show them crossing the line because this is how we think of their use. They are the main vehicle for processing from the threads library's point of view, so we show them in illustrations crossing that boundary, although they are, strictly speaking, in kernel space. The actual process structure is completely in kernel space.

As you can deduce, this definition of threads residing in a single address space means that the entire address space is seen identically by all threads. A change in shared data by one thread can be seen by all the other threads in the process. If one thread is writing a data structure while another thread is reading it, there will be problems (see *Race Conditions* on page 168).

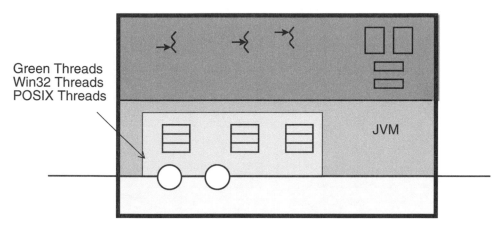

**Green Threads
Win32 Threads
POSIX Threads**

Figure 3–4 *How Java Is Built on Lower-Level Threads Libraries*

As threads share the same process structure, they also share most of the operating system state. Each thread sees the same open files, the same user ID, the same working directory; each uses the same file descriptors, *including the file position pointer*. If one thread opens a file, another thread can read it. If one thread does a `seek()` while another thread is doing a series of reads on the same file descriptor, the results may be surprising.

All of this is true no matter if you think of the running code as being native or as residing inside the JVM; the issues and consequences are the same. In some fashion, the JVM uses a threads library (possibly a native library such as POSIX or Win32, possibly its own library, green threads) to provide the infrastructure for your threads to run on. As far as you can tell, you're just running Java threads, but underneath you're running on the lower-level library (Figure 3–4).

The POSIX Multithreaded Model

In the POSIX multithreaded model (see Figure 3–5), threads are the portable application-level interface. Programmers write applications using the appropriate API. The underlying threads library schedules the threads onto LWPs. The LWPs in turn are imple-

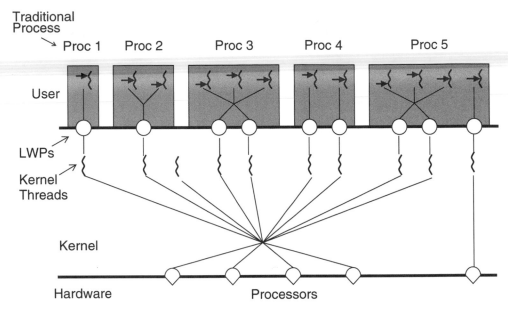

Figure 3–5   *POSIX Multithreaded Architecture*

mented by kernel threads[5] in the kernel. These kernel threads are then scheduled onto the available CPUs by the standard kernel scheduling routine, completely invisible to the user. This picture is accurate for POSIX threads. It is equally applicable for Win32 and Java threads, save that there are some limitations regarding the binding of threads to LWPs (see *Different Models of Kernel Scheduling* on page 72).

System Calls

A system call is the way that multitasking operating systems allow user processes to get information or request services from

---

[5]All the kernels are implemented using a threads library, often similar to Pthreads (Solaris kernel threads are very similar; DEC's kernel threads were based on Mach and are quite different). These *kernel threads* are used to implement LWPs. The kernel also uses them for its own internal tasks, such as the page daemon. The term *kernel thread* is not used uniformly, and many people use it to refer to LWPs (or logical equivalent). We will not deal with kernel threads at all.

the kernel. Such things as "Write this file to the disk" and "How many users are on the system?" are done with system calls. We divide system calls into two categories, blocking and nonblocking calls. In a *blocking system call,* such as "Read this file from the disk," the program makes the call, the operating system executes it and returns the answer, and the program proceeds. If a blocking system call takes a long time, the program just waits for it. (Usually, another process will be scheduled while this one is waiting.)

In a *nonblocking system call,* such as "Write this file to the disk without waiting," the program makes the call, the operating system sets up the parameters for the write, then returns, and the program continues. Exactly when the disk write actually occurs is not particularly important, and the program is able to continue working. A nonblocking system call may send the process a signal to tell it that the write is completed. Asynchronous I/O is important for many nonthreaded applications, as it allows the application to continue to work, even while there is I/O pending.

When a process makes a system call (see Figure 3–6), the following events occur:

1. The process traps to the kernel.
2. The trap handler runs in kernel mode and saves all the registers.
3. The handler sets the stack pointer to the process structure's kernel stack.
4. The kernel runs the system call.
5. The kernel places any requested data into the user-space structure that the programmer provided.
6. The kernel changes any process structure values affected.
7. The process returns to user mode, replacing the registers and stack pointer, and returns the appropriate value from the system call.

Of course, system calls don't always succeed. They can out-and-out fail or they can be interrupted. In C, when they fail they return a failure value and set `errno`. When interrupted by a signal the call is forced out of the kernel, the signal handler is run, and

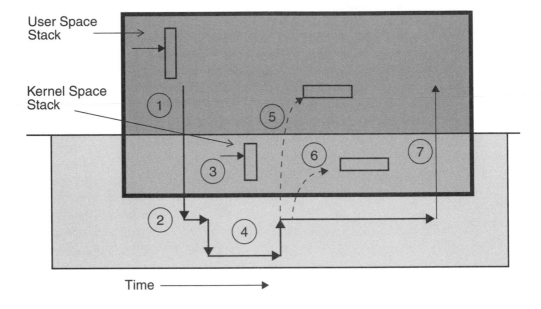

Figure 3–6 *Operation of a System Call*

the system call returns EINTR. (Presumably, the program will see this value and repeat the system call.) The Java model for handling these situations is to throw exceptions (there are a variety of exceptions for failing system calls and a special exception, InterruptedException, for interruptions).

What happens in a process with multiple LWPs? Almost exactly the same thing. The LWP enters the kernel, there's a kernel stack for each LWP, all the usual things happen, and the system call returns. And if several LWPs make system calls? They all execute independently and everything works as expected, with the usual caveats.

If several calls affect the same data, things could turn ugly. For example, if two threads issue calls to change the working directory, one of them is going to get a surprise. Or if two threads do independent calls to read(), using the same file descriptor, the file pointer will not be coordinated by either one of them, resulting in one thread reading from a different place than it expected. We'll deal with these issues later.

The really nice thing about different threads being able to execute independent system calls is when the calls are blocking system calls. Ten different threads can issue ten synchronous reads, all of which block, yet all the other threads in the process can continue to compute. Cool.

Signals

Signals are the mechanism that UNIX has always used to get asynchronous behavior in a program. With threads, we are able to get most asynchronous behavior without signals. Only interruptions need some signal-like mechanism in order to work. In Java, the UNIX signal model is not used at all (this is a good thing!) and interruptions are done by using the exception system.

Summary

Threads libraries can be implemented as self-contained user-level libraries or as kernel-based routines. The same program can be written in either, the difference often being quite minor. The main distinction of threads vs. processes is that threads share all process resources and data. The programming trade-offs, problems, and designs are the same for POSIX, Win32, and Java.

Lifecycle

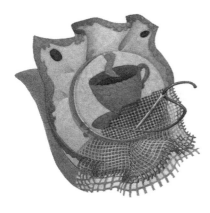

In which the reader is treated to a comprehensive explanation of the intricacies in the life of a thread—birth, life, and death—even death by vile cancellation. A small program that illustrates all these stages concludes the chapter.

Thread Lifecycle

The fundamental paradigm of threads is the same in all the libraries. In each, the program starts up in the same fashion as single-threaded programs always have—loading the program, linking in the dynamic libraries, running any initialization sections, and finally, starting a single thread running `main()` (the main thread). The main function will then be free to create additional threads as the programmer sees fit (Code Examples 4–1 to 4–3).

In Pthreads and Win32, you call the create function with a function to run and an argument for the function to run on. Java follows the same paradigm, but the API is rather distinct. In Java you subclass `Thread`, defining a `run()` method for it, then instantiate an instance of it and call `start()`. You can see how this maps directly onto the POSIX model. It is important to distinguish between the *thread object* that you've just created with `new Thread` and the *thread* as we've described it, which is created in the `start()` method.

```
error = pthread_create(&tid, NULL, start_fn, arg);

void *start_fn(void *arg) {
   doWork();
   pthread_exit(status);
}
```

Code Example 4–1   *Simple Call to Create and Exit a POSIX Thread*

```
public class MyThread extends Thread {
  public void run() {
      doWork();
    }
}

  Thread t = new MyThread();
  t.start();
```

Code Example 4–2   *Simple Call to Create and Exit a Java Thread*

```
handle = CreateThread(NULL, NULL, start_fn, arg, NULL, &tid);

void *start_fn(void *arg) {
    doWork();
    ExitThread(status);
}
```

Code Example 4–3 *Simple Call to Create and Exit a Win32 Thread*

Exiting a Thread

Conversely, a thread is exited by calling the appropriate thread exit function or simply returning from the initial function. Beyond the actual call to the create function, there is no parent/child relationship—any thread can create as many threads as it pleases and, after creation, there will be no relationship between the creator and createe.

In Java there is no thread exit function as there is in the other libraries, and the only way of exiting a thread is to return from the run() method. This seems a bit odd, but it is intentional. The basic idea is that only the run() method should make the decision to exit. Other methods lower in the call chain may decide that they are done with what they are doing, or they may encounter an error condition, but all they should do is pass that information up the call stack. They may return unique values to indicate completion or they may propagate an exception, but they shouldn't exit the thread.[1]

Moreover, even the run() method shouldn't be exiting the thread explicitly because it doesn't "know" that it's running in a unique thread. It is perfectly reasonable for a program to call the run() method in a new thread sometimes, and from an existing thread other times.

---

[1]In earlier programs we looked at this differently and even wrote a "thread exit" function for Java using thread.stop(). We recommend not doing that.

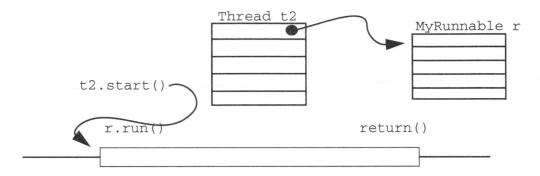

Figure 4–1   *Creating a Thread via a Runnable*

The Runnable Interface

There is a second method of creating a Java thread. In this method you write a class that implements the Runnable interface, defining a run() method on it (Figure 4–1). You then create a thread object with this runnable as the argument and call start() on the thread object. In simple examples, either method is fine, but we'll soon discover that the latter method is superior, and we'll use it in all our code (see Code Example 4–4). You will probably never use the first method yourself.

```
public MyRunnable implements Runnable {

    public void run(){
        doWork();
    }
}

Runnable r = new MyRunnable()
Thread t = new Thread(r);
t.start();
```

Code Example 4–4   *Simple Call to Run a Runnable in a Thread*

Finally, you can even use anonymous inner classes to define a thread's `run()` method (Code Example 4–5). You could even create a thread and pass it an inner class runnable, but that seems silly. We'll just define a `run()` method for the thread.

```
new Thread() {public void run() {doWork();}}.start();
```

Code Example 4–5   *Defining run() via an Inner Class in a Thread*

There are two reasons for using runnable. The first is that we are not changing the nature of the thread itself, we're only changing the `run()` method, so subclassing `Thread` isn't really appropriate. The second reason is that if we implement the `Runnable` interface, it's possible to subclass something else more useful. (True, it's unlikely that you'll ever subclass anything for your runnable; nonetheless, it's nice to have that option.) Still, the distinction between the two methods is quite minor. There are a few cases where we will subclass `Thread`, but in none of those will we ever define a `run()` method.

Moreover, we can consider a `Runnable` to be the work to be done, while the thread is the engine to do the work. From this point of view, it makes no sense to include the work inside the engine. On top of this, there is no reason to insist that the work be done in a unique thread. It is perfectly reasonable to execute the `run()` method of a `Runnable` in the current thread. This is exactly what we do in *Threads and Windows* on page 366.

What the `run()` method of `Thread` does by default is to look for a `Runnable` and call its `run()` method. You could both subclass `Thread` and define a `run()` method on it and then pass it a `Runnable` to run. In this case the `run()` method of the thread would be run. This would confuse the heck out of anyone reading your code. Don't do that.

In Pthreads and Win32 each thread has a thread ID (TID), which may be used to control certain aspects (scheduling classes, cancellation, signals, etc.) of that thread. (Win32 also defines a thread *handle,* which is a different version of a TID.) In Java, all of this is more conveniently handled simply by invoking methods on the thread object. (You will probably never call any methods on the runnable yourself.)

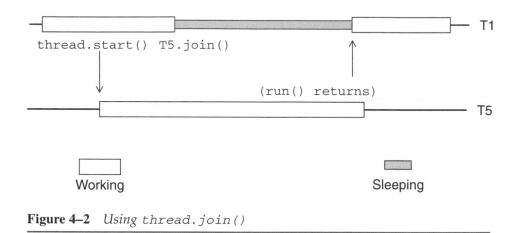

Figure 4–2   *Using* `thread.join()`

Waiting for Threads

Sometimes you specifically want to wait for a thread to exit (see Figure 4–2 and Code Example 4–6). Perhaps you've created 20 threads to do 20 pieces of a task, and you can't continue until they are all finished. One method is to call the wait function (called *join* in Pthreads and Java) on each of the desired threads. The caller will block until each of the specified threads has exited. The other way is to use normal synchronization functions. (We'll talk about this in *Using Barriers to Count Exiting Threads* on page 114.)

POSIX	Win32	Java
pthread_join(T5,...)	WaitForSingleObject(T5,...)	T5.join()

Code Example 4–6   *Waiting for Threads to Exit*

In addition to waiting for the threads to exit, the caller can receive a status from the exiting threads in Win32 and POSIX. In Java there is no such concept, but it's easy enough to build an ad hoc method should you need to. (You probably won't.) To ensure that no deadlocks occur, it makes no difference if the waiting thread calls the join function first or if the exiting thread calls the exit function first. Calling `return()` from the run method implicitly calls the thread exit function. Obviously, you should join a thread only once. It is legal in Java to join a thread more than once, but you're probably making a mistake if you do.

Who Am I?

Sometimes you want to know the identity of the current thread. In production programs this is pretty rare; most commonly you just want to print out some debugging information about which thread is running when. In any case, it's easy to do. All the libraries have a "current thread" function (Code Example 4–7). In Java you may also wish to know which Runnable is being run. You cannot find this out unless you build in a mechanism for it yourself (see *Java TSD* on page 180).

POSIX	Win32	Java
pthread_self()	GetCurrentThread()	Thread.currentThread()

Code Example 4–7 *Getting the Current Thread's Identity*

Don't Wait for Threads, Don't Return Status

When should you wait for a thread? Our *opinion* is never. Consider: Why do you care when a thread exits? Because you are waiting for that thread to complete some task, the results of which some other thread needs. By doing a join on that thread, you are implicitly assuming that the task will be complete when the thread exits. Although this may indeed be true, it would be conceptually cleaner if you simply waited for the task itself, using one of the synchronization variables discussed in Chapter 6. In many of our examples we simply count the number of threads that exit.

The only time you must join a thread is when you care about the thread itself (not the thread object). The only aspect of the thread that you have any kind of dependency on is the memory used for the thread's stack. In POSIX and Win32 it is possible to "touch" the stack directly. This is not possible in Java (a good thing), so the only possible interaction with the stack is the reuse issue. If you start a new thread, will it have to allocate new memory or can it use the newly freed memory from an exiting thread? Although it is possible to write a program where you can measure this effect, it would be quite artificial.

POSIX and Win32 can return a status value and the same argument applies. It isn't the thread that has status to return, it's the task that the thread was executing that has status, and that status may be handled without calling join. In all honesty, there are plenty of programs that don't take our advice and work just fine. You don't have to take our advice either, but you should consider it before making your decision.

Exiting the Process

The semantics of exit() [in Java, System.exit()] are retained in MT programs in all the libraries. When any thread in a process calls exit(), the process exits, returning its memory, system resources, process structure, all LWPs, etc. In Java, if main() "falls off the bottom" of the initial thread, the other threads will continue to run. [In the POSIX and Win32, the main thread will make an implicit call to exit(), also killing the process. This is a requirement for them to maintain compatibility with existing programs, not to mention the ANSI C spec.]

When any other thread in any of the libraries falls off the bottom of its initial function, it exits only that one thread. [In POSIX and Win32, if the main thread calls the thread exit function directly, that thread exits but does not call exit(), and the process continues.]

Finally, should all normal user threads exit (the library may create threads for its own use and they will not be counted; see *Daemon Threads* on page 234), the thread library will detect this and call exit() itself. This situation is not typical, however, as you will generally know when it's time to exit your process. Instead of letting the threads die one by one, you should call System.exit() explicitly.

Suspending a Thread

Win32 and Java have a function to force a thread to suspend its execution for an arbitrary length of time and a second function to cause the thread to resume [thread.suspend() and thread.resume()]. These functions were included for the purpose of allowing such things as garbage collectors and debuggers to gain full control of a process. As such, they are useful; however, for almost any other purpose they are the *wrong thing*. Because a suspended thread may hold locks that a controller thread needs, it is almost impossible to use suspension effectively. In Java these methods have been deprecated in JDK 1.2. In POSIX and UNIX98, they don't exist at all.[2]

Cancellation

It is possible for one thread to tell another thread to exit. This is known as *cancellation* in POSIX and simply as *killing a thread* in Java and Win32 (Code Example 4–8). In theory it's quite simple. T2 (Figure 4–3) tells T1 to exit, and it does. There is no relationship between the threads. Maybe T2 created T1, maybe T3 created both of them, maybe something else.

POSIX	Java	Win32
`pthread_cancel(T1);`	`T1.stop();`	`TerminateThread(T1);`

Code Example 4–8 *Cancellation in the Three Libraries*

How to make cancellation work correctly, in bounded time, and without corrupting any data is a different story. That part is highly complex and handled in Chapter 9. Moreover, `thread.stop()` has been deprecated in JDK 1.2. We'll discuss this in *Don't Call stop()* on page 190. Although deprecated, `stop()` will continue to be supported in Java for an unspecified amount of time. (It may never disappear.)

There is another technique that is more suitable for cancellation in Java. This is to interrupt the target thread and cause it to throw an `InterruptedException`. We can catch that exception and exit the thread on our own. This is what we'll do in *An Example: Create and Join* on page 59.

---

[2]They were to be included in UNIX98, and you may see reference to them, but they were dropped out at the last minute.

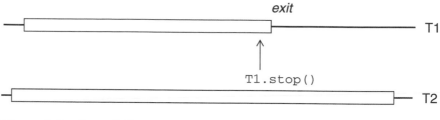

Figure 4–3   *Cancellation*

ThreadDeath

The stop() method is implemented by causing the target thread to throw an unchecked exception, ThreadDeath. That exception then percolates up to the run() method, where it causes the thread to exit. The original implementation of Java was not intended to expose ThreadDeath, but through some odd circumstances, it got out. You should consider it to be part of the implementation though, and not use it yourself. Yes, you could throw it yourself. You could even catch it yourself, but there are better ways of accomplishing whatever task you had in mind. Don't do that.

Garbage Collecting Threads

When do threads and thread objects get garbage collected? If you drop the last pointer to a thread, will it stop running and be garbage collected? No. When a thread is started, the thread object is entered into a thread group (see *Thread Groups* on page 224) and will remain there until it exits. The top-level thread group is one of the root GC nodes, so it never disappears.

As soon as a thread exits, its stack will be freed (this is an implementation detail), and some time after it exits and you drop the last pointer to the thread object, that thread object will be garbage collected. In other words, everything works the way you think it should and there's nothing to worry about.

Zombies

In POSIX, a *zombie*[3] thread is a dead thread whose memory has not yet been reclaimed. Reclamation occurs when that thread is joined. Java does not have this issue, so it is devoid of zombies; however, the underlying libraries may well use them to support Java. Nonetheless, imagining zombies in Figure 4–4 can help clarify the concept.

Is She Still Alive?

If you wish to know if a given thread is still running, you can call the method `thread.isAlive()`. This will tell you if the thread was running when you called it, but by the time you get around to using the information, it may have changed. In other words, between the time you find out that the thread is alive and the time when you find something for it to do, the thread may have exited. This is OK, because you don't really want to know that anyway. (If you think you do, you're wrong. You really want to know something else.)

If you want to know when a thread has exited, you join it. If you want to give a thread something new to do, you write the code so that the thread never exits, or so that the thread exits only on command.

In short, the method `isAlive()` is pretty useless. Several other methods are similar. The `activeCount()` method tells you how many threads were running when you called it. The `enumerate()` method promises to fill an array you supply with as many of the currently running thread objects as fit. By the time you use any of the information these methods supply, it may be out of date. Don't do that.

---

[3]In Haiti, a zombie is an "undead" person who has been cursed with voodoo. This inspired a classic American horror flick, *The Night of the Living Dead,* in which all these dead people crawl out of their graves and come after our heroes. This is the kind of thing that kernel hackers think about late at night.

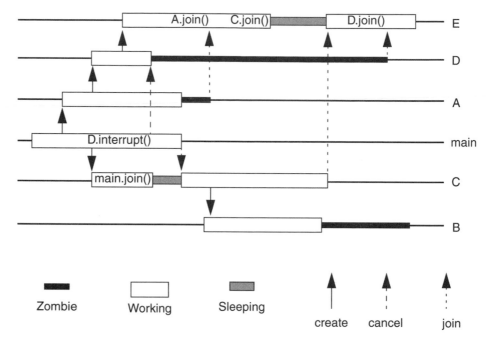

Figure 4–4 *Java Thread Create and Join*

Restarting Threads

Once a thread has exited, it is gone. The stack has been freed, the internal thread structures have been cleared, the underlying kernel resources have been returned. All that's left is the empty shell of the thread object. (If you extended the thread object and included your own instance variables, those will not be changed.) You cannot restart the thread; you cannot reuse the thread object. It's gone, dead, deceased, passed on, unrevivable.

If you created a thread using a `Runnable`, the `Runnable` is reusable. Indeed, if you did not specify any instance variables in the `Runnable`, you could simply create a single runnable object and create lots of threads that all used it. On the other hand, if you think you might change your program someday, or if someone else might end up maintaining it, this could be awkward. In all our programs we create a new `Runnable` for every thread.

An Example: Create and Join

In Figure 4–4 we show the operation of the program `Multi.java`, which makes a series of calls to create threads, stop them, and join them. The basic code is very simple and should require little explanation. A series of well-placed calls to `sleep()` arranges for the threads to execute in exactly the order we desire. Removing those calls (or setting breakpoints in the debugger) will cause the speed and order of execution to change, and some things will not work as intended. The program is not correct, per se, but it is a useful illustration of how to create and join threads without all that unsightly synchronization code.

The Main Thread Is Different

One slightly unusual aspect of this program is that we create a new thread which we call `threadMain` (Code Example 4–9, which follows). The actual main thread is identical to all the other threads, except for one thing. Because you did not create it, you do not know whether or not `main()` corresponds exactly to `run()`. In particular, just because `main()` returns does not imply that the main thread can then be joined.

```
//              Multi/Multi.java

/*
  Simple program that just illustrates thread creation, thread
  exiting, waiting for threads, and interrupting threads.

  This program relies completely on the accuracy of the sleep()
  method, something that is ill advised in a real program.
  For this example, that's OK. When you write programs,
  don't do that!
*/


import java.io.*;
import Extensions.*;


public class Multi {
    static Thread        threadA, threadB, threadC;
```

Code Example 4–9 *Java Create and Join*

```
  static Thread          threadD, threadE, threadMain;

public static void main(String[] args) throws Exception {
  threadMain = new Thread(new MyMain(), "threadMain");
  threadMain.start();
}
}


class MyMain implements Runnable {
  static long            startTime = 0;


public void run()   {

  startTime = System.currentTimeMillis();
  System.out.println();
  System.out.println("Time\tThread\t\tEvent");
  System.out.println("====\t======\t\t=====");
  System.out.println(time() + "threadMain\tStarted ");

  InterruptibleThread.sleep(1000);
  Multi.threadA = new Thread(new RunnableA(), "threadA");
  Multi.threadA.start();
  System.out.println(time() + "threadMain\tCreated threadA");

  InterruptibleThread.sleep(1000);
  Multi.threadC = new Thread(new RunnableC(), "threadC");
  Multi.threadC.start();
  System.out.println(time() + "threadMain\tCreated threadC");

  InterruptibleThread.sleep(2000);
  System.out.println(time() + "threadMain\tCancelling threadD");
  Multi.threadD.interrupt();

  InterruptibleThread.sleep(1000);
  System.out.println(time() + "threadMain\tExiting");
}

public static String time() {
  long time = (System.currentTimeMillis() - startTime)/1000 + 1000;
  return(time + "\t");
}
}


class RunnableA implements Runnable {
```

Code Example 4–9 *Java Create and Join (cont.)*

```
public void run() {

  System.out.println(MyMain.time() + "threadA\t\tStarting...");
  InterruptibleThread.sleep(1000);
  Multi.threadD = new Thread(new RunnableD(), "threadD");
  Multi.threadD.start();
  System.out.println(MyMain.time() + "threadA\t\tCreated threadD");
  InterruptibleThread.sleep(3000);
  System.out.println(MyMain.time() + "threadA\t\tExiting ");
}
}


class RunnableB implements Runnable {

public void run() {

  System.out.println(MyMain.time() + "threadB\t\tStarting... ");
  InterruptibleThread.sleep(4000);

  System.out.println(MyMain.time() + "threadB\t\tExiting ");
}
}


class RunnableC implements Runnable {

public void run() {

  System.out.println(MyMain.time() + "threadC\t\tStarting... ");
  InterruptibleThread.sleep(2000);

  System.out.println(MyMain.time() + "threadC\t\tJoining threadMain");
  try {
    Multi.threadMain.join();
  }
  catch (InterruptedException e) {System.out.println("CAN'T GET HERE.");}
  System.out.println(MyMain.time() + "threadC\t\tJoined threadMain");
  InterruptibleThread.sleep(1000);

  Multi.threadB = new Thread(new RunnableB(), "threadB");
  Multi.threadB.start();
  System.out.println(MyMain.time() + "threadC\t\tCreated threadB");
  InterruptibleThread.sleep(4000);

  System.out.println(MyMain.time() + "threadC\t\tExiting ");
}
}
```

Code Example 4–9 *Java Create and Join (cont.)*

```
class RunnableD implements Runnable {

public void run() {

  try {
    System.out.println(MyMain.time() + "threadD\t\tStarting... ");
    InterruptibleThread.sleep(1000);

    Multi.threadE = new Thread(new RunnableE(), "threadE");
    Multi.threadE.start();
    System.out.println(MyMain.time() + "threadD\t\tCreated threadE");
    Thread.sleep(5000);
    System.out.println(MyMain.time() +
                    "threadD\t\tSHOULDN'T REACH HERE!");
  }
  catch (InterruptedException e) {
    System.out.println(MyMain.time() + "threadD\t\tInterrupted. Exiting");
  }
}
}


class RunnableE implements Runnable {

public void run() {

  try {
    System.out.println(MyMain.time() + "threadE\t\tStarting... ");
    InterruptibleThread.sleep(3000);

    System.out.println(MyMain.time() + "threadE\t\tJoining threadA");
    Multi.threadA.join();
    System.out.println(MyMain.time() + "threadE\t\tJoined threadA");
    InterruptibleThread.sleep(2000);


    System.out.println(MyMain.time() + "threadE\t\tJoining threadC");
    Multi.threadC.join();
    System.out.println(MyMain.time() + "threadE\t\tJoined threadC");
    InterruptibleThread.sleep(2000);

    System.out.println(MyMain.time() + "threadE\t\tJoining threadD");
    Multi.threadD.join();
    System.out.println(MyMain.time() + "threadE\t\tJoined threadD");
    InterruptibleThread.sleep(1000);
```

Code Example 4–9 *Java Create and Join (cont.)*

```
   System.out.println(MyMain.time() + "threadE\t\tExiting ");
  }
  catch (InterruptedException e) {System.out.println("CAN'T GET HERE.");}
}
}
```

Code Example 4–9   *Java Create and Join (cont.)*

All code examples in this book are available from the Web (see *Code Examples* on page 410). They are all as nearly identical to the same programs written in C from *Multithreaded Programming with PThreads* as we could make them. In a few cases the Java code is a bit constrained because of this, but there are no significant issues.

The output from Code Example 4–9 (see Code Example 4–10) shows that indeed all the calls occur exactly when we expect them to.

```
bil@cloudbase[264]: java Multi

Time   Thread                      Event
====   ======                      =====
1000   threadMain                  Started
1001   threadMain                  Created threadA
1001   threadA                     Starting...
1002   threadMain                  Created threadC
1002   threadC                     Starting...
1002   threadA                     Created threadD
1002   threadD                     Starting...
1003   threadD                     Created threadE
1003   threadE                     Starting...
1004   threadMain                  Cancelling threadD
1004   threadD                     Interrupted. Exiting
1004   threadC                     Joining threadMain
1005   threadMain                  Exiting
1005   threadC                     Joined threadMain
1005   threadA                     Exiting
1006   threadC                     Created threadB
1006   threadB                     Starting...
1006   threadE                     Joining threadA
1006   threadE                     Joined threadA
1008   threadE                     Joining threadC
1010   threadC                     Exiting
1010   threadE                     Joined threadC
```

Code Example 4–10   *Output for Code Example 4–9*

```
1010   threadB                        Exiting
1012   threadE                        Joining threadD
1012   threadE                        Joined threadD
1013   threadE                        Exiting
bil@cloudbase[265]:
```

Code Example 4–10   *Output for Code Example 4–9 (cont.)*

There is nothing stopping you from starting the thread in the same line as the constructor (Code Example 4–11); we just don't do that very often.

```
new MyThread().start();
```

Code Example 4–11   *Construct and Start in a Single Line*

APIs Used in This Chapter

The Class java.lang.Thread

The class Thread defines thread *objects*. When the start() method is called, an actual running thread is created which the Thread object can control. It is important to distinguish between the object (which is just memory and a set of methods) and the running thread (which executes code). All static thread methods apply to the current thread.

Thread

```
public Thread()
public Thread(String name)
public Thread(Runnable runObj)
public Thread(Runnable runObj, String name)
          throws SecurityException,
          IllegalThreadStateException
```

These create a new thread object.

References: Chapters 4 and 10.

start

```
public void start()
        throws IllegalThreadStateException
```

> Calling the start() method on an instance of Thread will cause the appropriate run() method to execute in a new thread.

> *Reference:*   Chapter 4.

run

```
public void run()
```

> This is the method you define that actually executes the code you want. The base method simply looks to see if there is a Runnable and calls its run() method.

> *Reference:*   Chapter 4.

currentThread

```
public static Thread currentThread()
```

> This method returns the current thread object.

> *Reference:*   Chapter 4.

join

```
public final void join()
public final void join(long milliseconds)
public final void join(long milliseconds, long nanosec)
    throws InterruptedException
```

> This waits for the thread to exit.

> *Reference:*   Chapter 4.

> *Comment:*   Rarely used.

stop

```
public final stop()
public final stop(Throwable t)
```

> This kills the thread asynchronously.

> ***Reference:***   Chapter 4.

> ***Comment:***   It is deprecated in Java 2. Don't use it.

sleep

```
public static void sleep(long milliseconds)
public static void sleep(long milliseconds, long nanosec)
      throws InterruptedException
```

> This causes the current thread to go to sleep for the specified time. The precision of the wakeup is OS dependent. A typical minimum resolution is 10 ms. (Solaris defaults to 10 ms; root can set it to 1 ms. On Digital UNIX it's a mibisecond, 1/1024 second, 0.9765 ms.)

> ***Reference:***   Chapter 4.

> ***Comment:***   Fine for test programs. Probably will never use this in a real program.

destroy

```
public final void destroy()
```

> This causes the thread to exit immediately, running no `finally` sections, and releasing no locks. This was included in the Java spec to handle the extreme case of broken threads that ignore `stop()`. It is virtually impossible to use correctly and has never been implemented.

> ***Reference:***   Chapter 4.

isAlive

```
public final boolean isAlive()
```
> This returns true if the target thread is still alive.

Reference: Chapter 4.

activeCount

```
public static final int activeCount()
```
> This returns the number of currently active threads. (Sleeping and blocked threads are active.)

Reference: Chapter 4.

Comment: Deprecated in Java 1.1. See
`ThreadGroup.allThreadsCount()`.

enumerate

```
public static final int enumerate(Thread tarray[])
```
> This fills `tarray` with as many currently active threads as fit, returning that number.

Reference: Chapter 4.

Comment: Deprecated in Java 1.1. See
`ThreadGroup.allThreads()`.

getName setName

```
public String getName()
public void setName(String name)
          throws SecurityException
```
> This gets/sets the print name for the thread.

Reference: Chapter 4.

The Class Extensions.InterruptibleThread

This is one of the classes that we defined for this book to provide a consistent interface for dealing with certain problems.

exit

```
public void exit()
```

> This causes the current thread to exit. It is syntactic sugar for `Thread.currentThread().stop()`.

> *Reference:*   Chapter 4.

> *Comment:*   We wrote this method while trying to deal with the absence of such a function and the absence of any advice on this apparent oversight. We have subsequently been convinced that this is the wrong way to do things and that you should always return from the `run()` method (see *Exiting a Thread* on page 49).

The Interface java.lang.Runnable

This interface provides the building blocks for threads. You implement this interface, define a `run()` method on the class, and pass an instance of it to the thread.

run

```
public void run()
```

> This is the method you define that actually executes the code you want.

> *Reference:*   Chapter 4.

> *Comment:*   This is the only way to start anything.

Summary

The basic paradigm of thread creation in Java, POSIX, and Win32 is to build a new thread entity that will run a given function [in Java, `run()`] on a given argument (the implicit `this` argument). Threads can wait for each other, kill each other, or simply exit themselves.

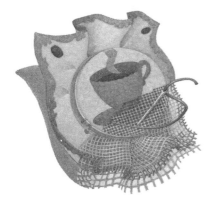

Chapter 5

Scheduling

- ▼ DIFFERENT MODELS OF KERNEL SCHEDULING
- ▼ THREAD SCHEDULING
- ▼ CONTEXT SWITCHING
- ▼ JAVA SCHEDULING SUMMARY
- ▼ WHEN SHOULD YOU CARE ABOUT SCHEDULING?
- ▼ APIS USED IN THIS CHAPTER
- ▼ THE CLASS JAVA.LANG.THREAD

In which we explain the myriad details of various scheduling models and alternative choices that could be made, describe context switching in detail, and delve into gruesome detail on various design options. There is light at the end of the tunnel, however.

Different Models of Kernel Scheduling

There are three primary techniques for scheduling threads onto kernel resources (and indirectly, onto CPUs). Two of them involve the use of LWPs (or something similar). These are the techniques from which the designers of the various operating systems had to choose. They wanted a model that would adequately support the complexity of the operating system and still meet the various demands of dedicated programmers. All three models are perfectly reasonable and give the programmer different sets of trade-offs, simultaneously building programs that do exactly the same things with different levels of efficiency. All three of these models are in use by different vendors.

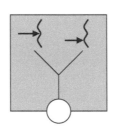

Many Threads on One LWP

The first technique is known as the *many-to-one model*. It is also known as *co-routining*.[1] Numerous threads are created in user space, and they all take turns running on the one LWP. Programming on such a model will give you a superior programming paradigm, but running your program on an MP machine will not give you any speedup, and when you make a blocking system call, the whole process will block. However, the thread creation, scheduling, and synchronization are all done 100% in user space, so they're done fast and cheap and use no kernel resources. This is how *green threads*[2] works. The DCE threads library also followed this model on HP-UX 10.20.

---

[1]The exact use of this term varies from book to book, but in broad terms, this is accurate.

[2]During the initial design phase of Java, Sun's native threading library wasn't complete and the "Green" group chose to implement a simpler library rather than wait. All of the early implementations of Java were based on green threads.

There is a clever hack[3] used for blocking system calls in some threads libraries (e.g., DCE threads in DEC OSF/1) that is worth mentioning. The library puts a *jacket routine* around each blocking system call. The jacket routine replaces the blocking system call with a nonblocking one. Thus, when a thread makes a blocking system call, the library can put that thread to sleep and allow another one to run. When the signal comes back from the kernel, saying that the system call is complete, the library figures out which thread made the call and wakes up that sleeping thread, and everything proceeds as if the thread had blocked in the first place. It's hassle-free async I/O!

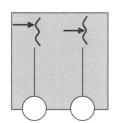

One Thread per LWP

The *one-to-one model* allocates one LWP[4] for each thread. This model allows many threads to run simultaneously on different CPUs. It also allows one or more threads to issue blocking system calls as the other threads continue to run—even on a uniprocessor.

This model has the drawback that thread creation involves LWP creation; hence it requires a system call, as does scheduling and synchronization. In addition, each LWP takes up additional kernel resources, so you are limited in the total number of threads you can create. Win32 and OS/2 use this model. Some POSIX implementations (DCE, IBM's early threads library, Xavier Leroy's LinuxThreads) also use it. Any JVMs based on these libraries also use this model, hence Java on Win32. (A JVM *could* build a two-level model on top of a one-to-one kernel model, but none currently do.)

---

[3]"Hassle-free for YOU, maybe. I had to code and debug the monster and I still have to explain it to users."—Dave Butenhof, reviewing this section.

[4]Remember, when you read about how a vendor implements this model, the vendor may not distinguish between the thread and the (possibly conceptual) LWP. The vendor may simply refer to the thread and expect you to understand that it's a single entity containing everything.

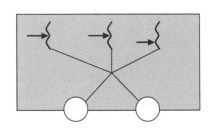

Many Threads on Many LWPs (Strict)

The third model is the strict *many-to-many model.* Any number of threads are multiplexed onto some (smaller or equal) number of LWPs. Thread creation is done completely in user space, as are scheduling and synchronization (well, almost). The number of LWPs may be tuned for the particular application and machine. Numerous threads can run in parallel on different CPUs, and a blocking system call need not block the entire process. As in the many-to-one model, the only limit on the number of threads is the size of virtual memory.[5] No native library actually uses this strict version, although Sun's implementations of Java 1.1 and 2 do use this.

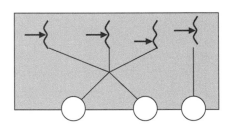

The Two-Level Model

The *two-level model* (known commonly as the *many-to-many model*) is a strict many-to-many model with the ability to specifically request a one-to-one binding for individual threads. This model is probably the best of the choices. Several operating systems now use this model (Digital UNIX, Solaris, IRIX, HP-UX, AIX). The JVMs on these OSs have the option of using any combination of bound and unbound threads.

The choice of the threading model is an implementation-level decision for writers of the JVM. Java itself has no concept of LWPs or threading models. This is a very reasonable choice by the

---

[5]On a 32-bit machine, this is roughly 2 GB (total virtual memory) / 8 kB (minimum stack size) = 256,000 threads.

Java designers; Java programs shouldn't be looking at this kind of low-level detail. Unfortunately, it brings in a very significant area of possible platform behavior difference.

Win32 Fibers   Win32 has a *fibers* library, which sits on top of its threads and gives a rough approximation of the two-level model. However, fibers have a completely different API and require explicit context switching, so it's best not to consider them to be threads. Indeed, you probably never want to work with fibers at all.

Thread Scheduling

As we have just seen, there are two basic levels to scheduling threads: process *local* scheduling (also known as *process contention scope*, or *unbound threads*—the many-to-many model) and system *global* scheduling (also known as *system contention scope*, or *bound threads*—the one-to-one model). These scheduling classes are known as the *scheduling contention scope*, and are defined concepts only in POSIX. In Win32 and in Java there is no such concept defined in the specs, no functions to select different models, no method of changing the default behavior at all. This is a limitation in some Java implementations and forces the user to call some native methods in order to get to the desired behavior (see *How to Get Those LWPs in Java* on page 87). Certain things cannot be done at all.

Process contention scope scheduling means that all of the scheduling mechanism for the thread is local to the process—the threads library has full control over which thread will be scheduled on an LWP. This also implies the use of either the many-to-one or many-to-many model. This is the scheduling method used for Java on Solaris. (Actually, POSIX allows PCS to be implemented as SCS, although we are not aware of any implementations that do so.)

System contention scope scheduling means that the scheduling is done by the kernel (i.e., one-to-one binding). POSIX allows both (it doesn't require both), whereas Win32 specifies only global scheduling. As it turns out, system contention scope scheduling is invariably what the programmer really wants on many platforms (e.g., Solaris). It provides the most predictable behavior and best performance.

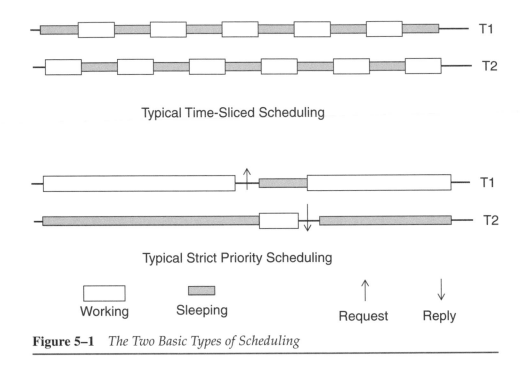

Typical Time-Sliced Scheduling

Typical Strict Priority Scheduling

Working	Sleeping	Request	Reply

Figure 5–1 *The Two Basic Types of Scheduling*

The entire subject of scheduling is fraught with problems. In all operating systems, both the scheduling of threads and the scheduling of processes themselves have problems that have never been resolved to everyone's satisfaction. In brief, there are two basic situations in which we find ourselves (see Figure 5–1).

The first case (the *independent* case) occurs when two processes (or threads) are running almost completely independently—neither ever has anything it wants from the other, and both would happily chew up every CPU cycle they could get. For example, consider two developers working on different projects on the same machine. Time slicing is necessary for both of them to get a fair share of the machine.

The other situation (the *dependent* case) occurs when the two processes depend directly upon each other. One process needs another to perform some task before it can continue—a text editor cannot do anything until the file system has delivered files to it to work on, and the file system has nothing to do until the text editor requests some services from it. In such a case, time slicing is of no use at all.

In Figure 5–1 we show two independent threads being time sliced and two dependent threads that require some resource. In the second case, T1 is allowed to run as long as it wants to. It could run forever if only it didn't need to exchange that resource with T2. A real machine is typically faced with both situations all the time, along with the judgments of users and system administrators as to the relative importance of the various processes.

We will not attempt to solve these problems here. Suffice it to say that the use of these techniques results in less than perfect scheduling algorithms, but we have done fairly well with them over the past 30–40 years nonetheless.

We will now go into some of the gory details of how scheduling is done. The major point we make is that most threaded programs are of the dependent case above, and scheduling is accomplished mainly by dependence upon the program's need for synchronization.

Process Contention Scope

PCS scheduling is done by the threads library. The library chooses which unbound thread will be put on which LWP. The scheduling of the LWP is (of course) still global and independent of the local scheduling. Although this does mean that unbound threads are subject to a funny, two-tiered scheduling architecture, in practice you can ignore the scheduling of the LWP and deal solely with the local scheduling algorithm.

There are four ways to cause an active thread (say, T1) to context switch. Three of them require that the programmer has written code. These methods are largely identical across all the libraries.

1. **Synchronization**. By far the most common means of being context switched (a wild generalization) is for T1 to request a mutex lock and not get it. If the lock is already being held by T2, then T1 will be placed on the sleep queue, awaiting the lock, thus allowing a different thread to run.

2. **Preemption**. A running thread (T6) does something that causes a higher-priority thread (T2) to become

runnable. In that case, the lowest-priority active thread (T1) will be pre-empted, and T2 will take its place on the LWP. The ways of causing this to happen include releasing a lock, and changing the priority level of T2 upward or of T1 downward.

3. **Yielding**. If the programmer puts an explicit call to the yield call [`Thread.yield()` `sched_yield()`] in the code that T1 is running, the scheduler will look to see if there is another runnable thread (T2). If there is one, that thread will be scheduled.[6] If there isn't one, T1 will continue to run.

4. **Time slicing.** If the vendor's PCS allows time slicing (like Digital UNIX, unlike Solaris), T1 might simply have its time slice run out and T2 (at the same priority level) would then receive a time slice.

A bit of reflection will show the reader that two of the methods can be executed entirely in user space, with the thread-level context switch requiring about 10 ms on a 167-MHz UltraSPARC. Preemption, however, is a bit more involved and requires a system call to execute (see *Preemption* on page 86).

In actual practice, you, the programmer, will spend very little time thinking about issues of scheduling. When a thread needs a common resource, it uses a lock. If it doesn't get the lock, it blocks, and another thread runs. Sooner or later the owner will release the lock and the first thread will become runnable again.

Priority Levels

The scheduler for unbound threads has a simple algorithm for deciding which thread to run. Each thread has an associated priority number. The runnable threads with the highest priorities get to run. These priorities are *not* adjusted by the JVM. The only way they change is if the programmer writes an explicit call to do so [`thread.setPriority()`]. This priority is an

---

[6]There are no guarantees about the behavior of `yield()`. It is legal for it to do nothing!

integer in Java, with value between MIN_PRIORITY (1) and
MAX_PRIORITY (10).

There are all sorts of details and exceptions related to Java priorities. On Windows NT there are only seven priority levels to
which the ten Java priority levels must be mapped. Native POSIX
libraries that use unbound threads don't necessarily propagate
those priority numbers up to the LWPs. Java does not *guarantee*
any behavior related to priority levels.

By default, Java threads will start with NORM_PRIORITY
(5). You can change that value as you please. We don't give you
any advice on how to choose the value, as we find that we don't
use it much ourselves. You probably won't, either. We are not
aware of any significant programs that set priority levels!

Nonetheless, there are plenty of programmers who love priorities. They carefully raise and lower levels to meet some criteria,
expecting to control the program's behavior closely. They are almost certainly fooling themselves. Don't use priorities.

Scheduling States

The natural consequence of the discussion above on scheduling is
the existence of four scheduling states for threads. (The astute
reader who has already figured this all out may skip this section.)

A thread may be in one of the following states:

Active: It is on an LWP.[7]

Runnable: It is ready to run, but there just aren't enough
LWPs for it to get one. It will remain here until an active thread
loses its LWP or until a new LWP is created.

Sleeping: It is waiting for a synchronization variable.

Suspended: A call to the suspension function
[thread.suspend()] has been made. It will remain in this
state until another thread calls the resume function on it.

---

[7]Whether or not the LWP is on a CPU is irrelevant.

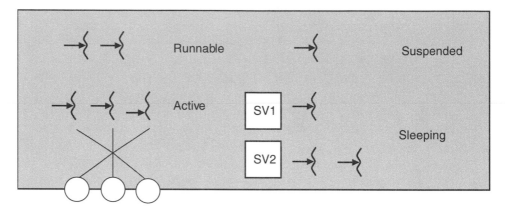

Figure 5–2 *Some Process Contention Scope Threads in Various States*

Zombie: It is a dead thread and is waiting for its resources to be collected. (This is not a recognizable state to the user, although it might appear in the debugger. This state does not appear in Java threads at all, although it may appear in the underlying native library. It is sometimes useful to use this concept for explaining behavior.)

Figure 5–2 shows a process with eight PCS threads and three LWPs. Five of the threads want to run, but only three can do so. They will continue to run as long as they want or until one of them makes a threads library call that changes conditions, as noted above. The two runnable threads are of equal or lower priority than the three active ones, of course. Should one of the sleeping or stopped threads be made runnable, whether they actually become active will be a question of priority levels. If the newly runnable thread is of higher priority than one of the active threads, it will displace the lowest-priority active thread. If it is of lower priority than all of them, it won't. If it is of *equal* priority, we make no guarantees. You should not write a program assuming anything about this condition. (It would actually be very difficult to write one that did depend on this.)

The LWPs that are to be used by the unbound threads are set up in a pool and are identical in all respects. This setup allows any thread to execute on any of the LWPs in this pool. You should not change any attributes of these LWPs (e.g., scheduling class, "nice" level), as you don't know which thread will be running on

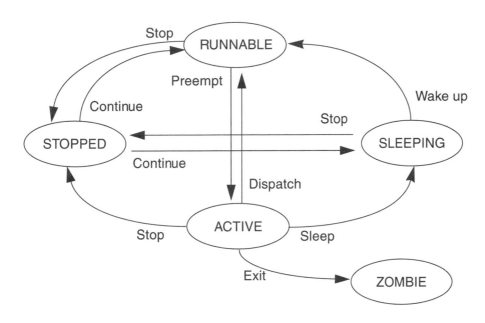

Figure 5–3 *Simplified View of Thread State Transitions*

them at any given time. Should you want a special LWP, you'd want a bound thread to run on it (not an option in Java).

When an unbound thread exits or goes to sleep (Figure 5–3), and there are no more runnable threads, the LWP that was running the thread goes to sleep in the kernel. When another thread becomes runnable, the idling LWP wakes up and runs it. Should an LWP remain idle for an extended length of time (5 minutes for Solaris 2.5), the threads library may kill it. You will never notice this. Should your application become more active later, more LWPs will be created for you.

When a bound thread blocks on a synchronization variable, its LWP must also stop running. The LWP does so by making a system call that puts it to sleep. When the synchronization variable is released, the thread must be awakened. This is done by making a system call to wake up the LWP. The LWP then wakes up, and the thread resumes running. Much the same thing happens when a locally scheduled thread blocks on a cross-process synchronization variable. In both cases the LWP goes to sleep in the kernel until the synchronization variable is released. This description is pretty much the same for Win32. Only the names are different.

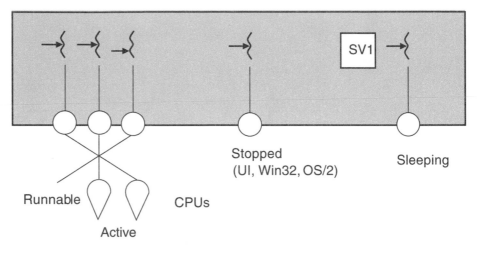

Figure 5–4   *Some System Contention Scope Threads in Various States*

System Contention Scope

An SCS thread is nothing more than a typical thread that is permanently bound to a specific LWP. The LWP runs only that thread and that thread runs only on that LWP. This means that this thread is never merely runnable, waiting for an LWP. It is always on an LWP, and that LWP is either sleeping on a synchronization variable, suspended, or active (Figure 5–4).

Win32 has only SCS scheduling, and it is handled completely by the normal kernel scheduler. There are a number of different scheduling classes for the different operating systems (batch, time sharing, interactive, realtime, etc.), which we will touch on later. Suffice it to say that with a SCS thread, you can set the kernel-level scheduling class and priority using the process-level API.

The primary conclusion in both cases is that you should see no particular differences between locally and globally scheduled threads as long as there are sufficient LWPs.

Context Switching

Context switching is a rather complicated concept and has many details of significance, so it is difficult to explain in just a few paragraphs. Nonetheless, we shall try. If you don't feel that you have a firm grasp of how it works, you should go bug a friend to explain all of the subtle nuances. Threads or no threads, you should understand this concept thoroughly.

A context switch is the act of taking an active thread off its LWP and replacing it with another one that is waiting to run. This concept extends to LWPs and traditional processes on CPUs also. We will describe context switching in traditional, process/CPU terms.

The state of a computation is embodied in the computer's registers—the program counter, stack pointer, and general registers—along with the MMU's (memory management unit) page tables. These, plus the memory contents, disk files, and other peripherals, tell you everything about the computer. When it's time to context switch two traditional processes, the register state must be changed to reflect the new process that we wish to run. It works approximately like this:

- All the current registers are stored into the process structure for P1.
- All the stored register values from the process structure for P2 are loaded into the CPU's registers.
- The CPU returns to user mode, and voila! P1 is context switched out and P2 is context switched in and running.

All the other data in the process structure (working directory, open files, etc.) remain in the process structure where it belongs. If a process wishes to use that data, it will reference it from the process structure. When two LWPs in the same process context switch, all of the above happens in much the same fashion.

Notice also that a context switch must be done by the CPU itself. One CPU cannot do the context switch for another. CPU1 can send an interrupt to CPU2 to let it know that it should context switch, but CPU1 cannot actually change the registers in CPU2. CPU2 has to want to context switch.

Finally, context switching for PCS threads involves much the same procedure. A thread (T1) decides that it has to context switch (perhaps it is going to sleep on a synchronization variable). It enters the scheduler. The CPU stores its register state into the thread structure for T1, then it loads the registers from another thread

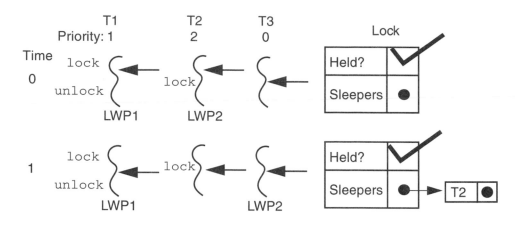

Figure 5–5 *How a Context Switch Works*

(T2) into the CPU and returns from the scheduler as T2. No system calls need be involved. It is possible that it happens completely in user space and is very fast.

It may be a bit unclear what the role of the LWP is when threads context switch. The role is invisible. The threads save and restore CPU registers with no regard to the LWP at all. The threads scheduler does not do anything to the LWP structure. Should the operating system decide to context switch the LWP, it will do so completely independently of what the LWP happens to be doing at that time. Should two threads be in the middle of context switching when the kernel decides to context switch the LWP, it still makes no difference. The threads' context switch will just take a little longer.

In Figure 5–5 we describe how context switching works for POSIX threads. (Java threads work exactly the same way, but the Java vocabulary for describing locks is a bit less clear for our purpose.) Three threads are runnable on two LWPs at time 0. Thread T1 holds a lock. Clearly, T1 and T2 will be the active threads, as they have the highest priorities. We'll imagine that T1 is on LWP1, T2 on LWP2 , and T3 on the runnable queue.

Approaching time 1, T2 attempted to lock the lock and failed. So, as part of the code for `pthread_mutex_lock()`, T2 put itself onto the sleep queue for the lock, then called the scheduler. The scheduler code ran (still as T2) and decided to run T3. Next,

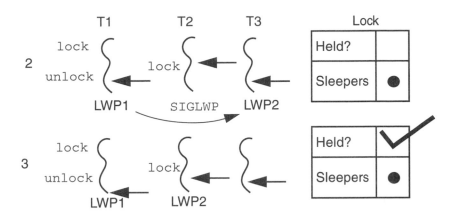

Figure 5–6 *How a Context Switch Works*

the scheduler stored away the CPU registers into T2's thread structure and loaded the registers from T3's. (At this particular instant, it's not defined which thread is running on LWP2, and it's not important, either.) At time 1, the scheduler code finishes its work and returns with T3 running on LWP2.

At time 2 (see Figure 5–6), T1 releases the mutex. As part of the code for `pthread_mutex_unlock()`, it takes the first thread off the lock's sleep queue (T2) and makes it runnable and releases the mutex. Finally, it calls the scheduler.

The scheduler notices that there's a runnable thread (T2) that has a higher priority than one of the active threads (T3). The scheduler then sends a signal in order to preempt the thread on LWP2. Now the scheduler has done its work. It returns, and T1 continues to run. This is the state of the world at time 2 (with a signal pending).

For some short period of time, T3 continues to run. When the signal arrives from the kernel, T3 is interrupted and forced to run the signal handler. That, in turn, calls the scheduler, which context switches T3 out and T2 in. And that's it! At time 3, T1 and T2 are both active, T3 is runnable, and T2 holds the lock.

There are a couple things to notice here. There's no guarantee that T2 will get the lock. It's possible that T1 could have reclaimed it; it's even possible that T3 could have snatched it away just before the signal arrived. If either of these events occurred, the net result is that a bit of time would have been wasted, but they would both work perfectly. This scenario works as described, irrespective of the number of CPUs. If this runs on a multiprocessor, it will work exactly the same way as it does on a uniprocessor, only faster.

In this example we have described two context switches. The first one was voluntary—T2 wanted to go to sleep. The second was involuntary (preemptive)—T3 was perfectly happy and only context switched because it was forced to.

Preemption

Preemption is the process of rudely kicking a thread off its LWP (or an LWP off its CPU) so that some other thread can run instead. (This is what happened at time 3.) For SCS threads, preemption is handled in the kernel by the kernel scheduler. For PCS threads, it is done by the thread library. Preemption is accomplished by sending the LWP in question a signal specifically invented for that purpose.[8] The LWP then runs the handler, which in turn realizes that it must context switch its current thread and does so. (You will notice that one LWP is able to direct a signal to another specific LWP in the case in which they are both in the same process. You should never do this yourself. You may send signals to threads but never to LWPs.)

Preemption requires a system call, so the kernel has to send the signal, which takes time. Finally, the LWP, to which the signal is directed, must receive it and run the signal handler. Context switching by preemption is involuntary and is more expensive than context switching by "voluntary" means. (You will never have to think about this while programming.)

The discussion of context switching and preemption above is accurate for all the various libraries. It is accurate for threads on LWPs and for LWPs (or traditional processes) on CPUs, substituting the word *interrupt* for *signal*.

---

[8]In Solaris 2.5 and below, it was SIGLWP. This is a kernel-defined signal that requires a system call to implement. Digital UNIX uses a slightly different mechanism, but the results are the same.

How Many LWPs?

The UNIX98 threads library has a call, `pthread_setconcurrency()`, which tells the library how many LWPs you'd like to have available for PCS threads. If you set the number to ten and you have nine threads, then when you create a tenth thread, you'll get a tenth LWP. When you create an eleventh thread, you won't get another LWP. Now the caveat. This is a *hint* to the library as to what you'd like. You may not get what you ask for! You might even get more. Your program must run correctly without all the LWPs you want, although it may run faster if it gets them. In practice, this becomes an issue only when your program needs a lot of LWPs.

You've got the power, but how do you use it wisely? The answer is totally application-dependent, but we do have some generalities. (N.B.: *Generalities*. If you need a highly tuned application, you've got to do the analysis and experimentation yourself.) We assume a dedicated machine.

- If your program is completely CPU bound, one LWP per CPU will give you maximum processing power. Presumably, you'll have the same number of threads.
- If your program is highly CPU bound *and* you do some I/O, one LWP per CPU and enough to cover all simultaneous blocking system calls[9] is called for.
- If your program is only I/O bound, you'll want as many LWPs as simultaneous blocking system calls.

How to Get Those LWPs in Java

And now we get to the specifics. This is the one area where things get very implementation and platform dependent. This is also an issue that has aroused great debate in the halls of

---

[9]Blocking system calls include all calls to the usual system calls such as `read()`, but any thread that blocks on a cross-process synchronization variable should also be counted. Bound threads are independent of this, as they each have their own LWP.

comp.programming.threads. Voices have been raised, enormous volumes of argument have been written, veritable fisticuffs have been exchanged over this!

First let's consider what we really want from our scheduler. We want all of our runnable threads to run as much as possible. We want to make as many blocking system calls as we feel like making, and we want them to execute concurrently.

One implementational technique for getting this effect is to use bound threads. Another is to ensure that the library creates a sufficient number of LWPs and guarantees that the runnable threads will be time sliced.

In Windows NT there is no issue with the number of LWPs available for a Java program. NT uses bound threads for everything, so you get all the LWP equivalents you need. Digital UNIX implements its library in such a fashion that you get one "virtual processor" (LWP equivalent) for each actual CPU and one more for every outstanding I/O request. So there are no such problems with Digital UNIX.

If you are running on a system that implements only PCS scheduling for Java threads (e.g., Solaris) there is no portable mechanism for specifying how many LWPs you'd like. Moreover, it is possible that you will want more LWPs than the system will give you automatically. This is one of those (very few) unfortunate places where the default is not what you want and you are forced to make a call to native code.

In Solaris you are provided with only one LWP by default. If all the LWPs in a process are blocked, waiting for I/O, Solaris will add another LWP if needed. This ameliorates the problem partially but still does not provide the full complement of LWPs if you either have multiple CPUs or don't make enough blocking calls. In most typical cases you will not get as many LWPs as you'd like. In Solaris, you are forced to make a native call to `pthread_setconcurrency()` to obtain the "expected" level of kernel concurrency. Obviously, this is not a good thing and makes a mess of your 100% pure Java program, but it is necessary for most high-performance MT programs. The technique for doing this is straightforward and shown in *Making a Native Call to pthread_setconcurrency()* on page 385.

Changing Scheduling Parameters for LWPs

Just because a thread is bound to an LWP does not imply that the LWP is going to be scheduled on a CPU immediately. Depending upon the nature of your application requirements, you may need to alter the kernel-level scheduling priority of that LWP. If you need merely to ensure that it gets a CPU within a second, then relying upon the normal time-slicing scheduler is probably sufficient.

nice()

If response is required on the order of 100 ms, the default may be sufficient, but it may not should there be a lot of contention for the CPU. In this case, simply raising the time-sharing class priority of the LWP is probably sufficient. The UNIX system call `nice()` will do this for you. Basically what `nice()` will do is add (or subtract) a fixed priority number to the level calculated by the kernel for an LWP, effectively making the LWP in question more "important" and ensuring that it gets the CPU when it wants it. In UNIX98, `nice()` is defined to act on the entire process. It is entirely implementation dependent and only gives you some vague control. In any case, this technique cannot be used with Java, as there is no way to bind a thread to any particular LWP.

Realtime LWPs

It's when you require response in the 2–100 ms range that things get interesting. You will need to put the LWP into the realtime scheduling class. You do all the typical realtime tricks—no blocking system calls, probably no I/O,[10] no paging (you'll need to lock down all the memory that your thread will use: functions, stack, data.), etc. ("Etc." means that there is plenty more involved that we haven't thought about, but that you'd better. Realtime

---

[10]For I/O, you'd typically set up the buffers in the realtime thread but then allow a normal thread to execute the I/O call on those buffers.

processing is a tricky thing; be very careful!) Java does not have realtime scheduling classes.

Avoid Realtime

You might require a realtime thread when you have the undivided attention of a user and are doing constant updating (e.g., mouse tracking, video or audio playback) or when you are doing machine feedback and control (e.g., autonomous vehicle navigation, robotics). Other instances include when you are doing realtime data collection with analysis.

You might think that you need a realtime thread, but don't, when you update displays with the *divided* attention of a human being (if you're 100 ms late in seeing the latest from the stock ticker, no big deal). *Avoid using the realtime class if you possibly can*.

Allocation Domains

POSIX recognizes the desire of some programmers for closer control over the scheduling of LWPs onto CPUs. Unfortunately, there is little convergence on the methods of doing so by the vendors, so there is little that POSIX can say about it. Basically, POSIX defines allocation domains, which are sets of CPUs. The programmer then specifies that certain LWPs are allowed to execute on the CPUs in the chosen domains. All of these functions are implementation specific.

Do allocation domains really gain you anything? In certain realtime applications, yes. Otherwise, probably not. Our *opinion* is that you are more likely to bog your program down with excessive complexity than to improve it if you use them in most programs. Java has no interface for allocation domains.

Binding LWPs to Processors

It's often possible to ensure that a given LWP will always run on a selected processor. It's also possible to ensure that a given LWP will run to the exclusion of all other LWPs in all processes by putting it into the realtime class. Doing both effectively binds the processor to the LWP as long as the LWP wants to run.

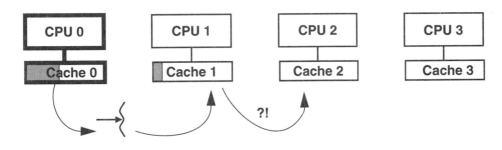

Figure 5–7 *Processor Affinity*

The question of when these things are useful has a somewhat tricky answer, and it changes with new operating system releases. If schedulers worked perfectly and had ESP, you would never bind an LWP to a CPU. In practice, it's *sometimes* otherwise. Java has no interface for binding LWPs to CPUs.

Happiness Is a Warm Cache

The main issue is that of cache memory latency. The current batch of PCs and workstations have external caches of significant size (typically, 1–4 megabytes). To replace the contents of such a cache completely can take a very long time (upwards of 100 ms, depending upon individual architecture). If an LWP is running on CPU 0 and it is context switched off for a short time, the vast majority of that cache will still be valid. So, it would be much better for that LWP to go back onto CPU 0.

The normal schedulers in the various OSs endeavor to do precisely that via *processor affinity* (Figure 5–7). Solaris, for example, will delay running an LWP on CPU 1, should that LWP previously have been on CPU 0. If CPU 0 becomes available relatively quickly (currently, 30 ms—three clock ticks), that LWP will be put back on CPU 0. If CPU 0 does not become available within that time frame, the LWP will be scheduled on whatever CPU is available.

We know of some instances where it has proven valuable to do processor binding of LWPs. If you are considering this, test first. *You should not even consider processor binding unless you already know that there's a clear problem of this nature.* And you must be aware that everything may be different on a different architecture or different OS release. The details of these issues are well beyond the scope of this book, and we wish to caution you that it is rare for anyone to have to address these issues.

Java Scheduling Summary

Java was designed for writing portable application code across many different types of systems—various types of UNIX (Solaris, SCO, AIX, Ultrix), Win32, Macintosh, OS/400, MVS, realtime systems, etc. Consequently, when it came to defining the threading and scheduling model to be used in Java, it needed to be one that could be supported relatively easily on all platforms. If we look at what all the primary Java platforms have in common with regard to thread scheduling, we find almost nothing! Other than having threads and thus needing to schedule them, all the systems are very different. This resulted in Java defining a very loose scheduling model:

- All Java threads have a priority and the scheduler will generally give preference to executing the highest-priority runnable thread (i.e., it is notionally priority preemptive). However, there is no guarantee that the highest-priority thread is always running.
- A system may apply time slicing to threads, but it is not required to. If time slicing does exist, whether it applies across all threads or only within priority levels, is not defined.

Given such a loose specification for scheduling, how can we write portable code? The answer is to never make optimistic assumptions about scheduling behavior but always assume the worst:

- You must assume that threads could be interleaved at any point in time.
- You must not require that threads be interleaved at some time. If you need to guarantee that different threads make progress, you will have to explicitly code things such that progress can occur.

How Many Threads in Java?

The Java spec does not state how many threads an implementation must support. The actual number is completely implementation dependent. Presumably, the number will be the same as the limit on the underlying native library. For JVMs based on POSIX threads (most UNIX implementations, Linux, VMS, AS/400), this will be a minimum of 64. The actual maximum is undefined, but probably at least 1000. On Solaris, for example, the limitation is strictly the amount of virtual memory you have, hence about 4000 threads on 32-bit Solaris, assuming minimal program and data size and the default 500k stack. On Windows NT the number of threads is more limited, as small as 64. (See NT documentation for details.) One implementation, BulletTrain from Natural Bridge Inc., actually builds a two-level model on top of NT, allowing Java to have more than 8000 threads simultaneously.

If you want more than a few hundred threads, be careful! You are probably doing something wrong.

When Should You Care About Scheduling?

There are times when you will want to deal with scheduling directly, but those times are few and far between for any of the libraries. If you find yourself thinking about this a lot, you're probably doing something wrong. Some examples follow.

It is possible to design a server program where each thread runs forever, picking up requests off the net, processing them, and returning for more. It is possible for an unbound thread to get starve for CPU time in this situation. In this case you should add LWPs for the purpose of effecting a time-slicing scheme.

A program that used a set of threads to produce data and another single thread to push that data out to some device in realtime needs to ensure that the output thread runs when it needs to. Here a higher priority would be in order. In the Delphax/Uniq case study (see *Vendor's Threads Pages* on page 410), where they built a high-speed printer driver, they found it worthwhile to make a bound thread and put the LWP into the realtime class.

In spite of all the attention we just paid to explaining it, you will not write much (if any!) code to deal with it. If the library writers did their job well, everything will "just work," without any effort on your part. In most MT programs, the different threads all depend upon one another, and it doesn't really matter which one runs first. Sooner or later, the running threads will need something from the other threads, and they will be forced to sleep until those other threads have produced that something.

APIs Used in This Chapter

The Class java.lang.Thread

yield

```
public static void yield()
```

This causes the current thread to give up its LWP (or CPU) to another thread at the same or a higher priority level (if any). It is legal for `yield()` to do nothing, so you must not rely on it.

Reference: Chapter 5.

Comment: You probably will never use this function.

setPriority getPriority

```
public final void setPriority(int newPriority)
       throws SecurityException, IllegalArgumentException
public final int getPriority()
```

These change (return) the priority level of the thread. The priority level must be between `MIN_PRIORITY` and `MAX_PRIORITY` if the thread group to which this thread belongs may set a lower bound than `MAX_PRIORITY`.

Reference: Chapter 5.

Comment: You probably will never use these functions.

suspend

```
public final void suspend()
```

> This causes the thread to stop running and wait until you call `thread.resume()`. Because suspension is asynchronous, you have no idea what the target thread was doing when you suspended it. For example, it may hold some locks that your other threads need. This makes it virtually impossible to use.
>
> *Reference:*   Chapter 5.
>
> *Comment:*   It has been deprecated in Java 2.

resume

```
public final void resume()
```

> This causes a suspended thread to resume.
>
> *Reference:*   Chapter 5.
>
> *Comment:*   It has been deprecated in Java 2.

MIN_PRIORITY MAX_PRIORITY NORM_PRIORITY

```
public final static int MIN_PRIORITY = 1;
public final static int MAX_PRIORITY = 10;
public final static int NORM_PRIORITY = 5;
```

> These are the minimum, maximum, and default priorities for normal threads.
>
> *Reference:*   Chapter 5.
>
> *Comment:*   You will probably never use these functions.

Summary

Several scheduling models exist, most of which are overkill. For all but truly exceptional programs, the normal vendor scheduler does a fine job and that, along with proper synchronization, means that we don't have to worry about scheduling at all. Realtime folks are on their own.

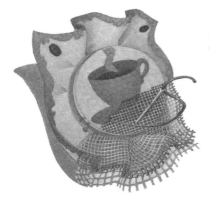

Chapter 6

Synchronization

- ▼ SYNCHRONIZATION ISSUES
- ▼ SYNCHRONIZATION VARIABLES
- ▼ APIs USED IN THIS CHAPTER
- ▼ THE CLASS JAVA.LANG.OBJECT
- ▼ THE CLASS EXTENSIONS.SEMAPHORE
- ▼ THE CLASS EXTENSIONS.MUTEX
- ▼ THE CLASS EXTENSIONS.CONDITIONVAR

In which the reader is led on a hunt for the intimidating synchronization variable and discovers that it is not actually as frightening as had been thought. Programs illustrating the basic use of the POSIX and Java primitives are shown.

Synchronization Issues

To write any kind of concurrent program, you must be able to synchronize the different threads reliably. Failure to do so will result in all sorts of ugly, messy bugs. Without synchronization, two threads will start to change some data at the same time; one will overwrite the other. To avoid this disaster, threads must reliably coordinate their actions.

In Code Example 6–1, your bank has one thread running, calculating the dividends on your bank account. If you're like me, that's about $10 @ 1%, giving a `newBalance` of $10.10. At exactly this instant, the end of the month arrives and a second thread decides to deposit your paycheck. As a well-paid, highly skilled programmer, that's probably about $20,000. The thread deposits the check and updates your account to $20,010. One microsecond later the first thread completes its work, overwriting your bank balance with $10.10. Too bad.

Thread 1	Thread 2
| ```
temp = your.bankBalance;
dividend = temp * InterestRate;
newBalance = dividend + temp;
your.bankBalance = newBalance;
``` | ```
temp = your.bankBalance;
newBalance = deposit + temp;
your.bankBalance = newBalance;
``` |

Code Example 6–1 *Why Synchronization Is Necessary*

Atomic Actions and Atomic Instructions

Implementation of synchronization requires the existence of an atomic *test and set* instruction in hardware. This is true for both uniprocessor and multiprocessor machines. Because threads can be preempted at any time, between any two instructions, you must have such an instruction. Sure, there might be only a 10-ns window for disaster to strike, but you still want to avoid it.

A test and set instruction tests (or just loads into a register) a word from memory and sets it to some value (typically, 1), all in one instruction, with no possibility of anything happening in between the two halves (e.g., an interrupt or a write by a different CPU). If the value of the target word *is* 0, it gets set to 1 and you are considered to have ownership of the lock. If it already is 1, it gets set to 1 (i.e., no change) and you don't have ownership. All synchronization is based upon the existence of this instruction.

In SPARC machines, the test and set instruction is `ldstub` ("load and store unsigned byte"), which loads a byte into a register while setting that byte to all ones. Code Example 6–2 shows how it can be used to create a basic lock. The important thing to understand here is that no matter how many different threads on how many different CPUs call `ldstub` at the same time, only one of them will get ownership. Exactly how the `go_to_sleep` function works is unimportant. Indeed, even if it did nothing at all and just jumped right back to `try_again`, the locking code would still work (see *Spin Locks* on page 148). Notice that there is no guarantee that a thread that goes to sleep will get the lock when it wakes up.

```
try_again:    ldstub address -> register
              compare register, 0
              branch_equal got_it
              call go_to_sleep
              jump try_again
got_it:       return
```

Code Example 6–2   *Pseudo-assembly Code for the Mutual Exclusion Lock*

Other types of atomic instructions are used on other machines, most of which are logically equivalent. The one type of instruction that is substantially different is the *compare and swap* instruction, which compares one word of main memory with a register and swaps the contents of that word with a second register when equal. This type of instruction allows some other types of atomic actions which are qualitatively distinct (see *LoadLocked/StoreConditional and Compare and Swap* on page 354), giving significantly superior performance for specific situations.

Critical Sections

A critical section is a section of code that must be allowed to complete atomically with no interruption that affects its completion.

We create critical sections by locking a lock (as in Code Example 6–2), manipulating the data, then releasing the lock afterward. Such things as incrementing a counter or updating a record in a database need to be critical sections. Other things may go on at the same time, and the thread that is executing in the critical section may even lose its processor, but no other thread may enter the critical section. Should another thread want to execute that same critical section, it will be forced to wait until the first thread finishes.

Critical sections are typically made as short as possible and often carefully optimized because they can significantly affect the concurrency of the program. As with all the code in this book, we rely upon the programmer to obey the rules for using critical sections. There is no external enforcement that prevents a sloppy programmer from manipulating data without holding the proper lock.

Lock Your Shared Data!

All shared data must be protected by locks. Failure to do so will result in truly ugly bugs. Keep in mind that all means *all*. Data structures that are passed to other threads and global variables are the obvious examples.[1] All data structures that can be accessed by multiple threads are included. *Static variables* are included.

Statics in Java are just global variables that are associated with a specific class. It was somewhat convenient to use these in the single-threaded programs of yore, but in MT programs they are disasters waiting to strike. You should reconsider your use of statics very carefully. If you do use 'em, lock 'em first!

Synchronization Variables

To provide synchronization, a system includes special data structures, and a set of functions manipulate them. POSIX defines three *synchronization variables* and the function `pthread_join()` to provide this functionality. (UNIX98

---

[1]It is, of course, possible to have global variables that are not shared, but this would be rather unusual. Be very careful if you think you have one. If you're wrong, you're going to be unhappy when something breaks.

makes it four.) Win32 provides synchronization variables of a slightly different nature. Java provides the same functionality by encapsulating synchronization variables within every object. These synchronization variables are manipulated by means of a keyword (synchronized), thread.join(), and several methods on Object. In all the libraries, these provide the only reliable means of coordinating the interactions of your threads. There are other tricky things you can do to coordinate your threads, but they won't work reliably because the hardware is designed assuming that you will be using synchronization variables (see *Bus Architectures* on page 346).

There are two basic things you want to do. The first is that you want to protect shared data. This is what locks do. The second is that you want to prevent threads from running when there's nothing for them to do. You don't want them spinning, wasting time. This is what semaphores, condition variables, wait sets, join(), barriers, etc., are for. Once again, we will describe how the simpler primitives in POSIX work, then show how Java maps onto them.

Mutexes

The mutual exclusion lock is the simplest and most primitive synchronization variable. It provides a single, absolute owner for the section of code (thus a critical section) that it brackets between the calls to pthread_mutex_lock() and pthread_mutex_unlock() (Code Example 6–3). The first thread that locks the mutex gets ownership, and any subsequent attempts to lock it will fail, causing the calling thread to go to sleep. When the owner unlocks it, one of the sleepers will be awakened, made runnable, and given the *chance* to obtain ownership. *It is possible that some other thread will call pthread_mutex_lock() and get ownership before the newly awakened thread does.* This is perfectly correct behavior and must not affect the correctness of your program.[2] It's unusual to write code that would be affected by this behavior (see *FIFO Mutexes* on page 145).

---

[2]In the absurd case of two threads trying to increment a counter, it is possible that only one of them will ever run, even though the program was written "correctly." The probability of T1 failing to get the mutex 1000 times in a row is normally tiny and is only of interest to the rarest of non-realtime programs.

POSIX	Win32	Java
pthread_mutex_lock(m)	WaitForSingleObject(m)	synchronized(o) {
...	...	...
pthread_mutex_unlock(m)	ReleaseMutex(m)	}

Code Example 6–3   *Using Mutexes in the Various Libraries*

In Figure 6–1, three threads all need a mutex. They have different priorities ("P:"), which determine the order in which they go onto the sleep queue. The threads have requested the lock in the order T1, T2, T3. As the first to try, T1 owns the lock, and T3 will be awakened as soon as T1 releases it, even though T2 requested the lock before T3.

Note that the mutex *doesn't* know who owns it.[3] Because mutexes protect sections of code,[4] it is not legal for one thread to lock a mutex and for another thread to unlock it. Depending upon the library implementation, this might not result in a runtime error, but it is illegal. The locking may occur in one function while the unlocking occurs in another; locks may overlap in their use (lock 2, unlock 1, lock 3, unlock 2, etc.), but under no circumstances should you ever release a lock from the wrong thread. If you think you need this kind of behavior, you should

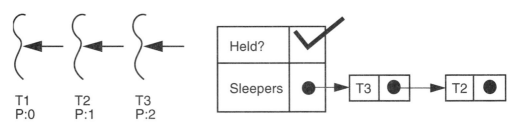

T1   T2   T3
P:0   P:1   P:2

Figure 6–1   *Mutex with Several Threads Sleeping on It*

---

[3]POSIX doesn't prevent a mutex from recording its owner, it just doesn't require it. Some implementations can be much faster if ownership is not recorded.

[4]To be more precise, a mutex protects itself. We trick it into protecting sections of code by placing the lock and unlock functions judiciously. By restricting data access to those functions, we manage to have mutexes protect our shared data, which is what we really want.

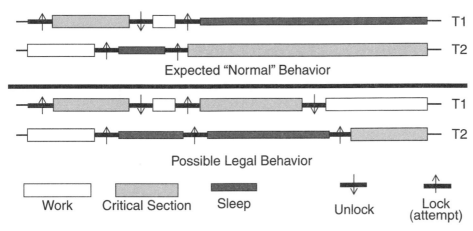

Figure 6–2 *Execution Graph of the Operation of a Mutex*

(1) think really hard about what you're doing, and (2) look at semaphores. This problem does not arise with Java synchronized sections, but we will be implementing a `Mutex` class a bit later for which this caveat applies.

In the execution graph for mutexes shown in Figure 6–2, we see the timing behavior of locks. The graph is shown for two threads on two CPUs, but for a uniprocessor the behavior will be identical, save that there will be gaps in each time line as the CPU context switches. Those gaps will affect neither the correctness of the code nor the probability of encountering race conditions in correctly locked code (see *Race Conditions* on page 168).

Figure 6–3 and Code Example 6–4 show the proper way to use mutexes while putting items onto a list (as thread 1 is doing) and taking them off (thread 2). Should two threads call `remove()` at the same time, one of them will get mutex ownership while the other will have to go to sleep. When the mutex is released, the sleeper will be awakened, but it is possible that either thread 1 or a third thread could slip in at just the right instant and get the lock. In this case the new thread, instead of the sleeper, would remove `Request2` from the list. Presumably all the threads will be executing the same code, so it won't make any difference which thread actually gets to process the request.

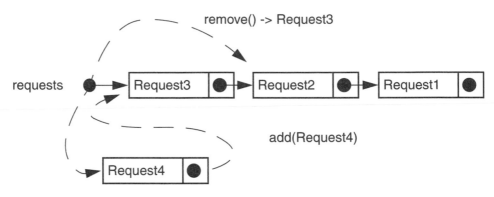

Figure 6–3 *Protecting a Shared List with a Mutex*

Thread 1	**Thread 2**

```
add(request_t *request)
{   pthread_mutex_lock(&lock);
    request->next = requests;
    requests = request;
    pthread_mutex_unlock(&lock);
}
```
```
                        request_t *remove()
                        {   pthread_mutex_lock(&lock);
                            ...sleeping...

                            request = requests;
                            requests = requests->next;
                            pthread_mutex_unlock(&lock)
                            return(request);
                        }
```

Code Example 6–4 *Protecting a Shared List with a Mutex (POSIX)*

The same lock must be used uniformly to protect data. Using one lock to protect the list in add() and a different lock in remove() would be a disaster, of course. Don't do that.

Now let's look at how Java implements mutual exclusion. The computational logic for Java is identical; the coding technique is different. In Java, a block of code marked synchronized will be protected by a mutex.

In Java every object has a mutex associated with it implicitly (Figure 6–4). There is no direct access to this mutex; rather, it is locked and unlocked through the use of synchronized state-

Type: Object   **int**

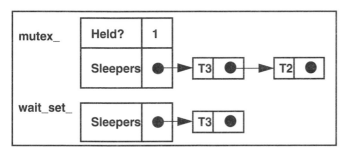

Figure 6–4 *All Objects Have Their Own Mutex and Wait Set*

ments. A synchronized statement has the form shown in Code Example 6–5.

```
synchronized(foo){
    // code to execute with foo's mutex held
}
```

Code Example 6–5 *Synchronized Statement*

When you enter the synchronized statement the mutex belonging to the object referred to by foo will be locked for you, and when you leave the statement, whether normally or via an exception, the mutex will be unlocked for you. Should the mutex already be locked, the thread will block, as with POSIX. This syntax makes it impossible to forget to unlock a mutex but also requires that all uses of mutexes are nested (i.e., you always release mutexes in the reverse order to which you acquire them). Unlike POSIX, in Java there is no defined wakeup order; even priority levels are ignored.

As a shorthand notation we can define a method to be synchronized, which has the same effect as placing the entire body of the method in a synchronized statement using the current object as the object to lock. The two bits of code shown in Code Example 6–6 behave identically.

Explicit Synchronization	Implicit Synchronization
``` public MyClass() { int count=0; void frob() { synchronized (this) { count++; }}} ```	``` public MyClass() { int count=0; void synchronized frob() { count++; }} ```

Code Example 6–6   *Using synchronized in Java*

The mutex that will be used is gotten from the object referenced, either the object the method is running on (for the implicit case) or from the object specifically mentioned (for the explicit case). The class Object (and hence any subclass, that is, every class) has two private instance variables.[5] One is a mutex, the other is a wait set, which we'll discuss soon. Primitive types (int, char, etc.) do not inherit from Object and hence do not have associated mutexes and wait sets.

It is important to realize that the mutex and wait set are per object, not per class; thus two different instances of class Foo will have two different mutexes (see Figure 6–5) and locking one will not protect data used by the other. So the code in Code Example 6–5 is correct because each instance of MyClass will have its own instance of count. If count had been declared to be static, the code would not have worked.

The *class object* itself is a subclass of Object; hence it too has a mutex and wait set. This mutex can be used to protect static data. It is used for static synchronized methods (see Code Example 6–7). The class lock may be used to protect class internals during instance creation, but this should not be an issue unless you're holding onto it for unusually long periods of time. In that case you may wish to use a different object (Code Example 6–8) to protect your static variables (probably not).

---

[5]It may seem rather expensive to allocate a few dozen bytes for every single object, especially when very few mutexes or wait sets ever get used. It would be if they were actually allocated every time. Clever systems programmers avoid this space overhead by a couple of tricks.

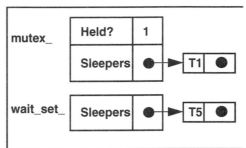

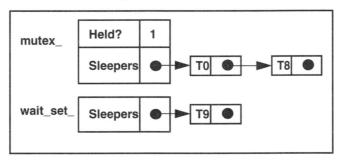

Figure 6–5 *Each Instance Has Its Own Mutex*

```
public class Foo
{   static int count = 0;

    static public synchronized void inc(int i)
    {count = count + i;}
}
```

Code Example 6–7 *Static Synchronized Methods Also Use the Class Lock*

```
public class Foo
{   static int count = 0;
    static Object o = new Object();
```

Code Example 6–8 *You May Use an Unrelated Object to Protect Static Data*

```
      public void inc(int i)
      {synchronized (o){count = count + i;}}
  }
```

Code Example 6–8 *You May Use an Unrelated Object to Protect Static Data (cont.)*

Notice that in Code Example 6–9 we use Foo.class to obtain the class object for Foo. Should you later define Bar, which subclasses Foo, a call to Bar.inc() will of course increment the same count variable as Foo.inc() (static variables are inherited by subclasses) and the lock from the Foo class will be locked, not the lock from Bar. This is, of course, what we want. If we had called getClass() instead of Foo.class, we would have locked the lock for Bar. That would have been a mistake and we would have been using two different locks to protect the same static variable. Don't do that.

```
public class Foo
{   static int count = 0;

    public void inc(int i)
    {synchronized (Foo.class){count = count + i;}}   // cf: getClass()
}
```

Code Example 6–9 *You May Use the Class Itself to Protect Static Data*

Now let's look at that shared list example implemented in Java (Code Example 6–10). No surprise, the code looks virtually identical to the POSIX code. (The two methods are part of a class Workpile, which we'll see a bit later.)

Thread 1   **Thread 2**

```
synchronized void add(Request r) {

    r.next = requests;              synchronized Request remove() {
    requests = r
}                                       ...sleeping...
```

Code Example 6–10 *Protecting a Shared List with a Mutex (Java)*

```
}
                                    r = requests;
                                    requests = requests.next;
                               }
                               return(r);
                          }
```

Code Example 6–10   *Protecting a Shared List with a Mutex (Java) (cont.)*

For the (rare) situation when you do not want to go to sleep, a trylock function is included in POSIX and Win32. In POSIX, `pthread_mutex_trylock()` returns 0 if you get the lock and `EBUSY` if you don't. (Win32 functions have timeouts for the same purpose.) If you get `EBUSY`, you'll have to figure out something else to do, as entering the critical section anyway would be highly antisocial. This function is used very rarely, so if you think you want it, look very carefully at what you're doing![6] [See *Making malloc() More Concurrent* on page 267.] There is no such functionality in Java. This is not a particular problem, as Java does not address itself to the kinds of low-level, realtime problems that `trylock` is useful for.

It is important to realize that although locks are used to protect data, what they *really* do is to prevent more than one thread from running the section of code they bracket (assuming that the same mutex is being used). There's nothing that forces another programmer (who writes another function that uses the same data) to lock his code—nothing but good programming practice.

Moreover, there is no automatic connection between the object's lock and the object's instance variables. Although it seems obvious that one would use the lock from `object1` to protect the instance variables of `object1`, it isn't a requirement and there are situations where you want to use the lock from `object2` to protect the data of `object1`! Nonetheless, it is a nice feature of object-oriented programming for the lock to be encapsulated with the data, making it that much less likely for you to make a mistake.

---

[6]We apologize if these warnings seem a bit much. We realize that *you* understand the issues involved. We just want to make it clear for that other programmer.

Win32 provides a mutex (which is a kernel object), along with a *critical section,*[7] which is more like a POSIX mutex. Win32 mutexes are recursive—meaning that the same thread can lock the mutex multiple times. Java-synchronized sections are also recursive. We'll discuss this in more detail in *Recursive Mutexes* on page 147.

Semaphores

In the nineteenth century, when trains were still advanced technology and railroad tracks were exotic and expensive, it was common to run single sets of tracks and restrict the trains to travel in only one direction at a time. *Semaphores* were invented to let the trains know if other trains were on the rails at the same time. A semaphore was a vertical pole with a metal flag adjusted to hang at either 45 or 90 degrees to indicate the existence of other trains.

In the 1960s, E. W. Dijkstra, a professor in the Department of Mathematics at the Technological University, Eindhoven, Netherlands, extended this concept to computer science. A *counting semaphore*[8] (a.k.a. *PV semaphore*) is a variable that can increment arbitrarily high but decrement only to zero. A POSIX sem_post() operation (a.k.a. "V"—*verhogen* in Dutch) increments the semaphore, while a sem_wait() (a.k.a. "P"—*proberen te verlagen*) attempts to decrement it. If the semaphore is greater than zero, the operation succeeds; if not, the calling thread must go to sleep until a different thread increments it.

A semaphore is useful for working with "trainlike" objects, that is, what you care about is whether there are either zero objects or more than zero. Buffers and lists that fill and empty are good examples. Semaphores are also useful when you want a thread to wait for something. You can accomplish this by having the thread call sem_wait() on a semaphore with value zero, then have another thread increment the semaphore when you're ready for the thread to continue (Code Example 6–11).

---

[7]We find it is somewhat confusing to use a generic term like *critical section,* which refers to a concept, for the name of a specific synchronization variable.

[8]The word *semaphore* has come to take on other meanings in computer science. System V semaphores, for example, are much more elaborate objects than counting semaphores.

POSIX	**Win32**	**Java** **(from Semaphore.java)**
`sem_wait(&s);`	`WaitForSingleObject(s,...);`	`s.semWait();`
`sem_post(&s);`	`ReleaseSemaphore(s,...);`	`s.semPost();`

Code Example 6–11   *Basic Use of Counting Semaphores*

In Figure 6–6 the semaphore started with a value of zero. The threads have executed their respective operations in the order T1, T2, T3, T4, T5. After T1 executed its `sem_wait()`, it had to wait (as the value was zero). When T2 did the `sem_post()`, T1 was awakened and decremented the value back to zero. T3 did a `sem_post()`, incrementing the value to one. When T4 did its `sem_wait()` it could continue without waiting at all. Finally, T5 called `sem_wait()`, and is still waiting.

Although there is a function `sem_getvalue()` which will return the current value of a semaphore, it is virtually impossible to use correctly because what it returns is what the value of the semaphore *was*. By the time you use the value it returned, it may well have changed. If you find yourself using `sem_getvalue()`, look twice; there's probably a better way to do what you want.

Java does not include semaphores as one of its base classes, but they are easily implemented and we have done so in our exten-

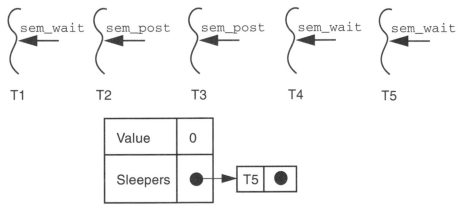

Figure 6–6   *How a Semaphore Operates*

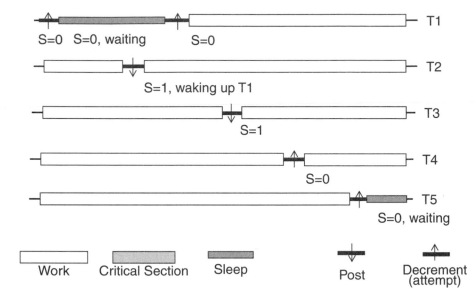

Figure 6–7 *Execution Graph of the Operation of a Semaphore*

sions package. Our Semaphore class behaves exactly as POSIX semaphores do (ignoring UNIX signal issues). Win32 implements counting semaphores with similar definitions.

In the execution graph (Figure 6–7) we see the operation of Code Example 6–11. Notice that when T1's decrement attempt fails, it simply goes to sleep and tries it again later. Another thread could jump in and decrement the value just as thread T1 was waking up, in which case T1 would have to go back to sleep. As with mutexes, this is usually not a problem.

A typical use of semaphores is in Code Example 6–12. This is a producer/consumer example in which one thread is continually receiving requests from the net, which it adds to a list, while the other thread is busy removing items from that list and processing them. It is particularly interesting to notice that the number of items on the list is contained in the semaphore, but the program never actually gets to look at that number. Should the producer place twenty items on the list all at once, the consumer function will be able to call sem_wait() twenty times without blocking. The twenty-first time, the semaphore will be zero, and the consumer will have to wait. Because the critical sections are so small,

the chance of any thread ever blocking on the mutex in
`get_request()` is very small.

In Code Example 6–12, the main things to notice are that
`get_request()` must allocate the memory for the request
structure that will be appended to the list, while
`process_request()` is responsible for freeing it. This code
may safely be run by any number of threads running the producer and any number running the consumer. In no case will a consumer ever attempt to remove a request from an empty list. The
semaphore actually encodes the minimum length of the list.
During the brief moments between the time a producer places a
request onto the list and the time the semaphore is incremented,
the semaphore value is one less than the actual length of the list.
For now, this is fine.

```
producer()
{request_t *request;
 while(TRUE)
    {request = get_request();
     add(request);
     sem_post(&requests_length);
    }
}

consumer()
{request_t *request;
 while(TRUE)
    {SEM_WAIT(&requests_length);
     request = remove();
     process_request(request);
    }
}
```

Code Example 6–12   *Classic Producer/Consumer Example*
(one_queue_problem.c)

The same problem done in Java (Code Example 6–13) is
quite similar again. Unlike C, there will be no issues surrounding allocating and freeing memory (ain't garbage collection
great?).

```
public class Consumer implements Runnable {
    Workpile workpile;
    Server server;

public void run() {
Item item;

while (true) {
    s.semWait();
    item = workpile.remove();
    server.process(item);
}
}


public class Producer implements Runnable {
    Workpile workpile;
    Server server;

public void run() {
Item item;

while (true) {
    item = server.get();
    workpile.add(item);
    s.semPost();
 }
}
}
```

Code Example 6–13   *Classic Producer/Consumer Example (OneQueueProblem)*

The list in both examples is unbounded and may continue to grow longer until memory is exhausted. This is a problem with our example code that must be solved. You should be able to come up with a solution yourself now. We'll get to it a bit later.

Using Barriers to Count Exiting Threads

Sometimes we do want to know when a set of threads have completed their work. One way of doing this is to use a *single barrier* (distinct from the *Barriers* on page 153). Each exiting thread will increment the barrier's value, and the thread waiting

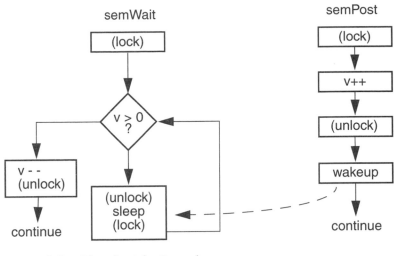

Figure 6–8 *Flowchart for Semaphores*

for them will wait until the value is the number of threads being waited for. This gives a convenient replacement for calling `thread.join()`. We'll be using single barriers regularly for this purpose.

We'll show the code in *Single Barriers* on page 154, but the gist of it is that worker threads call `barrier.barrierPost()` as they exit and the master thread calls `barrier.barrierWait()` (`barrier` has been initialized to the number of worker threads). Thus the master thread will wait until all the workers are done. (We don't actually care exactly when the worker threads exit.)

A Different View of Semaphores

Now let's look at a different picture of how a semaphore works. Figure 6–8 depicts the actual operation of `semWait()` and `semPost()` in our extensions package. As the value of the semaphore is a shared data item, it must be protected in a synchronized section (or logical equivalent). The first thing `semWait()` does is enter that synchronized section (locks the mutex). Then it checks the value. If it is greater than zero, the value is decremented, the mutex is released, and `semWait()` returns.

If the value of the semaphore is zero, the mutex will be released, and the thread will then go to sleep. Upon waking up, the thread must repeat the operation, reacquiring the mutex and testing the value.

The operation of `semPost()` is quite simple. It locks the mutex, increments the value, releases the mutex, and wakes up one sleeper (if there is one). The results are exactly what you expect. Even though you have no idea what the scheduling order might be, it is impossible to accidentally decrement the value below zero, and no thread can ever get "stuck" on the sleep queue when the value is greater than zero. There are timing gaps where things *look* momentarily inconsistent, and it is possible for a thread to be awakened by mistake, but the end results are always correct.

A semaphore is perfect for situations where you want to count things and have threads sleep when some limit is hit. If you wish to count *up* to some number, say for a list limited to ten items, you simply view the semaphore as counting the number of "spaces" in the list, initialize it to ten, and count down.

There are occasions when you want the same kind of sleeping behavior as with semaphores, but your test is more complex than just "Is $v > 0$?"

Condition Variables

Figure 6–9 shows a flowchart for a generalization on semaphores. Here the mutex is visible to the programmer and the condition is arbitrary. The programmer is responsible for locking and unlocking the mutex, testing and changing the condition, and waking up sleepers. Otherwise, it is exactly like a semaphore. We'll look at POSIX condition variables first, then see how Java implements the same concept.

Perhaps you want a thread to execute some code only if $X > 17$, Y is prime, and grandmother is visiting next Thursday. As long as you can express the condition in a program, you can use it in a condition variable. A condition variable creates a safe environment for you to test your condition, sleep on it when false, and be awakened when it might have become true.

It works like this: A thread obtains a mutex (condition variables always have an associated mutex) and tests the condition

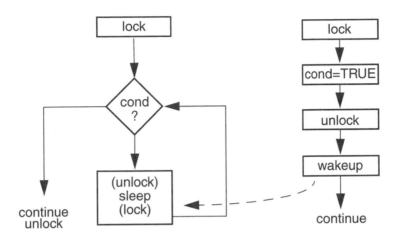

Figure 6–9 *Flowchart for Condition Variables*

under the mutex's protection. No other thread should alter any aspect of the condition without holding the mutex. If the condition is true, your thread completes its task, releasing the mutex when appropriate. If the condition isn't true, the mutex is released *for you*, and your thread goes to sleep on the condition variable. When some other thread changes some aspect of the condition (e.g., it reserves a plane ticket for granny), it calls `pthread_cond_signal()`,[9] waking up one sleeping thread. Your thread then reacquires the mutex,[10] reevaluates the condition, and either succeeds or goes back to sleep, depending upon the outcome.

You *must* reevaluate the condition! First, the other thread may not have tested the complete condition before sending the wakeup. Second, even if the condition was true when the wakeup was sent, it could have changed before your thread got to run. Third, condi-

---

[9]The term *signal* here is distinct from UNIX signals (SIGINT, etc.). *Wakeup* might be a better term.

[10]Obviously, when a thread sleeps on a condition variable, the mutex must be released (so other threads can acquire it) and reacquired upon waking. All of this is handled for you by `pthread_cond_wait()`.

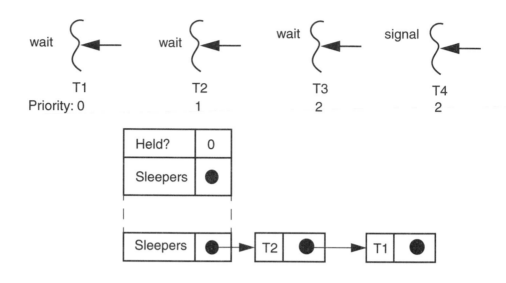

Figure 6–10   *Threads Using a Condition Variable*

tion variables allow for spurious wakeups. They are allowed to wake up for no discernible reason whatsoever![11]

In Figure 6–10, T1, T2, and T3 all evaluated the condition, determined it to be false, and went to sleep on the condition variable. T4 then came along, changed the condition to true, and woke up the first of the sleeping threads. T3 was awakened, reevaluated the condition, found it to be true, and did its thing, releasing the mutex when done. We'll assume that T3 also changed the condition back to false, so there was no reason to wake any other threads. If T3 hadn't changed the condition, it should have woken up another thread.

Depending upon your program, you may wish to wake up all the threads that are waiting on a condition. Perhaps they were all waiting for the right time of day to begin background work or were waiting for a certain network device to become active. A `pthread_cond_broadcast()` is used exactly like

---

[11] Due to some arcania in the hardware design of modern SMP machines, it proves to be highly convenient to define them like this. The hardware runs a little faster, and the programmer needs to reevaluate the condition anyway.

`pthread_cond_signal()` (Code Example 6–14). It is called after some aspect of the condition has changed. It then wakes all of the sleeping threads (in an undefined order), which then must all hurry off to reevaluate the condition. This may cause some contention for the mutex, but that's OK.

Thread 1	**Thread 2**

```
pthread_mutex_lock(&m);
while (!my_condition)
  pthread_cond_wait(&c, &m);
                              pthread_mutex_lock(&m);
... sleeping ...              my_condition = TRUE;
                              pthread_mutex_unlock(&m);
                              pthread_cond_signal(&c);
                              /* pthread_cond_broadcast(&c); */
do_thing();
pthread_mutex_unlock(&m);
```

Code Example 6–14 *Using a Condition Variable (POSIX)*

Presumably you are calling signal or broadcast any time that the condition has been changed such that it may have become true. In most cases you will have evaluated the condition completely before you signal or broadcast, but you do not have to. You certainly would want to signal any time that the condition became true.

There are several things you can do with condition variables that the compiler won't complain about but are guaranteed trouble. You could use the same condition variable with different mutexes (some POSIX implementations will detect this at runtime). You could have several functions that use one condition variable but that evaluate different conditions. (This latter is not illegal and is sometimes even useful, but not very often.) *Be careful!*

Java wait/notify

The Java equivalent to condition variables is wait/notify (Code Example 6–15). The behavior is virtually identical. You enter a synchronized section, evaluate a condition, continue on if true, and wait (releasing the synchronized section) if not. Another thread will enter a synchronized section, change the condition, and send you a wakeup. You reacquire the synchronized section, retest the condition, etc.

Thread 1	**Thread 2**

```
synchronized (object) {
   while (!object.my_condition)
       object.wait();

                                        synchronized (object) {
                                           object.my_condition = true;
                                           object.notify();
                                        // object.notifyAll();
                                        }
   do_thing();
}
```

Code Example 6–15   *Using wait/notify (Java)*

Whereas in POSIX mutexes and condition variables exist as separate data types that must be associated together by the programmer, in Java they are tightly integrated with each object. As we mentioned, every Java object has associated with it a mutex, and additionally every Java object has associated with it a condition variable. The class `Object` defines the methods `wait()`, `notify()`, and `notifyAll()` to manipulate the condition variable associated with that object. These correspond directly to `pthread_cond_wait()`, `pthread_cond_signal()`, and `pthread_cond_broadcast()`.

An object's condition variable is always associated with the object's mutex. Hence, before you can invoke `wait()` on the object, you must hold the mutex—that is you must be in a synchronized statement referring to that object. Unlike POSIX, Java also requires that you hold the object's mutex before doing a `notify()` or `notifyAll()`. This may make `notify()` and `notifyAll()` slightly less efficient due to the extraneous contention for the mutex (see below), but the extra cost is minimal.

It is legal to call `notify()` at any time whatsoever (as long as the mutex is held). It's not very useful to call it unless you have changed some aspect of the condition being tested, but it's never wrong. It will never cause a bug in your program.

Moreover, it is always legal to call `notifyAll()` instead of `notify()`. (The opposite is not true.) At worst, it will waste a bit of time while the extra threads wake up, realize there's nothing for them to do, and go back to sleep. We'll have more to say about this soon (see *Condition Variables vs. wait/notify* on page 160).

As with synchronized sections, there is no defined wakeup order for wait/notify. And also as with synchronized sections, it doesn't matter. You have a job and you want some thread to wake up and do that job—you don't care which thread.

Extraneous Contention

Because of the kind of interaction that exists between the condition variable and its associated mutex, it is possible to get some unwanted contention for the mutex. This is most evident when calling broadcast. Unfortunately, there is not much you can do about it, and your program may well suffer dozens of microseconds in wasted mutex blocks.

Figure 6–11 illustrates the problem. In the "Desired Behavior" case, the little bit of extra time it takes for T2 to wake up and try for the mutex is just long enough for T1 to release it. In the "Possible Behavior" case, the waiting threads wake up, try for the mutex, and have to go right back to sleep because the mutex hasn't been released yet. The most obvious solution for at least some of this problem is to make the call to signal or broadcast outside the critical section. This is what all of our POSIX code does.

InterruptedException

Now we need to deal with a little detail. For reasons we'll go into later (see *Defined Cancellation/Interruption Points* on page 193), a number of methods throw a special exception, `InterruptedException`. One of those methods is `object.wait()`, another is `Thread.sleep()`. We don't want to do anything with it yet, so we'll simply include a try/catch block and ignore it. Our code is shown in Code Example

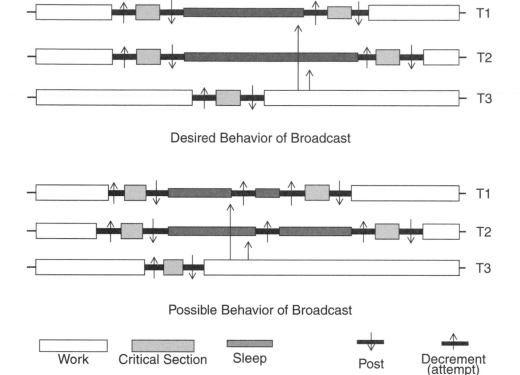

Desired Behavior of Broadcast

Possible Behavior of Broadcast

| Work | Critical Section | Sleep | Post | Decrement (attempt) |

Figure 6–11   *Extra Contention: When the Mutex Is Held by a Different Thread*

6–16. *In production code you should never ignore any exceptions.*

```
try {
   synchronized (object) {
   while (!object.my_condition)
      object.wait();
}
catch (InterruptedException(e) {}          // Ignore for now
```

Code Example 6–16   *Using wait/notify with*
InterruptedException

Controlling the Queue Length

So how do we prevent the queue from growing in the producer/consumer example? The simplest way is to initialize a second semaphore to the maximum allowed length and count it down.[12] This works quite well for simple programs, but you will probably never actually use this in a production program.

Often, you will find that you have more extensive demands on the program and will need to use a condition variable (wait/notify). Code Example 6–17 shows this situation. We will use the lock from `workpile` to protect both the length of the list and the list itself,[13] so we remove the locking from `add()` and `remove()` and do it in the producer and the consumer directly. (This code now looks a little bit ugly with so many references to `workpile`, but we'll deal with that later.) There is another little problem with this code, however.

```
public class Consumer implements Runnable {
...

public void run() {
   Item item;

   try {
     while (true) {
       synchronized (workpile) {
           while (workpile.empty()) workpile.wait();
           item = workpile.remove();
           workpile.notify();                         // Not quite right
       }
```

Code Example 6–17	*Classic Producer/Consumer Model (with a Tiny Bug)*

[12]One way to imagine this inverse use of a semaphore is to consider the queue to have some number of slots available. The semaphore encodes this number. When a producer places a new request onto the queue, there is one less available slot, so we decrement the semaphore. When a consumer takes a request off, there is one more, so we increment it.

[13]We are using one lock to protect two things that must be changed atomically with respect to each other. Any time we use either of those things, we must lock the same lock. You can never protect a variable using two different locks.

```
        server.process(item);
      }
  }

  catch (InterruptedException e) {}  // Ignore for now

}
}


public class Producer implements Runnable {

public void run() {
  Item item;

  try {
    while (true) {
      item = server.get();
      synchronized (workpile) {
          while (workpile.full()) workpile.wait();
          workpile.add(item);
          workpile.notify();                    // Not quite right
      }
    }
  }

  catch (InterruptedException e) {}  // Ignore for now
}
}
```

Code Example 6–17 *Classic Producer/Consumer Model (with a Tiny Bug) (cont.)*

You see, in this design, both consumers and producers will be sleeping on the same synchronized object. It would be unfortunate should a consumer take an item off the list and wake up another consumer instead of a producer, as intended.[14] With the right combination of list lengths, and number of producers and consum-

---

[14]This is *not* an obvious situation and requires some careful analysis to figure out. Moreover, it is possible that this program will work well on one platform while hanging on another. Part of the logic here relies on the order of wakeup for sleeping threads, something that is not guaranteed by the JVM. This, by the way, is a good thing, as the programmer should *never* rely on wakeup order.

ers, this code is likely to be inefficient, and it is even possible that it will deadlock.

The solution is simple: Consumers should only wake up producers, and producers should only wake up consumers. Unfortunately, the Java method `notify()` is linked specifically to the synchronized object, so there's no way to direct wakeups as we'd like. We could wake up everybody by calling `notifyAll()`. That would definitely give us a correctly working program, but it could[15] be abysmally inefficient. Let's consider a POSIX-style alternative.

POSIX-Style Synchronization in Java

What we're going to do is implement POSIX-style mutexes and condition variables in Java. Because POSIX mutexes and condition variables are separate, independent objects, it is possible to construct exactly the program logic that we really want. First, let's look at the classic POSIX solution to this problem, shown in Code Example 6–18.

```
void *producer(void *arg)
{request_t *request;

  while(1)
    {request = get_request();
     pthread_mutex_lock(&requests_lock);
     while (length >= 10)
       pthread_cond_wait(&producerCV, &requests_lock);
     add_request(request);
     length++;
     pthread_mutex_unlock(&requests_lock);
     pthread_cond_signal(&consumerCV);
   }
}

void *consumer(void *arg)
```

Code Example 6–18 *Classic Producer/Consumer in POSIX*

---

[15]*Would* it be abysmally inefficient? We'll take up this issue in *Condition Variables vs. wait/ notify* on page 160.

```
{request_t *request;

 while(1)
   {pthread_mutex_lock(&requests_lock);
    while (length == 0)
      pthread_cond_wait(&consumerCV, &requests_lock);
    request = remove_request();
    length--;
    pthread_mutex_unlock(&requests_lock);
    pthread_cond_signal(&producerCV);
    process_request(request);
  }
}
```

Code Example 6–18   *Classic Producer/Consumer in POSIX (cont.)*

The mutex protects both the list itself and the variable length. The distinction is that when the list is empty, the consumers will go to sleep on one condition variable (consumerCV) while the producers will go to sleep on another (producerCV) when the list is full. In this fashion the producers can be confident that they are waking up a consumer when they put a new item on the list, and the consumers know they are waking up a producer when they take one off. This is the behavior we want. Let's see how we can do this in Java.

POSIX-Style Mutexes in Java

Implementing mutexes is a snap. We need an object with one boolean and two methods, lock() and unlock(). To lock it, if the mutex is held by another thread, we wait. Otherwise, we set owned to true (Code Example 6–19). (Later we will use a slightly more elaborate version of mutexes which record the name of the owner, but right now we'll be simple.) To unlock, we'll just set owned to false, then call notify() to wake up one sleeper (if any). (A slightly more efficient version would count the sleepers.)

A sufficiently intelligent compiler could optimize this down to be identical to Pthread mutexes with identical performance. (I do not know of any compilers sufficiently intelligent, however, and the best code currently imaginable would be many times slower than Pthreads. A mutex class as part of the JVM would be a very good thing.)

Code Examples 6–19 and 6–20 are simplified and should not be used. We'll show the full, working versions of mutexes and condition variables in *Actual Implementation of POSIX Synchronization* on page 386.

```
// Don't use this code, it ignores exceptions.

public class Mutex {
boolean owned = false;

public synchronized void lock() {
while (owned) {
   try {wait();}
   catch (InterruptedException ie) {} // Ignore interrupts for now
   }
 owned = true;
}


public synchronized void unlock() {
 owned = false;
 notify();
}
}
```

Code Example 6–19   *Implementing POSIX-Style Mutexes in Java*

POSIX-Style Condition Variables in Java

Implementing a condition variable in Java is not particularly difficult, but there are a few subtle nuances (Code Example 6–20). The `ConditionVar` class itself requires just two methods, `condWait()` [equivalent to Java's `wait()`] and `condSignal()` [Java's `notify()`]. [Adding `notifyAll()` and a timed `wait()` is a simple exercise left to the reader.] The subtleties are in the `condWait()` method. The mutex must be released and the thread sent to sleep atomically with respect to the `condSignal()`, hence the synchronized section.

Consider what would happen if these were not done atomically. With a bit of (bad) luck, thread 1 could call `condWait()`, re-

```
// Don't use this code, it ignores exceptions.

public class ConditionVar
{

public void condWait(Mutex mutex) {
    try {
        synchronized (this){
            mutex.unlock();
            wait();
        }
    }
    catch (InterruptedException ie) {}// Ignore for now
    finally {mutex.lock();}          // *Always* lock before
returning!
}

public synchronized void condSignal() {
    notify();
}

}
```

Code Example 6–20 *Implementing Condition Variables in Java*

lease the mutex, and at just that instant thread 2 could be running on a different CPU. Thread 2 could then lock the mutex, change the condition to true, and call condSignal(). Thread 1 would not yet be asleep, so it wouldn't be awakened. It would subsequently go to sleep even though the condition is now true, and the wakeup from thread 2 would be lost. Having done its work, thread 2 might never send another wakeup (it might be waiting for thread 1 to finish!) and the entire program would hang. This would be a bad thing. It's known as the "lost wakeup problem" (see *The Lost Wakeup* on page 170).

The synchronized section in condWait() does not include the relocking of the mutex. This is also essential. Consider what could happen if it did (Code Example 6–21).

```
public void condWait(Mutex mutex) throws InterruptedException {
    synchronized (this) {
        mutex.unlock();
        wait();
```

Code Example 6–21 *condWait() Done Wrong*

```
    mutex.lock();
  }
}
```

Code Example 6–21 *condWait() Done Wrong (cont.)*

Running the producer/consumer code shown in Code Example 6–22, thread 1 might call `condWait()`, release the mutex, and go to sleep. Thread 2 could then lock the mutex and call `condSignal()`, waking up thread 1. Thread 1 could then reacquire the synchronized section for the condition variable and call `mutex.lock()`. At this time, thread 2 has released the mutex, hurried back to the top, and relocked that mutex. Thread 1 would have to go to sleep to wait for thread 2 to release it. Thread 2, however, needs to call `condSignal()` before it releases the mutex. To run `condSignal()`, it needs to obtain the synchronization for the condition variable, which is still held by thread 1. Deadlock.[16]

Code Example 6–22 shows how we'll write our producer/consumer model using condition variables. This code is perfectly correct and will work correctly on all platforms for any number of producers, consumers, and size limits. Note that we now are forced to use explicit mutexes instead of synchronized methods. The reason is that the data must be protected by the same lock in every instance. If we tried to use synchronized methods, we'd be unable to have our two condition variables both release that synchronization.

```
public class Consumer implements Runnable {
...

public void run()   {
Item item;
```

Code Example 6–22 *Producer/Consumer Model Using POSIX-Style Synchronization*

---

[16]By moving the `condSignal()` call in the P/C code outside the call to `mutex.unlock()`, this particular version of the problem could be resolved, but slightly more subtle versions of it would still be there for other situations. Consider having two consumers and one producer.

```
    while (true) {
        workpile.mutex.lock();
        while (workpile.empty()) {
            workpile.consumerCV.condWait(workpile.mutex);
        }
        item = workpile.remove();
        workpile.producerCV.condSignal();  //  Normally unlock first
        workpile.mutex.unlock();
    }
    server.process(item);
}
}


public class Producer implements Runnable {
...

public void run()  {
Item item;

    while (true)      {
        item = server.get();
        workpile.mutex.lock();
        while (workpile.full()) {
            workpile.producerCV.condWait(workpile.mutex);
        }
    workpile.add(item);
    workpile.consumerCV.condSignal(); //  Normally unlock first
    workpile.mutex.unlock();
    }
}
}
```

Code Example 6–22 *Producer/Consumer Model Using POSIX-Style Synchronization (cont.)*

A Stoppable Producer/Consumer Example

Let's use the ideas above to deal with a more complex situation. Say you like the operation of the producer/consumer model but you want to be able to start and stop at will. We'll use a shared variable, workpile.stop, which will control the threads. If it is true, all the producers and consumers will finish what they're doing and exit. Let's say further that we don't want the queue to be emptied at stop time. When we decide to start up the producers and consumers again, we'll require that the consumers empty the queue before any producers are started.

The only tricky part of this exercise is that some of the threads may be sleeping at the time we set `stop` to `true`, and we must ensure that they are awakened so that they can exit. We must also have the main thread sleep until the new consumers have emptied the queue. By having the threads wait on the condition (`work-pile.full() && (!workpile.stop)`), they can be awakened on a change of state for either the length or `stop` (Code Example 6–23).

```
public class Consumer implements Runnable {
...

public void run() {
  Item item;

  while (true) {
    workpile.mutex.lock();
    while (workpile.empty() & !workpile.stop) {
      workpile.consumerCV.condWait(workpile.mutex);
    }
    if (workpile.stop) break;
    item = workpile.remove();
    workpile.mutex.unlock();
    workpile.producerCV.condSignal();       // OUTSIDE the CS
    server.process(item);
  }

  workpile.mutex.unlock();                   // Unlock!
  barrier.barrierPost();                     // We're exiting
public class Consumer implements Runnable {
}
}


public class Producer implements Runnable {
...

public void run() {
  Item item;

  while (true) {
    item = server.get();
```

Code Example 6–23 *Stoppable Producer/Consumer Model*

```
  workpile.mutex.lock();
  while (workpile.full() && !workpile.stop) {
    workpile.producerCV.condWait(workpile.mutex);
  }
  workpile.add(item);
  if (workpile.stop) break;              // Put the Item on the list!
  workpile.mutex.unlock();
  workpile.consumerCV.condSignal();      // OUTSIDE the CS
}

workpile.mutex.unlock();                 // Unlock!
barrier.barrierPost();                   // We're exiting
}
}
```

Code Example 6–23 *Stoppable Producer/Consumer Model (cont.)*

Notice that we've moved the call to condSignal() outside the critical section. This is its normal position.

When we set stop to true, we will need to wake up all threads that might be sleeping. In Code Example 6–24, we spawn a thread to set stop true after 4 seconds. After it's set, the thread calls condBroadcast() to wake up all the worker threads. We would do the same if it were a button we were using, or any other method. Notice that we must lock the mutex before changing the value of stop; otherwise, we'll be subject to the lost wakeup problem.

```
public class Stopper implements Runnable {
...

public void run() {

    InterruptibleThread.sleep(delay);
    System.out.println("Stopping...");
    workpile.mutex.lock();
    workpile.stop = true;
    workpile.mutex.unlock();
    workpile.consumerCV.condBroadcast();
    workpile.producerCV.condBroadcast();
}


}
```

Code Example 6–24 *Stoppable Producer/Consumer Model*
(Stopper)

Finally, in this bit of code from main()
(Code Example 6–25), we see how we can synchronize on the exiting of the threads and the emptying of the queue. First we start them all up. Then we wait for all the threads to complete their work [they'll probably exit a couple of microseconds after they call semPost(); however, we don't really care]. After they have all completed their work, we can set stop back to false. (What if we didn't wait for all the threads to finish?) Then we create the consumers and wait for them to empty the queue. (Notice how we reuse the condition variable producerCV here. We could have used a third condition variable, but the extra efficiency we'd get would be absurdly small.) Once the queue is empty, we start up the producers again.

```
public static void main(String argv[]) {
...

   barrier = new SingleBarrier(nConsumers + nProducers);

    for (int j=0; j<3; j++) {

      System.out.println("Starting consumers...  List length: "
          + workpile.length());
      for (int i=0; i<nConsumers; i++) {
          t=new Thread(new Consumer(workpile, s, barrier));
          t.start();
      }

      workpile.mutex.lock();
      while (!workpile.empty())
      workpile.producerCV.condWait(workpile.mutex);
      workpile.mutex.unlock();

      System.out.println("Starting producers...List length: "
          + workpile.length());

      for (int i=0; i<nProducers; i++) {
          t=new Thread(new Producer(workpile, s, barrier));
          t.start();
      }
```

Code Example 6–25 *Stoppable Producer/Consumer Model [Starting Up and Shutting Down in* main()*]*

```
    new Thread(new Stopper(workpile, 5000)).start();

    barrier.barrierWait();
    System.out.println("Stopped! List length:" + workpile.length());
    workpile.stop = false;
    InterruptibleThread.sleep(2000);
}



    System.out.println("Finished!  Produced: " + s.pcounter
            + " Consumed: " + s.ccounter
            + " items. List length: " + workpile.length());
    System.exit(0);
}

}
```

Code Example 6–25   *Stoppable Producer/Consumer Model [Starting Up and Shutting Down in* main () *]   (cont.)*

A minor point: When we set `stop = false`, we don't have to lock the mutex. Why can we get away with this?

We can do this because we wrote the program and we happen to know that there are no other threads running by the time we get to this line, so for one brief moment, `stop` is not a shared variable. In production code it would be well advised to protect it anyway—no sense in making someone else wonder about it.

APIs Used in This Chapter

The Class java.lang.Object

---

synchronized

synchronized

This language keyword causes the current thread to obtain the hidden lock for the object. If the lock is already held by the current thread, it will essentially increment a counter for that lock (it's a recursive lock). If the lock is held by a different thread, this thread will go to sleep waiting for it to become available.

Reference: Chapter 6.

wait

```
public void wait()
   throws InterruptedException
```

This causes the current thread to block until it is awakened by either a call to notify(), interruption, or by a spurious wakeup. It will release the synchronization lock for the object as it goes to sleep and reacquire it before returning.

Reference: Chapter 6.

notify notifyAll

```
public void notify()
public void notifyAll()
```

These cause (one/all) of the threads that are in a wait() call for this object to wake up and return.

Reference: Chapter 6.

The Class Extensions.Semaphore

This is one of our classes. It implements POSIX-style semaphores. It is probably not useful except for demo programs.

semWait

```
public void semWait()
```

This attempts to decrement the value of the semaphore. If it succeeds, it simply returns. If the value is zero, this will cause the current thread to go to sleep until another thread increments it.

Reference: Chapter 6.

semPost

```
public void semPost()
```

This increments the value of the semaphore, waking up one thread (if any are sleeping).

Reference: Chapter 6.

The Class Extensions.Mutex

This is one of our classes. It implements POSIX-style (non-recursive) mutex locks. Use *only* when synchronized sections won't work, such as chained locking.

lock

```
public void lock()
```

This locks the mutex. If the lock is held by a different thread, this thread will go to sleep, waiting for it to become available.

Reference: Chapter 6.

unlock

```
public void unlock()
```

This unlocks the mutex, waking up one thread (if any are sleeping).

Reference: Chapter 6.

The Class Extensions.ConditionVar

This is one of our classes. It implements POSIX-style condition variables. Use *only* when synchronized sections and wait/notify won't work.

---

condWait

```
public void condWait(Mutex m)
```

This causes the current thread to block until it is awakened by either a call to condSignal() or by a spurious wakeup (not by interruption). It will release the mutex lock for the object as it goes to sleep, and reacquire it before returning.

Reference: Chapter 6.

---

condSignal condBroadcast

```
public void condSignal()
public void condBroadcast()
```

These cause (one/all) of the threads that are in a condWait() call to wake up and return.

Reference: Chapter 6.

Summary

The main issue in writing MT programs is how to get threads to work together. Locks (synchronized sections) and condition variables (wait/notify) are the fundamental building blocks from which anything can be built. Although there are many nonintuitive aspects of synchronization, most of them can be ignored, as things "just work."

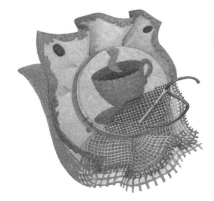

Chapter 7

Complexities

- ▼ COMPLEX LOCKING PRIMITIVES
- ▼ TIMEOUTS
- ▼ OTHER SYNCHRONIZATION VARIABLES
- ▼ VOLATILE
- ▼ PERFORMANCE
- ▼ SYNCHRONIZATION PROBLEMS
- ▼ APIS USED IN THIS CHAPTER
- ▼ THE CLASS EXTENSIONS.RWLOCK
- ▼ THE CLASS EXTENSIONS.BARRIER
- ▼ THE CLASS EXTENSIONS.SINGLEBARRIER

In which a series of more complex synchronization variables and options are presented and the trade-off between them and the simpler ones are discussed. Synchronization problems and techniques for dealing with them conclude the chapter.

139

Complex Locking Primitives

There are times when a simple mutex does not provide enough functionality. There are situations in which you can improve your program's efficiency or fairness by implementing more complex locking primitives. Keep in mind that the locks described below are more complex and therefore slower than normal mutex locks, generally by a factor of 2 or more. They are not generally useful, so be advised to consider your requirements closely before using them.

Readers/Writer Locks

Sometimes you will find yourself with a shared data structure that gets read often but written only seldom. The reading of that structure may require a significant amount of time (perhaps it's a long list through which you do searches). It would seem a waste to put a mutex around it and require all the threads to go through it one at a time when they're not changing anything. Hence, readers/writer locks.

With an RWlock, you can have any number of threads reading the data concurrently, whereas writers are serialized. The only drawback to RWlocks is that they are more expensive than mutexes. So you must consider your data structure, how long you expect to be in it, how much contention you expect, and choose between a mutex and an RWlock on those bases. As a rule of thumb, a simple global variable will always be locked with a mutex, while searching down a 1000-element, linked list will often be locked with an RWlock.

The operation of RWlocks is as follows: The first reader that requests the lock will get it. Subsequent readers also get the lock, and all of them are allowed to read the data concurrently. When a writer requests the lock, it is put on a sleep queue until all the readers exit. A second writer will also be put on the writer's sleep queue. Should a new reader show up at this point, it will be put on the reader's sleep queue until all the writers have completed. Further writers will be placed on the same writer's sleep queue as the others (hence, in front of the waiting reader), meaning that writers are always favored over readers. (Writer priority is simply a

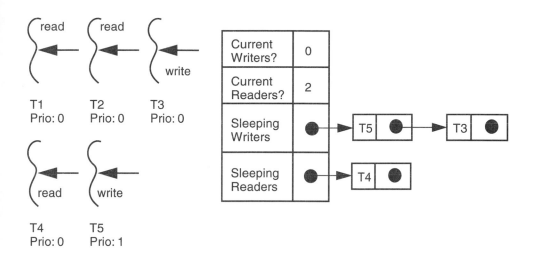

Figure 7–1   *How Readers/Writer Locks Work*

---

choice we made in our implementation; you may make a different choice.)

The writers will obtain the lock one at a time, each waiting for the previous writer to complete. When all writers have completed, the entire set of sleeping readers are awakened and can then attempt to acquire the lock. Should another writer show up before the readers get the lock, that writer will get priority.

"But," you may ask, "won't writer priority lead to starvation of readers in some cases?" Yup. And you can make a case for non-preferential RWlocks, or even reader-priority. However, we are concerned primarily with producing practical, well-performing programs, not proving theorems about degenerate cases. RWlocks are used primarily in situations where there are a great many read requests and very few write requests. If you have a large number of write requests, you shouldn't be using RWlocks.

In Figure 7–1, five threads all need an RWlock. They have different priorities, which determine the order in which they go onto the *writers'* sleep queue. The threads have requested the lock in the order T1, T2, T3, T4, T5. T1 and T2 own the lock, and T5 will be awakened as soon as they both release it, even though T3 and T4 requested the lock before T5. In Figure 7–2 we see exactly this happening. Note the overlapping read sections for T1 and T2.

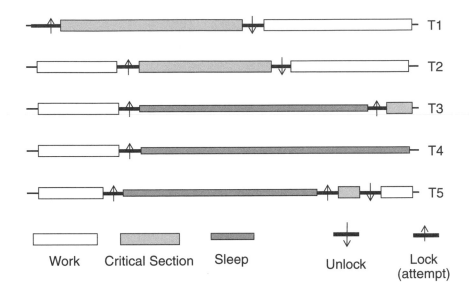

Figure 7–2 *Execution Graph for Readers/Writer Locks*

In the UNIX98 implementation of RWlocks, blocked threads are placed on the writer's sleep queue in priority order. (Priorities are uninteresting for readers.) We ignore priorities in our implementation, which is the right thing to do for most cases—better a faster, slightly unfair RWlock than a slower, fairer one.

You will be disappointed to discover that none of the three libraries define RWlocks. However, all is not lost. They can be built out of the primitives already available to you—mutexes and condition variables. We build them in our extensions library. RWlocks are also defined in UNIX98. A good example of using RWlocks is in *Global RWLock with Global Mutex to Protect Salaries* on page 273.

In our sample Java implementation (shown in Code Example 7–1), we use the explicit condition variables and mutexes. This allows us to send wakeups to only that set of waiters (either one writer or all readers) when we need to. If we had used native Java wait/notify, we would have had to wake up all sleepers at every wakeup point. In the vast majority of cases, that would not be a problem, as we've already assumed that writers are rare.

```
//                   Extensions/RWLock.java

package Extensions;

import java.io.*;


public class RWLock {
  Thread              owner = null;
  int                 nCurrentReaders = 0;
  int                 nWaitingWriters = 0;
  int                 nWaitingReaders = 0;
  Mutex               m =  new Mutex();
  ConditionVar        readersCV = new  ConditionVar();
  ConditionVar        writersCV = new  ConditionVar();


public String toString() {
  String name;

  if (owner == null)
    name = "null";
  else
    name = owner.getName();

  return("<RWLock: o:" + name + " r:" + nCurrentReaders + " ww:"
        + nWaitingWriters + " wr:" + nWaitingReaders + m + ">");
}


public void readLock() {

  m.lock();
  nWaitingReaders++;
  while ((owner != null) || (nWaitingWriters > 0)) {
    readersCV.condWait(m); }
  nWaitingReaders--;
  nCurrentReaders++;
  m.unlock();
}


public void writeLock() {
  m.lock();
```

Code Example 7–1 *Readers/Writer Locks in Java*

```
    nWaitingWriters++;
    while ((owner != null) || (nCurrentReaders > 0)) {
      writersCV.condWait(m);
    }
    nWaitingWriters--;
    owner = Thread.currentThread();
    m.unlock();
  }


public void unlock() {
  m.lock();
  if (owner != null) {
    owner = null;
  }
  else
    nCurrentReaders--;

  if ((nWaitingWriters > 0) && (nCurrentReaders == 0)) {
    writersCV.condSignal();
  }
  else
    if ((nWaitingWriters == 0) && (nWaitingReaders > 0)) {
      readersCV.condBroadcast();
    }
  m.unlock();
}

}
```

Code Example 7–1 *Readers/Writer Locks in Java (cont.)*

Priority Inheritance Mutexes

Should a high-priority thread (T2 in Figure 7–3) be blocked, waiting for a lock that is held by another thread of lower priority (T1), it may have to wait a longer time than seems reasonable, because a third thread (T3) of middling priority might be hogging the CPU. To do justice to overall system performance, it would be reasonable to elevate the scheduling priority of T1 to the level of the blocked thread (T2). This is not done for normal Pthread mutexes, so user programs may suffer from *priority inversion*. In POSIX, priority inheritance is an option during mutex initial-

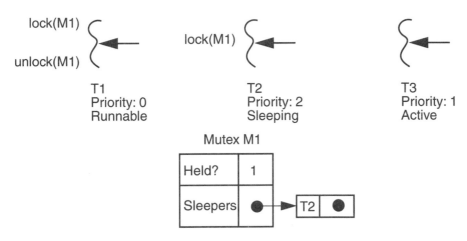

Figure 7–3 *Priority Inversion*

ization and is probably useful only in realtime situations. Java, by contrast, is very specifically not designed for realtime work, rendering the question of PI mutexes moot. You could write them, but it's very doubtful that they would be useful.

FIFO Mutexes

Every now and then, you come upon a program where you want to ensure that the thread that is blocked on a mutex will be the next owner of the mutex—something which is not in the definition of simple POSIX mutexes. Typically, this situation occurs when two threads both need a mutex to do their work: They hold the mutex for a significant length of time, they do their work independently of each other, and they have very little to do when they don't hold it. Thus, what happens is that T1 grabs the mutex and does its work (see Figure 7–4), while T2 tries for the mutex, and blocks. T1 then releases the mutex and wakes up T2. Before T2 manages to obtain the mutex, T1 reacquires it. This is illustrated in case 2.

Case 3 assumes that you have implemented FIFO mutexes, where the owner of the mutex automatically hands ownership over to the first waiter when releasing the mutex.

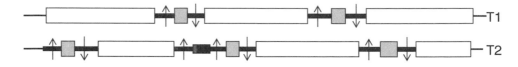

1: The common case: Very little contention, normal mutexes work well.

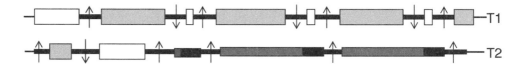

2: The uncommon case: T1 keeps reacquiring the mutex.

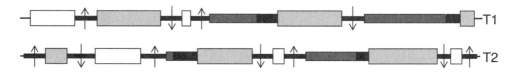

3: The uncommon case: Using a FIFO mutex.

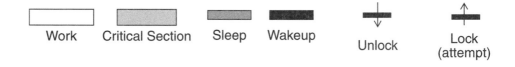

Figure 7–4 *When FIFO Mutexes Are Valuable*

This is a rare situation, and it merits reconsidering your algorithm before dealing with it. (If you contrast case 2 and case 3 against case 1, you will notice that the two threads are spending a lot of time sleeping on the job. This might run better with fewer threads!) But should you find yourself stuck with this kind of problem, it is a simple programming effort for you to implement guaranteed FIFO mutexes yourself. Once again, you almost certainly *don't* want FIFO mutexes.

Recursive Mutexes

Win32 mutexes are recursive—they can be locked multiple times from the same thread without deadlocking. POSIX mutexes cannot. Building a recursive mutex with POSIX is not at all difficult (an excellent exercise!) and indeed recursive mutexes are part of UNIX98. The real question is not if you can build them, but whether it's a good idea.

The chances are very high that if you have a situation where you want to use recursive mutexes in C, you'd be better off redesigning your code so that you don't need them. Why are you locking this mutex? To protect some shared data. Once you've done so, why would you ever want to lock it again? Because your code is structured poorly. Fix your code.

Once you've locked a recursive mutex three times, you will need to unlock it three times before any other thread can lock it. You *could* write an "unlock_all" routine, but it would probably just make your code even more confusing and very likely lead you to make mistakes.

In Java, synchronized sections are also recursive (Code Example 7–2). One synchronized method may call another synchronized method of the same object from the same thread without deadlocking.[1] A call to wait() will release the lock and when wait() returns, the lock will be reacquired at the same depth. The usual programming Java style almost makes it a requirement to have recursive mutexes. It would probably be a better thing if people wrote code such that they had public methods which were synchronized, which in turn simply called internal methods to do the real work, but this is unlikely to happen. Indeed, if we had a perfect programming language, this issue would not even come up.

---

[1]Java does not actually specify that locks are recursive, merely that synchronized calls may be made recursively. A sufficiently clever compiler could optimize most code so as to avoid actual recursive mutexes. I don't know of any such compilers.

```
void foo()                        public synchronized void foo() {
{pthread_mutex_lock(&m);
 bar();                              bar();
 pthread_mutex_unlock(&m);           ...
}                                 }

void bar()                        public synchronized void bar() {
{pthread_mutex_lock(&m);// Deadlock
 ...                                wait();    // works fine!
 pthread_mutex_unlock(&m);         }
}
```

Code Example 7–2 *Recursive Locking Calls in POSIX and Java*

Nonblocking Synchronization

All the POSIX synchronization variables have nonblocking calls associated with them. [For POSIX, `pthread_mutex _trylock()` and `sem_trywait()`. In Win32 there are timeouts associated with each call.] These functions can be used for things such as spin locks and complicated methods of coordinating threads while avoiding deadlock. It is very rare to ever use these functions. Java doesn't have nonblocking synchronized sections; however, it is a simple matter to write a nonblocking version of POSIX-style mutexes. But you probably don't want to do that.

Spin Locks

Normally, you should hold a lock for the shortest time possible, to allow other threads to run without blocking. There will occasionally be times (few and far between) when you look at the blocking time for a mutex (about 42 μs on an SS4, see Appendix C, *Timings*) and say to yourself "42 μs?! The other thread is only going to hold the mutex for 5 μs. Why should I have to block just 'cause I stumbled into that tiny window of contention? It's not fair!"

You don't. You can use a *spin lock* and try again. It's simple. You initialize a counter to some value and do a `pthread_mutex_trylock()`—that takes about 2 μs. If you don't get the lock, decrement the counter and loop. Another 2 μs. Repeat. When the counter hits zero, give up and block. If you get the mutex, you've saved a bunch of time. If you don't, you've only wasted a little time.

In Code Example 7–3 we show the construction of a simple spin lock. Although this is a good description of a spin lock, it's actually a poor implementation. We will discuss the issues and show a better implementation in Chapter 16.

```
                     /* Don't use this code! */
spin_lock(mutex_t *m)
{int i;
    for (i=0; i < SPIN_COUNT; i++)
        {if (pthread_mutex_trylock(m) != EBUSY)
            return; }              /* got the lock! */
    pthread_mutex_lock(m);        /* give up and block. */
    return; }                      /* got the lock after blocking!
*/
```

Code Example 7–3 *Simple Spin Lock*

Spin locks can be effective in very restricted circumstances. The critical section *must* be short, you *must* have significant contention for the lock, and you *must* be running on more than one CPU. If you do decide you need a spin lock, test that assumption. Set the spin count to zero and time your standardized, repeatable test case (you must have one!). Then set the spin count to a realistic value, and time the test again. If you don't see a significant improvement, go back to regular mutex locks. Spin locks are almost always the *wrong* answer, so be careful!

Adaptive Spin Locks

A refinement of spin locks, called *adaptive spin locks*, is used in many kernels. You can't build them yourself and they are not generally provided by the vendor, but you might be interested in knowing what they are.

If you could find out whether the thread holding the desired mutex was in fact currently running on a CPU, you could make a more reasoned judgment as to whether or not to spin. An adaptive lock can do this. If the mutex owner is running, the requestor spins. If the owner isn't, the requestor doesn't.

Unfortunately, in the user-level threads library, you generally cannot find out which thread holds a mutex, and even if you could, the system call required to find out whether the thread in question was on a CPU would be more expensive than just blocking. A clever trick in some operating systems does make this possible.

A fair (and unanswered) question is: "Will the time saved by not spinning make up for the extra time to use adaptive locks?" If you are using spin locks, you should know exactly how long a critical section can be held. It may well prove faster to spin for the known time and ignore run state entirely!

Java May Use Spin Locks

As the JVM is based on the underlying native threads library, it will use whatever type of mutex is provided. For example, on Digital UNIX, and on Solaris 2.6 and above, all mutexes are actually adaptive spin locks,[2] hence you will get them automatically. It is unlikely that you will ever notice the difference.

Timeouts

Condition variables and wait/notify also allow you to limit the sleep time. By calling `pthread_cond_timedwait()` [`object.wait(timeout)`], you can arrange to be awakened after a fixed amount of time, in case you're the impatient type. Should you know that the condition ought to change within some time frame, you can wait for that amount of time and then figure out what went wrong.

You can also use it simply as a thread-specific timer, although the standard timer functions [`sleep()`, `nanosleep()`; `Thread.sleep()`] are more appropriate and easier to use. Be aware that the system clock will limit the precision of the wakeup. A 10-ms resolution is typical. If you want 100-µs precision, you'll probably have to use something highly vendor specific, and you may have trouble getting such precision at all.

Once the wait time expires, the sleeping thread will be moved off the sleep queue and the wait will return. For POSIX, `pthread_cond_timedwait()` will return a value, `ETIMED-OUT`, so you know that it has timed out. In Java, there is no such in-

---

[2]If we claim that spin locks are not very useful, why do the OSs make them the default? Because a few programs will benefit a great deal and most programs don't really care.

dication and you are forced to keep track of the time yourself to determine that wait() timed out as opposed to having been awakened normally. (This is a bit of a hassle, and a wrapper function such as the one in Code Example 7–4 is quite convenient.)

Indeed, in Java it is impossible to know if you've actually timed out. You can find out if the current time is later than the timeout, but it's always possible that you received a spurious wakeup before the timer expired but didn't see the wakeup until after expiration. This shouldn't be a problem.

Elvis and the UFOs

In Code Example 7–4 we are faced with a serious situation. Evil space aliens are trying to kidnap Elvis in order to breed him with other Earthlings. To save him, we must eliminate the aliens quickly. If we fail to do so within a short time (10 seconds), they will escape with him and rock and roll will be lost.

```
public synchronized void saveElvis() throws InterruptedException {
  long timeRemaining, time = 10000;      // 10 seconds

  while (!eliminatedAliens()) {
    timeRemaining = timedWait(time);
    if (timeRemaining==0) return false; // Too late. Elvis kidnapped.
    time = timeRemaining;
  }
  return true; // Elvis lives!
}


public long timedWait(long waitTime) throws InterruptedException {
    long now, timeSoFar, startTime;

    startTime = System.currentTimeMillis();

    wait(waitTime);
    now = System.currentTimeMillis();
    timeSoFar = now - startTime;
    if (timeSoFar > waitTime) {return 0;}
    waitTime =  (waitTime - timeSoFar);
    return waitTime;
}
```

Code Example 7–4 *Recalculating Timeouts*

Our main method [saveElvis()] will sit in a while loop, waiting for us to eliminate the aliens. If we succeed, we'll return true from saveElvis(). If we time out, we'll return false. If our wait call returns before the time-out period and the aliens are not eliminated (perhaps some new aliens hatched from evil alien pods, perhaps we just suffered a spurious wakeup), we will go back and wait again. When this happens, we want to calculate the correct remaining time (instead of starting over with a new 10 seconds). Our timedWait() method will do this for us by returning the remaining time.

This method does the majority of the work. It records the starting time and calls wait() with the appropriate timeout. When wait() returns, it calculates how much time has elapsed. If it's more than the original timeout period, timedWait() returns ø. If it is less, timedWait() recalculates how much time is remaining and returns that, leaving it up to the caller to decide what to do. If the caller calls it again, it will wait again for the appropriate amount of remaining time. This is a bit awkward, but it does give the desired results.

It doesn't make any difference should another thread wake up the sleeper 1 ms after it has timed out. It also makes no difference should it subsequently take the ex-sleeper 16 hours to become active or acquire the lock. On the other hand, once the sleeper is awakened, it is taken off the sleep queue and the timer is turned off. If it takes another week before the wait function can get the required lock and returns, too bad. You will not get a timeout.

None of the wait functions will ever return without the lock being held—not on normal wakeups, not on timeouts, not on spurious wakeups, not even on cancellation or interruption. It is possible that right after waking up, a thread must go back to sleep because the lock is held by another thread!

Other Synchronization Variables

Join

The join functions are similar to synchronization variables in that they allow you to synchronize threads on the event of another

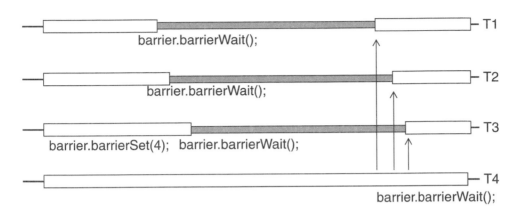

Figure 7–5 *Barriers*

thread exiting. You almost never actually care when a thread exits, and almost everything you do with join, you can do with the other synchronization variables (see *Don't Wait for Threads, Don't Return Status* on page 53).

Barriers

A barrier allows a set of threads to sync up at some point in their code. It is initialized to the number of threads using it, then it blocks all the threads calling it until it reaches zero, at which point it unblocks them all. The idea is that you can now arrange for a set of threads to stop when they get to some predefined point in their computation and wait for all the others to catch up. If you have eight threads, you initialize the barrier to eight. Then, as each thread reaches that point, it decrements the barrier and then goes to sleep. When the last thread arrives, it decrements the barrier to zero, and they all unblock and proceed (Figure 7–5).

Barriers are not part of any of the libraries, but they are easily implemented. They are also implemented in our extensions package and are part of the proposed extensions to POSIX.

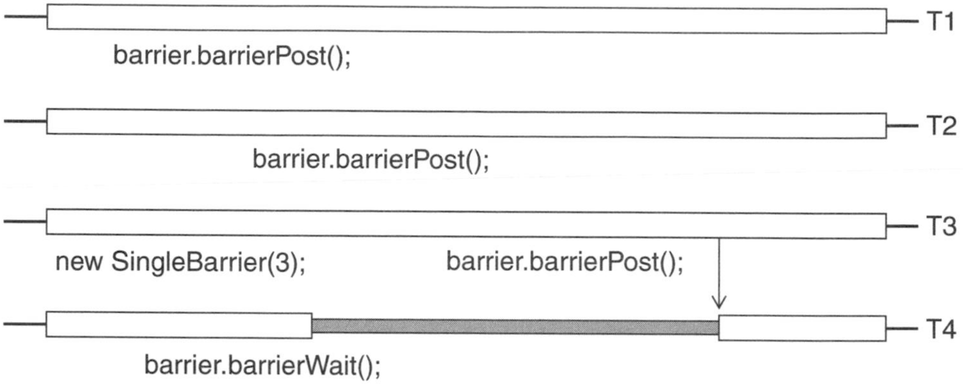

T1

barrier.barrierPost();

T2

barrier.barrierPost();

T3

new SingleBarrier(3);   barrier.barrierPost();

T4

barrier.barrierWait();

Figure 7–6   *Single Barriers*

Single Barriers

A single barrier is similar to a barrier, except that one (possibly more) thread will be waiting for the others (Figure 7–6). This is the synchronization technique we use in our programs to count threads as they exit (instead of joining them all). Basically, each thread increments the single barrier as it completes its work, while a single thread waits for them. When the last thread posts, the sleeper is awakened.

It's interesting to look at the design of a single barrier (Code Example 7–5). Notice in particular that the barrier must account for the situation where one waiter has been released but hasn't finished. (It's been awakened but hasn't gotten the CPU yet.) If one of the posters hurries around its loop and tries to use the single barrier again (before the waiter is done), there could be trouble! This is handled by counting both the number of posters and the number of waiters that have completed the code. When you write your own synchronization variables, you should carefully consider how those synchronization variables will work the *second* time around. Also notice how interrupted exceptions are handled. (We'll talk about this in detail in *Defined Cancellation/Interruption Points* on page 193.)

```
//              Extensions/SingleBarrier.java

/*
  Unlike a Barrier, where all threads wait until all are ready, with this
  Threads may indicate that they've completed their job by doing a
  barrierPost() and then continue.  Later, other threads (or the same)
  may wait until everyone has done a barrierPost() by doing a
  barrierWait().

  By default, assume a single waiter.  You must know the number of
  threads that will be posting and the number that will be waiting.

*/


package Extensions;

import java.io.*;


public class SingleBarrier {
  int          currentPosters = 0, totalPosters = 0;
  int          passedWaiters = 0, totalWaiters = 1;


public SingleBarrier (int i) {
  totalPosters = i;
}


public SingleBarrier (int i, int j) {
  totalPosters = i; totalWaiters = j;
}


public SingleBarrier () {
}


public synchronized void init(int i) {
  totalPosters = i; currentPosters=0;
}
```

Code Example 7–5 *Implementing Single Barriers in Java*

```
public synchronized void barrierSet(int i) {
  totalPosters = i; currentPosters=0;
}


public synchronized void barrierWait() {
  boolean interrupted = false;
  while (currentPosters != totalPosters) {
    try {wait();}
    catch (InterruptedException ie) {interrupted=true;}
  }
  passedWaiters++;
  if (passedWaiters == totalWaiters) {
    currentPosters = 0; passedWaiters = 0; notifyAll();
  }
  if (interrupted) Thread.currentThread().interrupt();
}


public synchronized void barrierPost() {
  boolean interrupted = false;

  // In case a poster thread beats barrierWait, keep count of posters.
  while (currentPosters == totalPosters) {
    try {wait();}
    catch (InterruptedException ie) {interrupted=true;}
  }
  currentPosters++;
  if (currentPosters == totalPosters) notifyAll();
  if (interrupted) Thread.currentThread().interrupt();
}

}
```

Code Example 7–5   *Implementing Single Barriers in Java (cont.)*

Win32 Event Objects

Win32 defines event objects, which are intended to handle the
same things as condition variables. Event objects have a
"signaled" state associated with them, however, making them
somewhat problematic to use. There is an interesting paper
showing the issues involved in constructing POSIX-style
condition variables from event objects (see *Threads Research* on

page 411). This paper also highlights the difficulties in using event objects correctly.

Win32 Critical Sections

In Win32 the term *critical section* is used to describe a simple mutex. The major distinction between Win32's mutexes and Win32's critical sections is that the former can be defined to be cross-process, whereas the latter cannot. All Win32 synchronization variables other than critical sections are kernel objects. Their handles must be closed before the kernel structures are released. They are also much slower than critical sections by about two orders of magnitude (!).

Multiple Wait Semaphores

In Win32 it is possible to wait for (1) any one of a set of synchronization variables or (2) all of that set. In POSIX and Java you would write the program differently and simply have a condition variable (wait/notify) waiting on a complex condition.

Interlocked Instructions

In Win32, several special functions are defined: `Interlocked-Increment()`, `InterlockedDecrement()`, and `InterlockedExchange()`. As their names suggest, they perform their tasks automatically without the need of an explicit lock. This makes them quite fast but limits their usefulness greatly. (Sure, you've incremented the value, but you don't know if someone else incremented it a microsecond later.) These are implemented by the Digital compiler as intrinsics using LockedLoad/StoreConditional instructions (see *LoadLocked/StoreConditional and Compare and Swap* on page 354).

The things you can do with them include reference counting, semaphores, and not much else. These types of operations are not part of either POSIX or Java, and the requisite instructions are not on all CPU architectures.

Message Queues

A question asked fairly often is how one can build message queues for threads—queues where one thread can line up requests for another thread to process. If this is truly what you need in your program, the answer is quite simple: Build a producer/consumer model with a queue as shown earlier. This gives you both complete control over your program and a simple programming model. What more could you ask for?

Win32 implements a kernel-level message queue that you can use for the same purpose. As it is part of the Win32 library, it makes sense to use it for cross-process communication, especially when you don't have control over all the source code. Otherwise, in a single process, it simply imposes too heavy a burden, in both CPU time and code complexity.

The ability to interrupt a thread and change what it's doing is a much different requirement and a far more difficult one to achieve. If you are thinking along these lines, reconsider your objectives very carefully! Why do you want to interrupt this particular thread? Could you get your work done by (1) polling from this thread, (2) waiting for this thread to complete its present task and then looking at a queue, or (3) simply creating a new thread to execute the task at hand? There is probably a simpler means of doing what you want. Find it.

Win32 I/O Completion Ports

An I/O completion port is Win32's answer to the producer/consumer problem. You create a completion port with a file handle and then have a number of threads waiting on that completion port. When a packet arrives on that handle, one of the waiting threads is awakened and given the packet to work on. Upon completion, the thread sends any reply it needs to send and goes back to wait on the port again. Windows NT hackers love these things.

Communicating via Streams

On occasion you will see discussions of communicating between threads via streams, pipes, sockets, or some other higher level of communication. There are valid reasons for doing this, but most of those reasons boil down to "to interface with existing code." If you're working with an interface that someone else defined, OK. Do it that way. Otherwise, forget it! What do you think you're doing? How often do threads want to exchange bytes? Practically never. They want to exchange objects. Even when they're using strings, what they want to communicate is the string, not the characters that make it up. So pass a string object.

Consider what a stream does. It supplies characters to a thread. If there are no characters in the stream, the caller blocks. When another thread writes into the stream, the first thread wakes up, removes the new characters, and starts over again. It's a producer/consumer model restricting the queue to bytes. And which one do you think is faster?

So you can communicate via streams, but... Don't do that.

Volatile

This keyword in C is used to indicate to the compiler that the variable in question changes independent of the local code. Hence, the compiler is not allowed to optimize away loads or stores. Indeed, loads must come from main memory, not be filled from cache. Stores should be expedited around the store buffer. The idea here is that memory-mapped I/O uses memory addresses as I/O registers and every read or write is meaningful. This is completely orthogonal to threads. Do not use volatile with threads, thinking that it will solve any threading problem. You won't like the results.

The Java spec says that volatile can be used instead of locking. It's right but misleading. Use locking. (See *Volatile: The Rest of the Story* on page 357.)

Performance

Condition Variables vs. wait/notify

As we've noted, there are two disadvantages of wait sets vs. condition variables: With condition variables it is clear from the code what you're waking up, whereas `notifyAll()` will potentially wake up a lot of threads unnecessarily and waste a lot of time.

The first point is unambiguous, but the second has that word *potentially* in it. What about the realities? We certainly have no problem in producing cases where performance is indeed abysmal, but how common are those cases?

Let's take a typical client/server program that has been optimized for a specific platform. Our primary concern is going to be obtaining maximum throughput on a dedicated machine. We'd like lower loads to be efficient also, but that is strictly secondary.

Let's assume that we have one producer thread listening to all clients. It will take 1 ms of CPU time to receive a request and enqueue it. Some number of consumer threads will dequeue those requests and process them as usual. We'll assume that all processing requires 4 ms of CPU and also requires one disk access averaging 15 ms latency. Further, we'll assume a sufficient number of disks and distribution of data to allow any number of overlapping requests to run completely simultaneously (i.e., 15 ms). Finally, we'll choose a 10-CPU machine.

We can conclude that the system will be 100% CPU-bound and that each request/reply will require 5 ms of CPU, allowing 200 requests/s on each CPU. Total latency will be 20 ms/request; thus each thread will be able to process 50 requests/s. To obtain maximum throughput, we'll need 4 threads per CPU—thus a total of 40 threads on our 10 CPUs, processing 2000 requests/s.

If we conveniently assume a very steady load with negative feedback from the buffer (i.e., a client who is waiting for a reply will not issue any new requests), the buffer will remain partially full at all times and no consumer threads will ever be waiting on an empty buffer, nor will the producer thread ever be waiting on a full one. The potential problem with excessive wakeups due to `notifyAll()` will be completely moot.

Now let's assume an overload. The buffer will remain full at all times and the producer will be blocking regularly, while the consumers will never block (the list is never empty). Once again, no excessive wakeup problem!

Finally, let's look at the underloaded case. Instead of the peak load of 2000 requests/s, let's look at 1000 requests/s. The buffer will be empty almost all the time and an average of 20 consumer threads will be sleeping. Each time the producer adds a request to the queue, it will wake up all 20. One consumer will get the request and the other 19 will have to go back to sleep. This is clearly a waste, but how much of one, and do we care?

On an SS4, a spurious wakeup costs about 100 µs. With a rate of 100 requests/s, this will cost us about 100 ms, roughly 1% of available CPU power (on our 10 CPUs). Do we care about a 1% waste on a non-peak load? Not very much. The conclusion is that on any similar program, the excessive wakeup problem is not a major performance problem at all!

By contrast, let's look at the extra CPU costs of using an explicit condition variable. A call to `condWait()`/`condSignal()` costs about 9 µs on an SS4, whereas wait/notify costs 3 µs. In our maximum throughput example we never block on the condition variable anyway, so there's no cost. In our overflow example, we'd be making 2000 calls/s, wasting 100 ms, 1% of CPU. In our underloaded example, we'd be saving 100 ms. None of these numbers is very large and the entire performance issue is completely moot for this kind of program (and indeed, probably for any "normal" program!).

The one perversely funny aspect of this entire issue is that wait/notify is implemented in terms on condition variables in the underlying POSIX library! If condition variables were included as part of the JVM, the performance numbers would turn around completely! Always use `wait()`/`notifyAll()` unless you have a very specific need for condition variables.

Coarse vs. Fine Grain Locking

At what level do you put your locks? You could have one big lock that covered everything, and then any time any thread wanted to access any shared data, it would need that one lock. This would be a good thing because you would not lock it very often. This would be bad because you'd be holding it for a long time.

You could do exactly the opposite and use a different lock for every set of variables, locking and unlocking them quite often. This would be a good thing because the locks would be free most of the time and you could get lots of concurrent operations. It would be bad because you would spend a lot of time in locking and unlocking overhead.

In small programs this may not be an issue. In larger programs it's quite likely that you'll choose different levels of granularity for different sections. In *Manipulating Lists* on page 270 we show a small search and update program that demonstrates this trade-off.

What to Lock

Closely related to the question of granularity is the question of what you want to protect. In the simple case, it's pretty obvious. You want to protect a queue? You lock the queue object every time you do anything with the queue. That's easy. Folks sometimes get confused when they're changing several things concurrently. What if you wanted to add items to your queue and you also wanted to change the pointer to the queue itself? In this scenario it is highly likely that your lock on the queue object would be counterproductive, because it would make you think you were protecting the queue (which of course you are), whereas what you really needed to do was to protect the variable that pointed to the queue.

Let's look at a more likely scenario. Let's assume that you have a queue of people and you want to do very fine grained locking on that queue by locking each individual element of that queue (instead of having one big lock protecting the entire queue). This is a perfectly reasonable thing to do and in some cases is the most efficient method of locking a structure. (We'll look at the perfor-

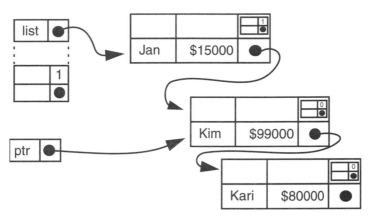

Figure 7–7 *Friends/Enemies with Only One Local Mutex Lock*

mance of this design in more detail in *Manipulating Lists* on page 270.)

The question we want to answer here is "What should I lock?" We can point you to many examples of programs where people have locked the wrong thing. In Figure 7–7 we see a queue of people and their salaries. Each person object also contains a lock. What does that lock protect? It can protect pretty much anything you want it to (you're the programmer), except for itself or the object that contains it.

The most obvious things for the lock in Jan's object to protect are the data for Jan, along with Jan's "next" pointer. A better choice is to have that lock protect the data in Kim's object along with Jan's "next" pointer. What that lock cannot protect is the pointer list, because the only way to find Jan in the first place is to follow list. So even though you may hold Jan's lock, another thread will still be able to come in and take Jan off the queue by changing list. This is why it's better to have Jan's lock protect Kim's data. You need to hold Jan's lock anyway in order to access Kim, so why complicate matters?

What if you have another thread which has a pointer (ptr) to Kim? You'd better not. Only the thread that holds Jan's lock is allowed to access Kim's object, except for data that is constant or data that might be out of date and you don't mind. Now if you remove Kim from the list, things change. Jan's lock will no longer protect Kim (it will now protect Kari) and you will be able to do anything you want with Kim's object because the thread that removes Kim from the list will be the only thread that has access to Kim. If you then pass Kim to another thread, you will need to come up with another method of protecting Kim.

The main point here is that when manipulating complex data structures you need to consider your locking scheme carefully.

Double-Checked Locking

In a small number of very restricted cases, it is reasonable and legal to look at shared data values without holding any locks. Obviously, anything that's a constant may be used without a lock. In Java this includes objects that also contain shared variables and that may be moved onto or off of shared lists. [This is a different situation than in C/C++, where you explicitly return unneeded structures to the heap via `free()`. In Java, the garbage collector will take care of that.]

The other situation where you may look at unprotected shared data is when you don't mind if that data is out of date. A monitor that runs a periodic display of the current value of some variable is always going to lag behind the actual value of that variable. You could reasonably look at the value in question without locking *as long as that value is guaranteed to change atomically*. So values of type `int`, `char`, and `float`, along with pointers, are fine. Depending upon your hardware, 64-bit values such as `double` and `long` may also be legal. Of course, you will not know how much the value of that variable changes while you're displaying it. If it has a sudden peak to 10 times its previous value, is that important? You're the programmer.

Display of a value is a good example because it's simple. It's a bad example because it doesn't gain you anything. Displaying something is an expensive operation, requiring hundreds to thousands of microseconds. Saving 1 μs by skipping a lock is not going to make a difference in performance, but it will make your code a little uglier.

A better example of this situation is what's come to be known as *double-checked locking* (Code Example 7–6). This is useful in situations where a value is going to be initialized dynamically exactly once. The naive way of doing this is to have each thread lock a lock and then check to see if the data has been initialized yet, doing the initialization if not. With double-checked locking you can skip the lock and look directly at the value in question. If the value is valid, you know it has been initialized and that you can use it. If the value is invalid (presumably `null`), you lock the lock, recheck, and initialize. It is essential that you lock and recheck, as it is always possible for another thread to be running the same code at the same time.

```
void foo() {
    if (!object.initialized) {
        synchronized (object) {
            if (!object.initialized) {
                object.initialize();
                object.initialized = true;
                }
        }
    }
    use object
}
```

Code Example 7–6 *Double-Checked Locking*

You will probably never have use of this technique, as its use is so limited. Dynamic initialization like this is generally avoidable as you normally do initialization statically at load time or possibly directly from `main()` before any threads are started. Be very careful when doing this, as it's easy to do wrong.

Synchronization Problems

A number of things can go wrong when you try to coordinate the interactions of your threads. Not using synchronization variables is the most obvious and most common. But even when you've been careful to lock everything in sight, you still may encounter other problems. All of them have solutions; none of them have perfect solutions.

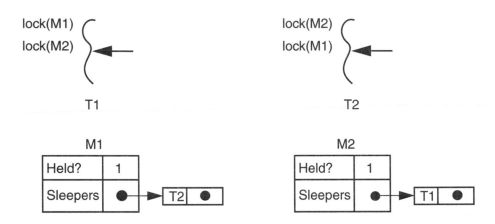

Figure 7–8   *Typical Deadlock*

Deadlocks

A deadlock is a kind of catch-22 in which one thread needs another thread to do something before it proceeds, and the other thread needs something from the first. So they both sit there, doing nothing, waiting for each other, forever. This is a bad thing.

A typical deadlock (Figure 7–8; Code Example 7–7) occurs when thread T1 obtains lock M1, and thread T2 obtains lock M2. Then thread T1 tries to obtain lock M2, while thread T2 tries for lock M1.

Thread 1	**Thread 2**
``public void frob() {
synchronized (one)
synchronized (two) {...}
}```	```public void tweek() {
synchronized (two)
synchronized (one) {...}
}```

Code Example 7–7   *Deadlock in Java*

Although typically a two-thread problem, deadlocks can in-volve dozens of threads in a circle, all waiting for one another.

They can involve a single thread that tries to obtain the same (non-recursive) mutex twice, and they can involve a thread that holds a lock dying while another thread is waiting for it.

Deadlocks can always be avoided simply by using careful programming practices. If you declare a lock hierarchy and always acquire locks in the same order—A before B before C, etc.—then there is no chance of a deadlock. When you want to do out-of-order locking, you can use the trylock functions to see whether you can get all the locks you need, and if not, then release them all and try again later (Code Example 7–8).

```
pthread_mutex_lock(&m2);
...
        if (EBUSY == pthread_mutex_trylock(&m1))
              {pthread_mutex_unlock(&m2);
               pthread_mutex_lock(&m1);
               pthread_mutex_lock(&m2);
              }
do_real_work();                              /* Got 'em both! */
}
```

Code Example 7–8 *Locking Mutexes Out of Order*

A typical instance of this out-of-order locking is the Solaris virtual memory system, which must lock access to pages. There is an official hierarchy which says that page 1 must be locked before page 2, etc. Occasionally, the VM system will lock page 2 and then discover that it also wants page 1. It will then execute a trylock on page 1. If that succeeds, all is well and it proceeds. If it fails, it releases the lock on page 2 and requests the locks in proper order.[3] This is a simple optimization that saves a bit of time in the normal case and is always correct.

Obviously, this kind of design is not possible using Java's synchronized sections. You could extend our Mutex class to behave like this, but the overhead is so large that it is very unlikely to be worth the effort.

---

[3]Note that you must release lock m2. Just spinning, waiting for m1 to become available, will not work.

Race Conditions

Races are instances of indeterminacy in otherwise deterministic programs. The result a program will give in a race condition depends upon the luck of the draw—which thread happens to run first, which LWP happens to get kicked off its processor by the page daemon, etc. Race conditions are generally bad things, although there are times when they are acceptable. Certainly, one would be upset if 1414.60/2.414 came out to be 586 on one run of a program and 586.001 on the next.

Most commonly, race conditions come around in programs in which the programmer forgot to write proper locking protection around some shared data or when locks were taken out of order. Still, it is certainly possible to write code that is perfectly correct, yet suffers from races. Consider Code Example 7–9; if v starts with the value one, the result will either be one or zero, depending upon which thread runs first.

Thread 1	Thread 2

```
synchronized (one) {          synchronized (one) {
    v = v - 1;                    v = v * 2;
}                             }
```

Code Example 7–9 *Simplistic Race Condition*

It is worth noting that some instances of indeterminacy in a program are acceptable. If you write a program that searches for a solution to a chess problem by creating lots of threads to consider lots of different possible moves, you may get different answers depending upon which thread completes first. As long as you get one good answer ("Checkmate in three!"), you don't really care if you move your pawn or your rook first.

Recovering from Deadlocks

A common question is, "What if a thread that is holding a lock dies? How can I recover from this?" The first answer is, "You can't." If a thread was holding a lock, it could legitimately have changed portions of the data that the lock protected in ways impossible to repair. If it was in the midst of changing the balance of your bank account, there is no inherent way for you to know whether or not it had credited the deposit it was working on. This is, of course, a very bad thing.

Pthreads makes no provision for this situation. Only the owner of a mutex can release it, and should that owner die, the mutex will never be released. Period. This is not really a problem for well-written programs. The only way for a thread to die is for the programmer to write the code that kills it. Thus, the proper answer here is, "Fix your code!"

You can, however, build arbitrarily complex "recoverable" locks from the primitives in all the libraries. Using them properly is the trick. Win32 and UI *robust* mutexes do allow recovery should the owner thread die. This is nice functionality if you need it, but it makes mutexes more expensive to use when you don't.

In a single-process, multithreaded program, recovering from deadlocks is not too much of an issue. You have complete control over your threads, and if your process dies, all the threads die with it. In a shared memory, multiple-process program, it is more problematic, as it is possible for one process to die while leaving others running.

It is somewhat reasonable to consider recovering from a deadlock in the case of a process dying unexpectedly. In other deadlock situations, where threads are waiting for each other, you really shouldn't be looking at recovery techniques. You should be looking at your coding techniques.

System V-shared semaphores do make provision for recovery, and they may prove to be the solution to your problem. They provide room for a system-maintained "undo" structure, which will be invoked should the owner process die, and they can be reset by any process with permission. They are expensive to use, though, and add complexity to your code.

Both Win32 and UI robust mutexes have built-in "death detection" also, so that your program can find out that the mutex it was waiting for was held by a newly dead thread.

Still, just having to undo structures that can reset mutexes does not solve the real problem. The data protected may be inconsistent, and this is what you have to deal with. It is possible to build arbitrarily complex undo structures for your code, but it is a significant task that should not be undertaken lightly.

Database systems do this routinely via *two-phase commit strategies,* as they have severe restrictions on crash recovery. Essentially, what they do is (1) build a time-stamped structure containing what the database will look like at the completion of the change; (2) save that structure to disk and begin the change; (3) complete the change; (4) update the time stamp on the database; and (5) delete the structure. A crash at any point in this sequence of events can be recovered from reliably.

Java does not have anything similar to these recoverable mutexes, nor does it need them. Java programs are either single process programs (in which case a deadlock is a programming bug) or they use RMI or some other kind of remote method invocation (in which case the RMI package is responsible for dealing with dead processes).

Be very, very careful when dealing with this problem!

The Lost Wakeup

If you simply neglect to hold the lock while testing or changing the value of the condition, your program will be subject to the fearsome *lost wakeup problem.* This condition occurs when one of your threads misses a wakeup signal because it had not yet gone to sleep. Of course, if you're not protecting your shared data correctly, your program will be subject to numerous other bugs, so this is nothing special. In Java it is not possible to suffer the lost wakeup problem just using `notify()`/`wait()` directly because you must hold the lock before you can call `notify()`. However, you can create constructs in Java that will have this problem. The `Mutex` and `ConditionVar` classes that we just built are subject to lost wakeup.

In Code Example 7–10 (slightly modified from our `Stop-Queue` example), it is possible for the stopper (which has failed to use the lock) to decide that it's time to stop and broadcast right at the instant between when the consumer checks the condition and when it goes to sleep. This code will promptly hang.

The probability that the stopper would get to run at exactly the right (er, wrong) instant is very small. (In 1000 test runs of this code it did not occur once.) If we insert a slight delay in the consumer between the test and the call to `condBroadcast()`, we

Thread 1 (The Consumer)	Thread 2 (The Stopper)

```
while (true) {
  mutex.lock();
  while (empty() & !stop) {          Thread.sleep(delay);
    Thread.sleep(delay);             System.out.println("Stopping")
                                     //    mutex.lock();
                                     stop = true;
                                     //    mutex.unlock();
                                     consumerCV.condBroadcast();
                                     producerCV.condBroadcast();


    consumerCV.condWait(mutex);
  }

  if (stop) break;
  item = remove();
  mutex.unlock();
  producerCV.condSignal();
  server.process(item);
}
```

Code Example 7–10   *The Lost Wakeup Problem*

can get it to happen. (In the example code on the Web, the program `LostWakeup` allows you to vary the sleep time (`delay`) to see how often it occurs on your machine.)

InterruptedException

Exceptions are a wonderful mechanism to handle unusual situations. They allow you to write your code in a simple, straightforward fashion and still be able to have special code for those special situations. Moreover, should those special situations occur in many diverse locations in your code, you are able to place a single exception handler at an appropriate location in your code, obviating the need for large amounts of repeated code. Finally, because you can allow an exception to propagate up through the call stack, it also provides you with a convenient method of executing "indirect jumps" [by means of C's `longjmp()` or Lisp's `catch`/`throw` blocks].

This is fine when you intend to handle these exceptions, but what if you don't intend to handle them? What about when you know there won't be any exceptions? What about Interrupt-

edException when you know you are never going to call interrupt ()? Or when you know you're simply going to ignore it?

So far, our code has been sprinkled with bits that look as
shown in Code Example 7–11.

```
try {wait();}
catch (InterruptedException ie) {}
```

Code Example 7–11   *Ignoring InterruptedException*

The obvious alternative, propagating the InterruptedException up the call chain, is viable, but a hassle. Just about every
major method in your program will be propagating InterruptedException, and should you be making lots of changes to your
code, you'll be inserting and removing "throws InterruptedException" regularly (Code Example 7–12). What a pain for
something that you won't be using.

```
public void foo() throws InterruptedException {
  wait() or sleep() or read() etc.
}
```

Code Example 7–12   *Propagating InterruptedException*

We solved this dilemma in our code for sleep() by writing a
method InterruptibleThread.sleep() which simply
caught InterruptedException and then interrupted the
thread again as it exited. The same general technique can be used for
wait() or any other method that throws InterruptedException (Code Example 7–13).

```
public static void sleep(long time)  {
 boolean interrupted = false;

  try {Thread.sleep(time);}
  catch (InterruptedException ie) {interrupted=true;} // Forget
timeout
  if (interrupted) Thread.currentThread().interrupt();
}
```

Code Example 7–13   *Ignoring InterruptedException*

This technique is nice when you don't want to handle interrupts at all the places they can occur. It is perfectly reasonable to have an interruptible program that pays attention to these interrupts only at certain points. We'll go into greater detail in *Implementing enableInterrupts()* on page 215.

APIs Used in This Chapter

The Class Extensions.RWLock

This is one of our classes. It implements POSIX-style readers/writer locks. RWLocks are useful only in very limited circumstances. Time your program carefully first!

readLock writeLock

```
public void readLock()

public void writeLock()
```

This locks the RWLock in either reader or writer mode. If a read lock is held by a different thread, this thread will be able to get another read lock directly. If a write lock is requested, the current thread must go to sleep, waiting for it to become available.

Reference: Chapter 7.

unlock

```
public void unlock()
```

This unlocks the RWLock (both for readers and for writers). If this is the last reader, it will wake up one writer thread (if any are sleeping). If this is a writer, it will wake up one writer thread (if any are sleeping); otherwise, it will wake up all the sleeping threads with reader requests.

Reference: Chapter 7.

The Class Extensions.Barrier

This is one of our classes. It implements barriers.

Comment: You won't use these very often, but if you're implementing something like a simulation, these might come in useful.

Barrier

    public Barrier (int i)

This creates a barrier object with a `count` of `i`.

Reference: Chapter 7.

barrierSet

    public synchronized void barrierSet(int i)

This resets the barrier `count` to `i`.

Reference: Chapter 7.

barrierWait

    public synchronized void barrierWait() {

This causes the calling thread to block until `count` threads have called `barrierWait()`.

Reference: Chapter 7.

The Class Extensions.SingleBarrier

This is one of our classes. It implements barriers with a divided set of waiters and posters.

Comment: You won't use these very often, perhaps only for example programs.

SingleBarrier

    public SingleBarrier (int i)

            This creates a single-barrier object with a count of i.

        Reference: Chapter 7.

barrierSet

    public synchronized void barrierSet(int i)

            This resets the single barrier count to i.

        Reference: Chapter 7.

barrierWait

    public synchronized void barrierWait() {

            This causes the calling thread to block until barrierPost() has been called count times.

        Reference: Chapter 7.

barrierPost

    public synchronized void barrierPost() {

            This increments the counter for how many times barrierPost() has been called.

        Reference: Chapter 7.

Summary

A wide variety of more complex synchronization is possible, but probably not useful. Building your own synchronization variables is not terribly difficult, but it can be quite subtle. Deadlocks can always be avoided; race conditions are more problematical. Trying to recover from deadlocks is very, very tricky. Interruptions are a real pain.

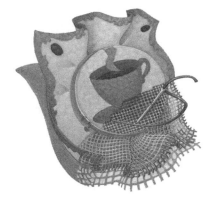

TSD

▼ THREAD-SPECIFIC DATA

▼ JAVA TSD

▼ APIS USED IN THIS CHAPTER

▼ THE CLASS JAVA.LANG.THREADLOCAL

In which explanations of thread-specific data, their use, and some implementation details are provided.

Thread-Specific Data

Sometimes it is useful to have data that is globally accessible to any function, yet still unique to the thread. Two threads that are printing out data, one in French and the other in Danish, would find it most convenient to have a private global variable, which they could set to the desired language. Any function at any depth could then access this variable without the hassle of passing it at every call.

TSD provides this kind of global data by means of a set of function calls. The techniques used by POSIX and Java provide the same functionality with one major distinction.

In POSIX, TSD is implemented by creating an array of *key* offsets to *value* cells, attached to each thread structure (Figure 8–1). To use it, you first create a new key, which is then added to the TSD arrays for all threads.[1] Keys are just variables of type `pthread_key_t` (which are opaque data types, most commonly integers), and key creation (*initialization* is a more descriptive term) consists of setting the value of the key to the next location. Once the key has been created, you can access or change the value associated with the key via calls to `pthread_getspecific()` and `pthread_setspecific()`.

TSD is typically used to declare all the keys globally, initialize (er, "create") them in `main()`, then create threads and start the program for real. If you are creating some TSD in a library, you must arrange for that library to do the initialization before use. In Code Example 8–1, `bar()` in the first thread will see $\sqrt{2}$,[2] and in the second thread will see π.

---

[1]Adding the new element to the array need not be done at creation time. It can be more effective to add the element at first access time for each thread.

[2]One of my best friends, a math wiz, purchased a small farm in rural Minnesota. His address was 1414, rural route 2.

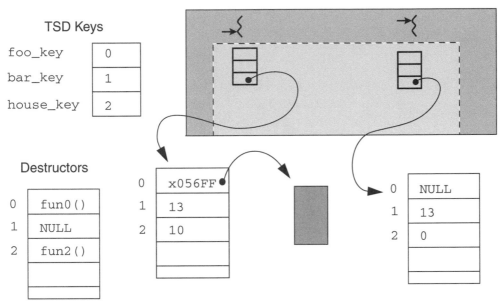

Figure 8–1 *Thread-Specific Data in POSIX*

```
pthread_key_t house_key;

foo((void *) arg)
{
    pthread_setspecific(house_key, arg);
    bar();
}

bar()
{float n;
    n = (float) pthread_getspecific(house_key);
}

main()
{...
    pthread_keycreate(&house_key, NULL);
```

Code Example 8–1 *Use of POSIX TSD*

```
    pthread_create(&tid, NULL, foo, (void *) 1.414);
    pthread_create(&tid, NULL, foo, (void *) 3.141592653589);
...}
```

Code Example 8–1   *Use of POSIX TSD (cont.)*

In Win32 there is a different version of TSD. Win32 calls it *dynamic thread local storage* and its use is virtually identical to TSD in POSIX (Code Example 8–2). Other than the lack of destructors, you may use it in the same fashion as TSD.

```
key = TlsAlloc();
TlsSetValue(key, data);
data = TlsGetValue(key);
```

Code Example 8–2   *Dynamic TLS in Win32*

The actual implementation of TSD is different from vendor to vendor, but in general they're all the same. When accessing a TSD item, we first need to know which thread we're running on. Think about this for a moment. How does a thread find out who it is? How does it find its own thread structure? On SPARC machines, there is one register (g7) reserved for special use. Compiler writers are instructed not to use it. Here the threads library places a pointer to the thread structure of the running thread. The thread first dereferences g7 to find the structure [this is what `pthread_self()` and `Thread.currentThread()` do], then it dereferences an element of the structure to find the TSD array. Finally, it looks up the appropriate element in the array.

Java TSD

Java did not provide for TSD directly until Java 2. This was not a problem, however, as the ability to extend the thread class meant that you could simply add an instance variable to a subclass *if* you were in control of thread creation (Code Example 8–3).

This technique is fairly straightforward, efficient, and gives you most of the functionality that POSIX TSD does. It does require you to declare the TSD as part of the thread, versus the more dynamic nature of POSIX TSD, but this is unlikely to be a problem. (In this simple example we do not provide any protection to

```
public MyThread extends Thread {
    float transcendental;
}

public MyRunnable implements Runnable {

    public run() {
        ((MyThread)Thread.currentThread()).transcendental = 3.1415926535;
        ...
        bar();
    }

    public bar () {
        meditateOn(((MyThread)Thread.currentThread()).transcendental);
    }
}

Thread t = new MyThread(new Myrunnable());
t.start();
```

Code Example 8–3 *Implementing TSD by Subclassing Thread*

ensure that only the current thread can access the TSD, but clearly no other thread should.)

Nonetheless, in Java 2, a TSD class (actually called TLS—*thread local storage*) is provided that will give you a more dynamic, POSIX-like functionality (Code Example 8–4). In this version you create an instance of the ThreadLocal class, then when you call the set() and get() methods, you will be manipulating a thread-specific value. This is essentially just a hash table indexed on the current thread. The values stored by ThreadLocal do need to be of type Object, so primitive types must be contained in the appropriate wrapper type (e.g., Integer for int).

```
public MyObject {
    static ThreadLocal transcendental = new ThreadLocal();
}

public MyRunnable implements Runnable {
```

Code Example 8–4 *Using ThreadLocal in Java*

```
public void run() {
    MyObject.transcendental.set(new Float(3.1415926535));
    ...
    bar();
}

public void bar () {
    meditateOn((Float) MyObject.transcendental.get());
}
}

Thread t = new Thread(new Myrunnable());
t.start();
```

Code Example 8–4 *Using ThreadLocal in Java (cont.)*

You still have the problem of figuring out how to pass the ThreadLocal object around. Here, we have chosen to make it a static instance variable of MyObject. When you are creating all the threads yourself, you can use the first method, subclassing Thread, but when you are using threads that someone else created, you will need to use thread local storage. Clearly, any kind of TSD is going to be slower than accessing simple global variables. Note that the current performance of ThreadLocal is significantly worse than using our home-built thread-local variables! (See *Timings* on page 419.)

The other missing piece of functionality is the lack of a specific TSD destructor. The primary use of a TSD destructor in POSIX is to reclaim dynamically allocated data, something the Java garbage collector will do automatically. The other, more general use of a destructor is to return a specific resource (e.g., to replace an object onto a list of free objects, close a file descriptor, socket, etc.). There is no direct parallel for this in Java. If you find yourself with this kind of problem (very unlikely!), you will need to write an ad hoc method to take care of it at thread exit time.

Should you wish to know what Runnable your thread is, you can use a thread local variable or thread local storage to record that information (Code Examples 8–5 and 8–6).

```
public class MyThread extends Thread {
Runnable runnable;

public MyThread(Runnable r) {super(r); runnable=r;}
}
```

Code Example 8–5 *Recording the Runnable in the Thread*

```
public class MyThread extends Thread {
    static ThreadLocal runnable = new ThreadLocal();

public MyThread(Runnable r) {super(r);
MyThread.runnable.set(r);}
}
```

Code Example 8–6 *Recording the Runnable in Thread Local Storage*

APIs Used in This Chapter

The Class java.lang.ThreadLocal

This class implements thread local storage by defining an object that can hold different values for different threads.

ThreadLocal

```
public ThreadLocal()
```

This creates a new thread local object.

Reference: Chapter 8.

get set

```
public Object get()
public void set(Object o)
```

These functions set/get a thread-local value for this object.

Reference: Chapter 8.

Summary

We described the basic design of thread-specific data storage, its use, and some of the implementation details.

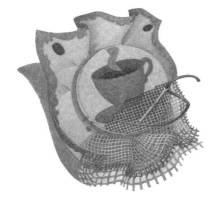

Chapter **9**

Cancellation

In which we describe the acrimonious nature of some programs and how unwanted threads may be disposed of. The highly complex issues surrounding bounded time termination and program correctness are also covered. A simple conclusion is drawn.

What Cancellation Is

Sometimes you have reason to get rid of a thread before it has completed its work. Perhaps the user changed her mind about what she was doing. Perhaps the program had many threads doing a heuristic search, and one of them found the answer. Perhaps it's time to shut down a server. In such cases you want to be able to have one thread kill the other threads. This is known as *cancellation* (a POSIX term; see Figure 9–1).

No matter how you choose to deal with the issues of cancellation, be it in Java, Win32, or POSIX threads, the primary issues remain the same. You must ensure that any thread that you are going to cancel releases any locks it might hold, frees any memory it may have allocated for its own use, and leaves the world in a consistent state (Code Example 9–1).

Java	POSIX	Win32
T1.stop()	pthread_cancel(T1)	TerminateThread(T1)

Code Example 9–1   *Asynchronous Thread Cancellation*

The fundamental operation is quite simple: You call the cancellation function with the target thread, and the target thread dies sometime "soon." The ramifications of doing this are, however, quite complex, making cancellation one of the most difficult operations to execute correctly.

Polling for Cancellation

There are three basic techniques of cancelling threads. The simplest is to do it ad hoc. You set a flag and let all the target threads continue to run until they see it. This is what we did in our `StopQueue` example. This is great unless one of your threads is blocked waiting for I/O, in which case it may never notice that the flag has been set.

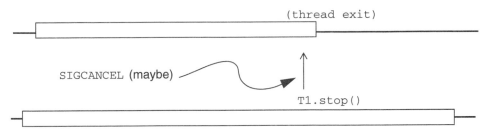

Figure 9–1 *Thread Cancellation*

Asynchronous Cancellation

The second method is known as *asynchronous cancellation*. This is what most people think of first. You call the cancel function and the target thread dies "soon."[1] If the thread is sleeping or blocked on I/O, it will be awakened in order to die.

This is the only type of cancellation that Win32 provides. You call `TerminateThread()` and the target thread dies. Unfortunately, should that thread own some resource, hold some lock, or have malloced some memory, your program will be in trouble. This type of cancellation is known as *unrestricted asynchronous cancellation,* and it is the responsibility of the killer to know that the victim can be safely eliminated at the time of cancellation—a difficult task at best, impossible at worst.

In POSIX you get this behavior by calling `pthread_cancel()` with the cancellation type set to asynchronous. In Java, the method `thread.stop()` behaves similarly, save that any synchronized sections will be released and any `finally` clauses will be executed.

---

[1]The actual delivery time of a stop request is not specified. The most obvious implementation for a truly asynchronous stop is to use UNIX signals or NT's equivalent. Signals in UNIX are indeed asynchronous, but not as immediate as you might imagine. The usual implementation of signals is for the caller to mark a bit in the target's process structure, and for the caller to look at that bit only when context switching on the system clock. Thus delivery of signals, hence stop notifications, occurs only at clock ticks. Perfectly legal but not intuitive.

Deferred Cancellation

The third type of cancellation is known as *deferred cancellation*. In this type of cancellation, a thread exits only when it polls the library explicitly to find out if it should exit. When the thread blocks in a library call which is a *cancellation point* [e.g., sem_wait()], the thread will be awakened in order to exit. POSIX defines a set of standard library functions that must call it (see *Defined Cancellation/Interruption Points* on page 193).

In POSIX, there's a function pthread_testcancel(), which checks to see if a bit has been set. If the bit is set, it exits the thread; otherwise, it returns, and the thread continues normally.

Using interrupt() for Deferred Cancellation

In Java, InterruptedException and Interrupted-IOException are used in much the same fashion as POSIX deferred cancellation. One thread may call interrupt() on another thread, and when that thread hits an interruptible point (the Java analogue to POSIX cancellation points), that method will then throw an InterruptedException or InterruptedIOException, and you may then handle that exception as you see fit. If your objective is to kill the thread, you may simply have the exception handler exit the thread. If you merely wanted the thread to quit what it was doing and start doing something else, you can do that. (This is rather nicer than POSIX cancellation, as you may choose to do other things upon interruption.)

Progressive Shutdown

There are those who suggest that a progressive shutdown scheme is more appropriate than cancellation. By *progressive*, they mean first set a flag and wait. If that doesn't do the trick, reduce the scheduling priority. If that's not enough, restrict permissions and hope the target thread hits a security violation. Then try interrupt(), then try stop(), then try destroy(). This just doesn't seem like a terribly great idea.

interrupt()

Basically, a call to interrupt() sets a flag and looks to see if the target thread is blocked. If it is blocked, it is forcibly awakened. When it sees the flag, it throws an exception. You may also test to see if a thread has been interrupted via Thread.interrupted() (for the current thread, this also resets the interrupted flag) or thread.isInterrupted() (for an arbitrary thread, this does not reset the flag). Once the flag is cleared, no method will throw InterruptedException until interrupt() is called again (Code Example 9–2). Catching the exception will also reset the flag.[2]

Thread 1	Thread 2

```
try {                            t1.interrupt()
    ... lots of work ...         if (t1.isInterrupted()) {
    while (!ready()) {wait();}       System.println(t1+"int'd")
    ... more work ...
    if (Thread.interrupted() {
        exit threaAd or whatever
        }
    }
catch (InterruptedException e) {
    exit thread or whatever
    }
```

Code Example 9–2   *Using thread.interrupt()*

In POSIX deferred cancellation and in Java interruption, a thread may run for an arbitrary amount of time after a cancellation (interruption) has been issued, thus allowing critical sections to execute without having to disable/enable cancellation. This is good because you know that the thread will exit synchronously. This is bad because you must do extra work if you wish to ensure bounded cancellation times. An interrupted thread could go off and run in a

---

[2]This "interrupt flag" was not part of the Java 1.1 specification per se, nor was its behavior with respect to being cleared well defined. But it is defined in Java 2 and this is how it works in both 1.1 and 2.

loop for hours before hitting an interruption point. Of course, this might be OK.

There is no pat answer to these issues, and you, as the responsible programmer, must resolve them on a program-by-program basis. In POSIX you may select asynchronous for one program, deferred for a second, and a mixture of both for a third. Java does not officially give you this option because the method `stop()` has been officially deprecated in JDK 1.2. But as `stop()` will continue to be supported for some amount of time into the future, you *could* continue to use it. Don't.

Don't Call `stop()`

So what was the problem with the `stop()` method? Why has it been deprecated in JDK 1.2? Basically, it has proven just too difficult to use correctly. Just like POSIX's asynchronous cancellation, `stop()` will interrupt a thread in the middle of whatever it's doing and leave no options for proper recovery of system state.

Yes, you can write a `finally` section to reestablish invariants, but you need to know which invariants to reestablish (perhaps your code is complex and only half of it ran). You also have to deal with the fact that the stop message can arrive in the middle of the `finally` section, in which case that will be stopped. In other words, `finally` sections don't help.

About the only thing you can do is to write a stop protocol (similar to Code Example 9–6) yourself in which the killer thread and the target threads agree on exactly when a stop request may be issued. Basically, you would write a new class of threads `StoppableThread`, which would have two new methods: `enableStop()` and `disableStop()`. You would then write a method, `myStop()`, which would check the stoppable state of the target thread and call `stop()` only if it were enabled. All threads that you intend to stop would have to be of class `StoppableThread`. (We show this technique for interruption in `InterruptibleThread`.)

So it's possible to use `stop()` for cancellation. It's just very difficult and you probably don't want to do this. (And of course, it's deprecated in JDK 1.2.) On top of all that, there is no clear statement of exactly when a thread that has been stopped will actually exit. If it's sleeping, will it be awakened? Maybe. Can it be forced to pop out of a JNI call? Maybe.

ThreadDeath

The way stop() works is that it throws an unchecked runtime exception, ThreadDeath. This exception then propagates up the call stack, running all finally sections and unlocking all locks that it encounters. When it gets to the initial run() method, it pops out of that, too, and the thread exits.

When Java was being designed, ThreadDeath was not supposed to be an exposed interface; you weren't supposed to know about it. But it did become public and is now officially supported. That's very interesting, but now forget it.

It is possible for you to throw ThreadDeath yourself. It is possible for you to catch ThreadDeath and deal with it yourself. You will even find books that give you snippets of code that do so. But they never give you enough to create a robust program. Yes, it is possible to use ThreadDeath. Don't do that.

Using stop() to Implement Thread.exit()

There is a second use for stop(). You can use it as the Java equivalent to pthread_exit() (Code Example 9–3). This use of stop() does not have any deadlock or data corruption problems noted above because you call it synchronously and you can ensure that it is called only when everything is consistent and safe. Unfortunately, even this use of stop() is deprecated. What to do?

```
public class InterruptibleThread extends Thread {

public static void exit() {
  Thread.currentThread().stop();
}

...
```

Code Example 9–3 *Implementing exit()*

For a long time in our programs we simply put a little syntactic sugar over it and included it in our `InterruptibleThread` class as below. You will find examples of code like this in many of our older example programs. We have subsequently been convinced that this is the wrong way to do things. Indeed, we have been convinced that even `pthread_exit()` is the wrong way to do things!

Never Exit a Thread!

More accurately, never try to exit a thread explicitly. The argument goes like this: A runnable should be viewed as a package of work to be done. As such, you never know for sure just who is going to do that work. It could be a new thread, it could be an old thread, it could be the current thread. As such, neither the `run()` method nor any of the methods it calls (most certainly not any library objects you bought from Joe's Object Factory) should cause a thread to exit. They don't know anything about the thread that's running them.

If there is a problem, they should either deal with it directly or throw an exception to be handled by a higher-level method. The run method itself has no idea which thread is running it, so at most it should simply return. If returning happens to exit the thread running it, that's OK. This way, runnable objects are free to be used by any thread in any fashion it chooses.

In our ThreadedSwing example (Code Example 9–4; see also *Threads and Windows* on page 366), we do exactly this. In the snippet below, when we run the program with threads turned off, the work is performed by the current thread in-line. When we turn threads on, the work is farmed out to a new thread.

Don't Call `destroy()`

There is another method, `destroy()` which stops a thread but doesn't unlock locks or run `finally` sections. It was intended as a thread killer of last resort (in case you were in an unstoppable loop or if there were a bug in the JVM). If you use this method to kill a thread, you should expect the rest of your program to either crash or hang sooner or later. This method is

```
public void actionPerformed(ActionEvent event) {
                ThreadedJButton          currentButton         =
    (ThreadedJButton)event.getSource();

  System.out.println("Pressed " + currentButton);
  currentButton.setEnabled(false);
  System.out.println(currentButton + " disabled.");
  DoWorker w = new DoWorker(currentButton);

  if (ThreadedSwing.useThreads)
    new Thread(w).start();
  else
    w.run();
}
```

Code Example 9–4   *From ThreadedSwing Example:*
NumericButtonListener.java

not deprecated in Java 2, but neither is it implemented in any of the JVMs.

Defined Cancellation/Interruption Points

POSIX *requires* that a set of 25 library functions be cancellation points and that they must be interruptible should they be blocked at cancellation time. They are *required* to test for cancellation even if they don't block. These are functions such as (pthread_cond_wait, pthread_testcancel, read, sem_wait, write). It allows about 60 more, but leaves it to the vendor's discretion.

Java faces the same set of issues for its interruptible points, and in JDK 1.2, a set of methods are defined to throw InterruptedIOException. (They must throw the exception if they have received an interrupt.) Unfortunately, Java does not specify exactly which functions these are, nor does it actually require that they throw the exception from the middle of a blocked system call. Among the calls that do throw InterruptedIOException are read() and accept(), which we illustrate in *A Robust, Interruptible Server* on page 389. Unlike catching InterruptedException, catching InterruptedIOException does *not* clear the interrupt flag.

The Problem with I/O

This problem is even more insidious than it appears at first glance. Not only are the interruption points not specified, not only are they not required to wake up from blocking calls to throw the exception, it is not even well defined what happens when they do! In particular, if a thread is blocked, waiting on a `read()` from a socket, it is legal for it to read in an unspecified number of bytes from the socket and then throw `Interrupt-edIOException`. This would leave the socket stream in an undefined state. The only thing that you could do would be to close the socket.

Writes to sockets can also block for an unbounded time if the socket buffer in the kernel fills up. Typically, this buffer is around 64k, so it's unlikely to fill unless the client is asleep.

Not Cancelling upon Interruption

Interruptions in Java are just exceptions and nothing says that you have to exit a thread simply because it's been interrupted. For example, you may have a thread running Dungeon Of Doom '99, which is waiting for the user to vaporize an evil space Dalique (Code Example 9–5). If the user fails to do so, you may interrupt that thread after 2 seconds and declare him "eliminated," but only if he's already injured. If you want to use interruption for more than one purpose, you'll need to set a (protected!) variable to indicate what the interrupted thread should do.

Handling Interrupts

In writing your own libraries, it would be nice to have all of your functions interruption safe. You can ensure this by never calling any interruptible functions, or by properly handling interruptions when you do call some. There are a variety of methods for handling this.

Disabling Interrupts

You might simply ensure that no interruptions will be sent while your function runs. This requires a bit of coordination between

```
public synchronized boolean justInjured() {
    if (health > 1)
        return true;
    else
        return false;
}

public void attack() throws LiquidatedException {
...
try {
    vaporizeDalique();
    }
catch (InterruptedException ie) {
    if (justInjured())
        synchronized (this) {health--;}
    else
        throw new LiquidatedException();//Eliminate Eliminate Eliminate
    }
}
```

<hr>

Code Example 9–5   *Testing a Variable from an Exception Handler*

your libraries and the user of your library to establish a "disabled" protocol such as that used in Code Example 9–6. You probably don't want to do this, as it binds your library too close to the application. In Code Example 9–6, the interruptible thread states a request that no interruptions be sent by setting inCriticalSection to true. That variable must be protected, of course, and it must be tested at each entry to any code that is either interruptible or that issues interrupts.[3] (Ugly, eh? Compare to *Implementing enableInterrupts()* on page 215, where this technique is cleaned up a bit.)

Ignore Interrupts

You could install interruption handlers that do nothing and assume that either the programmer will never call interrupt or that

<hr>

[3]As a matter of fact, even this code is not flawless by the definition of interruption. It is theoretically possible for the interrupter thread to get the lock, send an interrupt to the target thread, and release the lock; the target thread could then lock the lock and Thread.interrupted() could still return false. It's difficult to imagine an implementation of the JVM for which this could happen, but it is possible according to the official definition.

The Interruptible Thread

```
public void doDatabaseThing() throws InterruptedException {
    InterruptibleThread t = InterruptibleThread.self();

    synchronized (t) {
      if (Thread.interrupted()) {throw new InterruptedException();}
      t.inCriticalSection = true; // Don't cancel in critical section!
    }

    try {
       incrementDatabase(1);
       Thread.sleep(10);           // Or some other interruptible method
       incrementDatabase(-1);
       }
    catch (InterruptedException ie) { } // Impossible

    synchronized (t) {
      t.inCriticalSection = false; // Now it's OK to cancel
      t.notify();
    }
}
```

The Interrupter Thread

```
    synchronized (t) {
      while (t.inCriticalSection) {
          try { t.wait(); }
          catch (InterruptedException ie) { } // Impossible
      }
      t.interrupt();
    }
```

Code Example 9–6   *Inventing an InterruptDisabled Protocol*

---

she will keep calling it until the thread disappears. Most sample code you see in other books and articles does this. This is too much for a library to assume. Don't do that.

Exit on `interrupt()`

You could install interruption handlers that will exit the thread right there and then, assuming that the programmer always intends interruption to be cancellation and that all data is consistent anytime your library is called. This is also too much for a library to assume. Don't do that.

Propagate `InterruptedException`

You could propagate the exception. By propagating, you shift the burden of dealing with the exception to the callers, who must then treat your libraries as throwing `InterruptedException`. Propagating the exception is certainly the right thing to do for many library functions.

The value of this is that if your library makes unbounded blocking calls, anyone who used it would want to be able to interrupt it. If you make bounded-time blocking calls, it's not so vital. It's generally OK if your library call takes 40 ms and you don't interrupt it.

Reinterrupt

You may wish to avoid dealing with `InterruptedException` at all. In such cases you can set a flag, reenter whatever code you were running, wait until that code returns normally, and then call interrupt on yourself before leaving.

The point here is that (1) you don't want your code to do anything with interrupts at all, (2) you don't want the caller to have to deal with `InterruptedException` being thrown from your code, and (3) you really wish that you could have called a method that didn't throw that exception at all, but there was no alternative. This is a common thing to do.

The mutex class shown in Code Example 9–7 (this is the actual code we use) exemplifies this situation. In this code we don't want to be bothered with interrupts and we don't want the caller of `mutex.lock()` to be forced to catch `InterruptedException` all the time. So we simply call `interrupt()` on the current thread again, trusting that it will be seen in the caller's code somewhere else.[4] This way, the exception will never be lost.

---

[4]If the programmer doesn't deal with `InterruptedException`, what the heck is he doing calling `interrupt()`?

```
public synchronized void lock() {
  boolean interrupted = false;

  while (owner != null) {
    try {wait();}
    catch (InterruptedException ie) {interrupted=true;}
  }
  owner = Thread.currentThread();
  if (interrupted) owner.interrupt();
}
```

Code Example 9–7   *Calling* interrupt() *upon Return*

Of course, this code could block forever and that could be a problem. This is what the designer of the program needs to deal with. He needs to guarantee that another thread will do whatever is necessary to make this method return. (For a mutex or synchronized section, he must guarantee that the owner releases it.)

So this is a good thing. We're not dropping interrupts. But we're still not out of the woods. What if you have a method which calls one of these methods and that method doesn't know about you reinterrupting? It could get nasty. Consider the naive code (shown in Code Example 9–8) for condition variables and RWlocks.

What happens if we're blocked waiting to get a read lock and we get interrupted? Well, our condition variable class doesn't want to throw InterruptedException, so it just schedules a reinterrupt and returns as if from a spurious wakeup. Unfortunately, our lock code views the return as spurious and just calls condWait() again. Which promptly sees the new interrupt and throws InterruptedException again, etc. (Code Example 9–9). Don't do that.

So if we wanted to use that design for condition variables, we would need to keep that in mind and play the same tricks in the readers/writer lock. Ugh!

Now, what we really want is for InterruptedException to work correctly and simply and any synchronization variables we build on top of Java to be equally simple to use. By sticking with our original version of condWait(), which doesn't treat InterruptedException as a spurious wakeup, we get the best of both worlds (Code Example 9–10). This is also almost certainly what you want to do in any of your code. If you want to get fancy, be careful!

```
public void condWait(Mutex mutex) {
  boolean        interrupted = false;

    try {
      synchronized (this) {
        mutex.unlock();
        wait();
      }
    }              // NB: There is no 'while' loop
    catch (InterruptedException ie) {interrupted=true;}

    mutex.lock();
    if (interrupted) Thread.currentThread().interrupt();
}


public void readLock() {

  m.lock();
  nWaitingReaders++;
  while ((owner != null) || (nWaitingWriters > 0)) {
    readersCV.condWait(m); }
  nWaitingReaders--;
  nCurrentReaders++;
  m.unlock();
}
```

Code Example 9–8   *Naive Condition Variable and Readers/Writer Lock*

```
public void readLock() {
  booleaninterrupted=false;
  m.lock();
  nWaitingReaders++;
  while ((owner != null) || (nWaitingWriters > 0)) {
    if (Thread.interrupted()) interrupted=true;
    readersCV.condWait(m); }
  nWaitingReaders--;
  nCurrentReaders++;
  m.unlock();
  if (interrupted) Thread.currentThread().interrupt();
}
```

Code Example 9–9   *Handling Interruptions from condWait() the Hard Way*

```
public void condWait(Mutex mutex, long timeout) {
  boolean       interrupted = false;


  while (true) {
    try {
      synchronized (this) {
        mutex.unlock();
        wait(timeout);
        break;
      }
    }
    catch (InterruptedException ie) {interrupted=true;}
  }

  mutex.lock();
  if (interrupted) Thread.currentThread().interrupt();
}
```

Code Example 9–10   *The Right Way of Implementing condWait()*

The vast majority of programs don't deal with interrupts at all. Computational programs don't care. Interactive programs usually are fine doing "dirty" shutdowns ["Who cares if there are open file descriptors, sockets, etc.? System.exit() will close them and any clients can deal with it on their end."] It's the more serious server and database programs that need to do clean shutdowns.

Cancellation State

POSIX has a more elaborate version of cancellation. It defines a *cancellation state* for each thread that will enable or disable cancellation for that thread. Thus you can disable cancellation during critical sections and reenable it afterward. Neither Win32 nor Java defines this state, although it would not be too difficult for you to write it yourself [*Implementing enableInterrupts()* on page 215]. Cancellation state makes it (just barely) feasible to use asynchronous cancellation safely, although there are still significant problems to be dealt with.

A Cancellation Example

Code Example 9–11 uses cancellation via interruption to get rid of unneeded search threads. This program has the objective of finding a certain number by using a heuristic. The desired number is the process ID, and the heuristic is to generate random numbers, checking to see if they happen to be the PID (Figure 9–2). Admittedly, this is not a very clever heuristic, but the concept is solid. You can reasonably replace the problem and heuristic with more meaningful ones, such as a chess position and an alpha-beta search. The cancellation issues won't change.

The main thread gets the PID and creates 10 threads to search for it. Each of the searcher threads proceeds to generate a random number, checking to see if that happens to be the PID. When one thread finds the number, it interrupts all the other threads, then returns itself. The main thread will do a join on all the searcher threads, printing out the answer when all have exited.

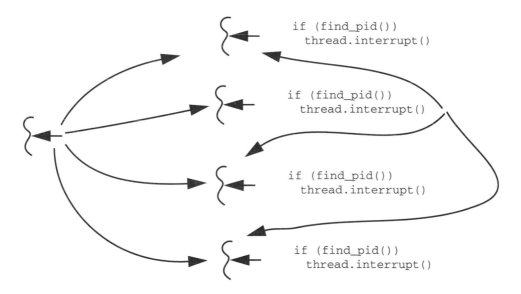

Figure 9–2 *Cancellation Example Program*

```
//              CancellationInterrupt/Cancellation.java


/*
   A very simple example to run which illustrate cancellation.
   Choose a target number, then create a bunch of threads to search
   for using a heuristic [call rand()!].  The first to find it cancels
   the others.

   A database is included to illustrate typical problems.  The database
   should always by 0 at the end of every transaction.  Observe how
   much effort that takes.


 */



import java.io.*;
import Extensions.*;

public class Cancellation {
   int            answer = 0;
   int            target = 9;
   boolean        found = false;
   int            nSearchers = 10;
   TSDThread      threads[] = new TSDThread[nSearchers];
   Object         databaseBalancedLock = new Object();
   int            databaseBalanced = 0;
   Object         nGuessesLock = new Object();
   int            nGuesses = 0;
   static         boolean DEBUG = false;


public static void main(String argv[]) throws InterruptedException {
   Cancellation c = new Cancellation();

   if (System.getProperty("DEBUG") != null) DEBUG = true;
   for (int i=0; i<2; i++) {
     c.run();
   }
}


public void incrementGuesses() {
```

Code Example 9–11 *Using interrupt() to Cancel Searcher Threads*

```
    synchronized(nGuessesLock) {
      nGuesses++;
    }                // Cannot synchronize on cancel. Why?
  }

  public void incrementDatabase(int i) {

    if (DEBUG)
      System.out.println(Thread.currentThread().getName()
                        + " incrementing "
                        + databaseBalanced + " by " + i);

    synchronized(databaseBalancedLock) {
      databaseBalanced += i;
    }      // Cannot synchronize on cancel. Why?
  }


  public void run() throws InterruptedException {
    Thread t;
    nGuesses = 0;
    found = false;

    synchronized(this) {
      for (int i=0; i<nSearchers; i++) {
        threads[i] = new TSDThread(new Searcher(this, i));
        threads[i].start();
      }
    }
    for (int i=0; i<nSearchers; i++) {
      threads[i].join();
      System.out.println(threads[i].getName() + " joined.");
    }

    System.out.println("The answer is: " + answer + ", it took: " + nGuesses
                        + " guesses, and the database is...");
    if (databaseBalanced == 0)
      System.out.println("Consistant.");
    else
      System.out.println("Inconsistant!");
  }

}
```

Code Example 9–11   *Using* `interrupt()` *to Cancel Searcher*
Threads (cont.)

```
//                 CancellationInterrupt/Searcher.java

import java.io.*;
import java.util.*;
import Extensions.*;


public class Searcher implements Runnable {
  int           target;
  Cancellation  cancel;
  int           seed;


public Searcher(Cancellation c, int s) {
  target = c.target;
  cancel=c;
  seed = s;
}


public void doDatabaseThing() throws InterruptedException {
  TSDThread self = (TSDThread) Thread.currentThread();

    synchronized (self) {
      if (Thread.interrupted()) {
        System.out.println(self.getName() +
                          " before DoDatabaseThing, interrupted.");
        throw new InterruptedException();
      }
     self.inCriticalSection = true;  // Don't cancel in critical section!
    }
    try {
      cancel.incrementDatabase(1);
      Thread.sleep(10);                      // Use normal sleep() here.
      cancel.incrementDatabase(-1);
      synchronized (self) {
        self.inCriticalSection = false;
        self.notify();
      }
    }
  catch (InterruptedException ie) {
    // Should never get here!
    System.out.println(self.getName() +
                      " BUG in DoDatabaseThing, interrupted.");
    cancel.incrementDatabase(-1);  // Fix it up.
```

Code Example 9–11   *Using interrupt() to Cancel Searcher Threads (cont.)*

```
      throw ie;
  }
}


public void run() {
  TSDThread self = (TSDThread) Thread.currentThread();
  Random r = new Random(seed);
              int guess;

  System.out.println(self.getName() + " is searching...");

  for (int i=0; true; i++) {
    try { doDatabaseThing(); }
    catch (InterruptedException ie) {return;}
    guess = r.nextInt()% 10;
    cancel.incrementGuesses();

    if (guess == target) {
      synchronized(cancel) {
      System.out.println(self.getName() + " got the answer: " + guess);
      if (cancel.found) {
          System.out.println(self.getName() + " too late! Exiting");
        return;        // If someone else already found it...
        }
        cancel.found = true;
        for (int j=0; j<cancel.nSearchers; j++) {
          TSDThread t1 = (TSDThread) cancel.threads[j];
          if (!t1.equals(self)) {            // Don't kill yourself
            synchronized (t1) {
              while (t1.inCriticalSection) {
                try  {
                  t1.wait();
                }
                catch (InterruptedException ie) { } // Impossible
              }
              t1.interrupt();
              if (Cancellation.DEBUG)
                System.out.println(self.getName() + " cancelling "
                                   + t1.getName());
            }
          }
        }
        cancel.answer = guess;
        System.out.println(self.getName() + " done.");
```

Code Example 9–11 *Using* `interrupt()` *to Cancel Searcher Threads (cont.)*

```
        return;
      }
    }
  }
}


}
```

```
//                  CancellationInterrupt/TSDThread.java

/*
  Add a bit of Thread-Specific Data.
  */

import java.io.*;
import java.util.*;
import Extensions.*;


public class TSDThread extends Thread {
 boolean inCriticalSection = true;


public TSDThread(Searcher o) {
  super(o);
}


}
```

Code Example 9–11 *Using* `interrupt()` *to Cancel Searcher*
Threads (cont.)

The method `doDatabaseThing()` uses the technique described in Code Example 9–7 to ensure that it runs atomically. In addition, you will notice that when the answer is found, the finder locks a synchronized section for the `cancel` object. In case some other thread already found the answer, our thread will enter this critical section, see that `cancel.found` is `true`, and exit by itself. [It is perfectly possible for two threads to find the answer independently and the interruption which the first sends to the second not to be seen by the second thread until later. So we need to check this variable. Alternatively, we could reasonably have called `Thread.interrupted()`.]

Each of the searcher threads calls doDatabaseThing() during the loop, so you don't have to worry about them never seeing the interruption. The main thread looks for the result in the global variable answer. It prints out success, noting the number of attempts required, then waits for all the searchers to exit. When they have all exited, it repeats the process.[5] Simple? Well…

Using Cancellation

You've seen the definition of *cancellation*. Now how can you use it effectively? The answer is, "not easily!"

First, let us consider your objectives in using cancellation. You created some threads to accomplish a task, and now you don't need them to work on it any longer. Perhaps the task has already been accomplished, or perhaps the user has changed her mind. Normally, we use cancellation to stop threads because we don't want them to waste time on something unnecessary. This is the best case. Sometimes we want to use cancellation to prevent threads from doing something that we no longer desire. This is harder.

In cancelling a thread, what do you want? Do you want to:

1. Kill it instantly?
2. Kill it in bounded CPU time?
3. Prevent it from making any more global changes?
4. Prevent it from wasting CPU time?

Presumably you want goal 4, generally implying goal 2. After all, if you don't care whether the CPU time is bounded, why bother cancelling the thread at all?

If you think you need goal 1, you'd best do some rethinking. First, it isn't possible; second, it isn't even well defined.[6] So, instead of goal 1, what is it that you really want?

---

[5]This is pretty ugly code. We'll fix it up in a bit.

[6]If nothing else, special relativity denies the concept of objective synchronisity. Practically speaking, it will take at least 1 μs to send an interrupt anyway.

If it was goal 3 you were thinking of, you're in much the same boat. It really isn't possible and not very meaningful. Now if you're satisfied with "not very many more global changes," we can put that in with goal 4 and proceed.

Ensuring Bounded CPU Time

The exact time of cancellation (interruption) is not guaranteed by POSIX, Java, or Win32. The target thread will become aware of a pending cancellation request some time after the function has been called. If you are using asynchronous cancellation [i.e., stop()], the thread should indeed spend very little extra time processing. No assurances here, but you can reasonably expect that it will be gone within a few milliseconds of CPU time (who knows how long it might sleep for if it needs a lock!). With deferred cancellation, the timing situation is more complex. The main point to remember is that you cannot rely upon the target thread exiting at any specific time. If you need to know when it has exited (you usually do!), you must use some sort of synchronization (either call join or use a barrier).

As an example of a long wall-clock delay in cancellation, consider the case of a low-priority target thread and a high-priority killer on one LWP. The cancellation will be sent, but as the high-priority thread continues to run, the target thread will not get a chance to exit any time soon. If the killer is running in realtime mode, the target might never exit! (Of course, in that case, you have lots of other problems to deal with.)

Deferred cancellation is a polling scheme when a thread is running, and more like asynchronous cancellation when the thread is blocked. For running threads, the polling is essentially as shown in Code Example 9–12. Thread T2 cancels T1 by calling interrupt(), which in turn sets a variable in the thread structure. When T1 enters a cancellation point such as read(), that function then checks to see if the thread has been cancelled, and exits if so.

To ensure bounded cancellation time with interruptions, it is up to you, the programmer, to insert calls to interruption points within every unbounded code path. In other words, for every loop

```
      interrupt()                        read()
void interrupt() {           read(...)
   T1.interrupted = true;     {...
   ...                            if (self.interrupted)
}                                     throw new InterruptedIOException();
                             }
```

Code Example 9–12   *Deferred Cancellation as Polling*

that might run longer than your declared time limit, you must
make sure that there is an interruption point in that loop. The obvious method is simply to include in the loop a call to
`Thread.interrupted()`.

Interrupting Computational Loops

In a tight loop, the overhead of `Thread.interrupted()` may
prove excessive, even though it is very fast (about 3 μs on a 110-
Mhz SS4). You can test only once every 1000 iterations, or
something similar (Code Example 9–13).

```
for (i=0; i < N; i++) {
   a[i] = b[i];
   if (i%1000 == 0)
      if (Thread.interrupted()) {throw new InterruptedException();}
   }
```

Code Example 9–13   *Testing Once Every 1000 Iterations*

So how long a latency can you afford for cancellation? That's a
decision for you to make. Most likely the answer is going to be
something like, "I want the target thread gone within 10 ms of CPU
time after the call to cancel, with a probability of 99.999%."[7] With
any sort of normal program, you'll have no problems. Analyze
your program carefully, then test it.

---

[7]What if you want 100% probability? Forget it. There is no such beast. When the probability of
program failure drops below the probability of the computer being hit by a meteorite (about 1E-11 per
year), you can relax.

What if you want bounded wall-clock time? Things get a bit stickier. We are now talking about realtime processing and an entirely different set of issues. The basic answer is, "Don't do that!" If you are going to do it, you'll need to know more than we do about realtime.

Interrupting Blocked Threads

Now that we've taken care of the CPU-bound programs, what about the I/O-bound programs? We've already stated that all blocking methods are intended to be interruptible. Is that enough? Or is it too much?

The thing we want here is the same as above—we want a time bound for when our thread will see the interruption. Moreover, we can generally be fairly generous about that time bound. In particular, the amount of time it takes to read a block from disk (about 20 ms) is not going to be a problem. We are not going to be concerned with interrupting local disk I/O. Unfortunately, if we are reading remote files via NFS, we don't have that assurance. What do we want to do if NFS fails? Can we treat that differently from waiting for clients? Perhaps.

Interrupting Sockets

Still, the most common issue is sockets, because we have no idea when a client might send the next request. Taking the canonical case of wanting to shut down a server, we are concerned primarily with forcing threads that are blocked, waiting on a read from a socket to pop out of that read and see the shutdown request. In some systems it is actually possible for us to write into that socket from the local program. This would make things much easier, but this is not generally the case; certainly it is not the case with Java. With Java we need to use interruption.

What Should Throw `InterruptedException`*?*

That part is fine. Waiting for a socket? Throw an interruption and exit. The problem that occurs is that many other methods may receive that interruption instead. If our thread is calling `wait()`

somewhere, that `wait()` will be the one to receive the interruption and we'll be forced to deal with it there. We don't really want that. We can control the `wait()` code more directly and more easily by using flags as in our `StopQueue` example. We would really prefer to use the `StopQueue` technique everywhere except when blocking on the socket.

The point is that we don't want to have to catch `InterruptionException` all the time, and we particularly don't want to have to write exception handlers that clean up the world all over the place. As long as we know we have a time bound on our code, we don't want to deal with these exceptions at all. Unfortunately, this is the way that Java works and we have to deal with them anyway.

Obviously, there are many options here and the issues are quite complex. We have yet to see a sufficiently complete solution to them. Our opinion is that simplicity is best. Maximal simplicity. If we could, we would use the `InterruptibleThread` to disable `InterruptedException` everywhere except in unbounded blocking reads. If we didn't have control over the threads, we would use the reinterrupt technique in our libraries and require the program to unblock our waits explicitly, as with `StopQueue`.

So, should our explicit Mutex class throw `InterruptedException` or should it catch it and reinterrupt later? We chose the latter for exactly the same reason that POSIX and Java chose it. With hundreds of locks scattered throughout our code, it would be a nightmare to catch exceptions at every call. (Consider the extreme example of requiring every call to new to catch an `OutOfMemoryException`!)

This is why none of our synchronization variables throw `InterruptedException`. The programmer can always ensure that they don't block forever and is thus freed to deal with `InterruptedException` in fewer places in the code. Fewer is better. If you really wanted to, of course, you could write your own versions of Mutex, etc., that did throw `InterruptedException`.

When should you write a method that throws `InterruptedException`? Probably never.[8]

---

[8]This is bound to be a topic of debate, and we don't claim any special knowledge. We just haven't seen any better suggestions.

Interrupting Sleeping Threads

A thread that is waiting for a synchronized section lock to be released is not at an interruptible point, and it will continue to sleep until that lock is released. Once it acquires the lock, it must proceed until it hits an interruptible point (ditto for POSIX mutexes). This can be a serious sticking point when you are concerned about elapsed wall-clock time. Just be sure that you don't hold any locks that the interrupted threads might need.

Interruption in wait()

While wait() is an interruption point,[9] there is an additional issue that must be addressed. Upon a normal return, it always re-locks the synchronized section. Upon interruption, it must also re-lock said synchronized section! Any exception handlers will be run with the lock held as appropriate. This means that if you're interrupting a thread to kill it quickly, you'd best be sure that no one is holding that lock for a long time.

In Code Example 9–14 both the exception handler and the finally section will run with the lock held. If the synchronization had been inside the try clause, the exception handler and the finally section would have run without the lock being held. The throw from wait() still would have had to relock, even though the lock would be released promptly.

```
synchronized (this) {
    try {wait();}
    catch (interuptedException ie) {cleanUpAndExit();}
    finally {doWhatEver();}
    }
doWhatEverElse();
```

Code Example 9–14   *Interrupting a* wait()

---

[9]Should wait() be an interruption point? A strong case can be made for it not being one, but in as much as we don't have any say on the matter, we'll just accept it as is. [If a thread is blocked on wait(), the programmer has complete control over it and can wake it up and have it see that it's exit time, the way we did in the StopQueue example. It's only when a thread is blocked on something that we don't have control over (e.g., I/O) that we need to be able to interrupt it.]

The Morning After

Well, now that we've done all that, we're ready to get back to some useful work, right? Not quite.

Threads are rather particular about how they're treated after cancellation. They want to be pampered. They want to be joined or at least waited for after they clean up.

The point here is that you don't want to be starting up new threads until the old ones are truly gone. What if you have global variables that you need properly initialized? What if there is shared data that you don't want old and new threads sharing? If nothing else, it's nice to clean up memory before making new demands. (We're assuming that you'll run the same code again in your program. If you really only ran it once, you wouldn't need to be so careful.)

In the searcher example (Code Example 9–15) we have one global array of threads. It would not do to start creating in new threads while the successful searcher was still busy killing off the old losers. Instead, we must wait for all the threads to exit before we reinitialize and start over again.

```
synchronized(this) {                        // Protect threads[]
    for (int i=0; i<nSearchers; i++) {
      threads[i] = new Thread(new Searcher(this, i));
      threads[i].start();
    }
  }

  for (int i=0; i<nSearchers; i++) {
    synchronized(this) {t = threads[i];}//
    Searcher may use threads[]
    t.join();
  }
```

Code Example 9–15 *From the* main() *Method for Searcher Example*

We don't actually need the threads to exit. We merely need the threads to reach a point where they will never change any shared data and we will never use them again. Instead of using join(), the same effect could be accomplished by using a SingleBarrier.

Multithreaded Programming with Java Technology

Another detail to note in this code is the joining code. We first lock the lock, get the next thread object, then unlock it again before calling `join()`. Why? Well try it! Just move the `join()` inside the synchronized section. Deadlock again! (The main thread is holding the lock, blocking on a join, while the successful searcher needs to lock the lock before it can cancel the other searchers.)

This is actually a very interesting bit of code. As soon as the main thread has created the last searcher thread and released the lock, the array can be treated as a constant—no other changes will be made to it until all searcher threads exit. This means that the main thread, which knows that the array is a constant, could dispense with locking the array in the join code. The searcher threads, which don't know when the array becomes a constant, must synchronize on that state somehow. (What if one of the searchers found the PID before the main thread had finished creating the rest? It might execute the cancellation loop and miss the not-yet-created threads.)

Cleanup

When a thread is cancelled, POSIX provides a way to clean up the thread's state through a set of cleanup handlers that are called upon the exiting of a thread. These are functions of one argument, which you define and then push onto a thread's cleanup stack. Should the thread exit [either via cancellation or a call to `pthread_exit()`], the functions on the stack will be run on the argument supplied. Should the thread not be cancelled, you may pop the functions off when they are no longer required (Code Example 9–16).

```
pointer = malloc(100);
pthread_cleanup_push(free, pointer);
use(pointer);
free(pointer);
pthread_cleanup_pop(0);
```

Code Example 9–16 *How POSIX Cleanup Handlers Are Used*

The general idea for cancellation is that programmers will write their programs such that sections of code that allocate resources, obtain locks, etc., are preceded (or followed) immediately by cleanup handler pushes. The cleanup handlers will be responsible for freeing resources, reestablishing data invariants, and freeing locks.

Java provides a neater solution to this problem. First, because Java has a garbage collector, there is no need to free memory, as in C/C++. Second, in those instances where you do need to release specific resources (close file descriptors, remove entries from lists, etc.), you can use the existing Java constructs of exception handlers and `finally` sections to ensure that the exit code is executed (Code Example 9–17).

```
try {
    open_file();
    try {
        do_stuff();
    }
    catch (InterruptedException ie) {
        clean_up_stuff();
    }
}
finally {
    close_file();
}
```

Code Example 9–17 *How InterruptedException Handlers Clean Up*

Implementing `enableInterrupts()`

Thus far we've been dealing with these issues by writing snippets of ad hoc code—sufficient to the immediate problem but not easily reused. In Code Example 9–18 we show a subclass of `Thread` that deals with these problems more neatly. Because the methods are synchronized, there are no race conditions. If a thread has not disabled interrupts, `interrupt()` will call the method for the superclass [the normal `interrupt()`]. That interrupt will remain pending until either the programmer's code clears it [via calling `interrupted()` or catching `Inter-`

ruptedException] or disableInterrupts() is called.[10] If disableInterrupts() gets called, the flag will be cleared and our interruptPending flag will be set. This ensures that a subsequent call to enableInterrupts() will reinterrupt the thread so that the interruption does not get lost.

```java
public class InterruptibleThread extends Thread {
private boolean interruptsEnabled = false;
private boolean interruptPending = false;


public static void enableInterrupts() {
  InterruptibleThread self = InterruptibleThread.currentThread();

  synchronized (self) {
    self.interruptsEnabled = true;
    if (self.interruptPending) self.interrupt();
    self.interruptPending = false;
  }
}

public static void disableInterrupts() {
  InterruptibleThread self = InterruptibleThread.currentThread();

  synchronized (self) {
    if (interrupted()) self.interruptPending = true;
    self.interruptsEnabled = false;
  }
}

public synchronized void interrupt() {
  if (interruptsEnabled)
    super.interrupt();
  else
    interruptPending = true;
}


}
```

Code Example 9–18   *Implementing enableInterrupts()*

---

[10]These are static methods (as it only makes sense to call them from the current thread), but they must be called from an InterruptibleThread. You will get a runtime error otherwise.

The most interesting piece of this code is where it deals with a race condition for `interrupt()`. Imagine that t1 has called `t2.interrupt()`. Soon afterward, t2 calls `disableInterrupts()` with no intervening interruptible calls. That could leave the interrupt flag set after `disableInterrupts()` returned. To prevent this, `disableInterrupts()` checks for that condition, clears the flag [`interrupted()` does this automatically] and sets the `interruptPending` flag so that a subsequent call to `enableInterrupts()` will notice this and reissue the interrupt. Thus, the code following `disableInterrupts()` will never see an interrupt and any interrupts issued previously to `disableInterrupts()` will not be lost.

A similar design could be used to disable `thread.stop()`, and indeed we do so in our extensions package, but only as an illustration. It has been degradated—don't use it.

A Cancellation Example (Improved)

Using the `InterruptibleThread` from above, we can now write a cleaner version of our search program (Code Example 9–19). The two ugly portions of the program were `doDatabaseThing()` and the cancellation code in `searcher.run()`. Using the disable/enable code, the first function becomes simpler and the latter gets to eliminate all of its checking code and simply call the `interrupt()` method with no further concerns.

```
public void doDatabaseThing() {
try {
    InterruptibleThread.disableInterrupts();
    cancel.incrementDatabase(1);
    Thread.sleep(10);
    cancel.incrementDatabase(-1);
    InterruptibleThread.enableInterrupts();
    }
catch (InterruptedException ie) {InterruptibleThread.impossible(ie);}

}
```

Code Example 9–19 *Cleaner Version of doDatabaseThing()*

Simple Polling

In a program of any complexity, using cancellation is very difficult. A program that will be ported to other languages will be even harder to write correctly. A strict polling scheme would be vastly superior in almost every respect, as long as we don't have to worry about blocked threads. In the code for `CancellationNot` (Code Example 9–20), we see the same searcher program written using polling. (Note that where we test for `cancel.found`, we could use double-checked locking.)

```
public void run() {
  Random r = new Random(seed);
  int guess;

  System.out.println(t.getName() + " is searching...");

  for (int i=0; i<1000000; i++) {// Better never hit 1000000!
    doDatabaseThing();
    synchronized(cancel) { if (cancel.found) break; }
    guess = r.nextInt() % 1000;
    cancel.incrementGuesses();
    if (guess == target) {
      System.out.println(t.getName() + " got the answer:" +
                cancel.answer);
      synchronized(cancel) {
          if (cancel.found) break;
          cancel.answer = guess;
          cancel.found = true;
          break;
      }
    }
  }
  cancel.barrier.barrierPost();
  return;
}
```

Code Example 9–20   *Implementing the Searcher with Polling*

This polling example sure looks a lot simpler compared to the complexity of the previous examples, and it is. But it is also much less generally useful because many interesting programs involve unbounded blocking calls. Thus any kind of server program will invariably be calling `read()` on a socket, and there is no guarantee if or when that call will return. So use polling if you can, but you'll probably be stuck with using interruption.

APIs Used in This Chapter

The Class java.lang.Thread

interrupt

    public void interrupt()

This sets the interrupt flag and causes the target thread to throw an `InterruptedException` if it is blocked on (or as soon as it executes) an interruptible method or `InterruptedIOException` if it is blocked on I/O.

Reference: Chapter 9.

interrupted

    public static boolean interrupted()

This returns the value of the interrupt flag for the current thread and clears it.

Reference: Chapter 9.

isInterrupted

    public boolean isInterrupted()

This returns the value of the interrupt flag for the thread.

Reference: Chapter 9.

Comment: You will probably never use this.

The Class Extensions.InterruptibleThread

This is one of the classes that we defined for this book to provide a consistent interface for dealing with certain problems. Some of those problems are artificial, a product of trying to write uniform example code in both POSIX and Java.

exit

```
public void exit()
```

This causes the current thread to exit. This is just syntactic sugar for: `Thread.currentThread().stop()`.

Reference: Chapter 4.

Comments: This is not the right way to do things. Don't exit from threads; return from the `run()` method, instead.

interrupt

```
public void interrupt()
```

This causes the target thread to throw an `InterruptedException` as soon as it executes an interruptible method when interrupts are enabled. If disabled at the time, the actual interrupt will be issued as soon as the interrupts are reenabled.

Reference: Chapter 9.

disableInterrupts

```
public void disableInterrupts()
```

This causes the current thread to set a flag indicating that it is not interruptible. The method `interrupt()` will look at this.

Reference: Chapter 9.

enableInterrupts

```
public void enableInterrupts()
```

> This causes the current thread to set a flag indicating that it is interruptible. The method `interrupt()` will look at this. If the flag indicates a pending interrupt, that interrupt will be reissued at this time.
>
> *Reference:*   Chapter 9.

Summary

Cancellation is the method by which one thread can kill another. Because of issues surrounding shared resources, held locks, and dynamically allocated storage, cancellation is extremely difficult to use correctly.[11] Cancellation can be avoided completely by implementing a polling scheme in any of the libraries, as long as we don't have to worry about blocked threads. In Java, `interrupt()` with exception handlers makes it merely difficult to use cancellation.

Avoid cancellation if at all possible.

---

[11]Just spelling *cancellation* is an issue! Webster's allows it to be spelled with either one "l" or two.

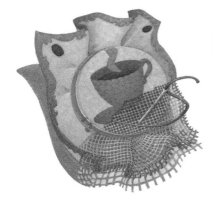

Chapter 10

Details

In which a number of minor details are covered.

Thread Groups

A thread group is a group of threads, or more precisely, a group of threads (possibly empty) and other thread groups (also possibly empty). The *raison d'être* for thread groups is security. Java needs some method of allowing you to download untrusted foreign code and run it without it being able to affect the rest of your program.

The idea was that you run the foreign code in its own thread group and tell that thread group that it is not allowed to start, stop, suspend, etc., any threads outside that group. This way, your threads are safe from the foreign code, but the foreign code is still able to create new threads of its own. Clever, eh?

Unfortunately, they changed the security model for Java, and thread groups no longer provide this kind of protection; rather, security is handled in a different fashion. So of what use are thread groups now? You could use thread groups as a general container to keep track of your own threads, but you'll probably find it easier simply to keep a list or an array of thread objects and manipulate your threads with those. Because of the way MT programs are written, about the only thing you'll ever do with a list of threads is to wait for them to exit, or to interrupt them. Thread groups don't help you with this.

When you create a thread, it is placed in a thread group. You can specify a particular thread group if you wish. That thread group can now restrict the new thread to creating threads only in that group or subgroups. You can place a small number of restrictions on threads in a particular thread group (set a maximum priority level), and you can call `stop()`, `suspend()`, `resume()`, or `interrupt()` on all threads in a group, but none of these are particularly useful. You can also do the usual set operations to find the parent of a group, the children, etc.

You will probably never use thread groups.

Thread Security

Thread security in Java is really rather simple—at least it was until Java 2 came along. First we will explain how security worked prior to Java 2 and then go into some of the details of the new security features of Java 2.

Prior to Java 2 the primary focus of security was the `Secu-rityManager` class. The `SecurityManager` class is used to enforce a security policy for Java programs and in most cases is never modified by programmers. The `SecurityManager` class is usually defined and activated when a Java VM starts. When a Java method tries to access a vulnerable resource in the Java VM, one of the check methods in the `SecurityManager` class is called. If the check method permits the requested action, the check method will return silently. However, if the check method does not permit the requested action, the method throws a security exception. Using the Thread class as an example, when the `checkAccess()` method is called from the `Thread` class, it calls into the `SecurityManager` class and executes the `checkAccess()` method. If the calling thread is allowed access, the `checkAccess()` method simply returns. If the calling thread is not permitted, the `checkAccess()` method throws a `SecurityException`. Code Example 10–1 shows how the code would look in the calling thread.

```
Thread A;
try {
   A.checkAccess();
   }
catch (SecurityException se) {
  System.out.println("Thread access error: " + se.getMessage());
   }
```

Code Example 10–1 *Checking for Security Violations*

This may seem rather trivial; well, it is. The `SecurityManager` class defines the security to be implemented for the entire Java VM. In most cases the `SecurityManager` class has been defined for you. For example, when you are using the Netscape browser to execute Java code, the developers at Netscape have defined the `SecurityManager` for you. In this case, you can't modify or remove the `SecurityManager`. In most cases the `SecurityManager` will be defined and installed for you; this is the case when the Java VM is started for you. For example, the Java VM is started for you when you run code via a browser or appletviewer. If you start the Java VM yourself, for example from a command line, you are responsible for defining and installing a `SecurityManager`.

By default, a `SecurityManager` is not installed in the Java VM. Depending on how you execute Java code, you may have to install your own `SecurityManager`. If some other program controls the Java VM, in most cases that program will install a `SecurityManager`. This is the case with browsers; since the browser controls the Java VM, it will probably install a `SecurityManager`. If the Java VM is not controlled by another program, in most cases you will have to install a `SecurityManager`. This is the case when you write your own Java applications. If you don't define a `SecurityManager` in your application, your program will have full reign of the Java VM.

The main problem with the security mechanism in previous versions of Java is that you do not have fine-grained control over the security of your program. The other side of this is that users could not define what level of security they were willing to accept. For example, if a Java application was executed on your machine, it had full access to the machine just as a traditional C application would. The security mechanisms in Java 2 have solved these problems.

Now that we have a bit of history, let's talk about how security works in Java 2. Java 2 exploits the concept of protection domains. Java has always had the concept of protection domains. That is, different code in the Java VM can have different levels of security. The simple case of this is the fact that Java applications have access to the entire Java VM, whereas Java applets do not. The major difference with protection domains in Java 2 is the flexibility and control you have over how security is implemented. Although complete coverage of Java security is beyond the scope of this book, we will give you a general idea how security works in Java as it relates to threads.

First we should mention that the `SecurityManager` class still exists in Java 2 and is also backward compatible with previous versions of the JDK. The `SecurityManager` in Java 2 is just a wrapper for compatibility where all security actions are forwarded on to the new protection domain infrastructure. This means that you could continue to use the `SecurityManager` class in a way that you may be familiar with, but its internal workings are far different. In fact, the interface for security is the same for both the `Thread` and `ThreadGroup` classes, but the implementation of security has changed.

The new security mechanism is based on the concept of having a set of permissions. A `Permission` object in Java is really just an object that represents access to a protected resource. All permissions in Java have a name as well as semantics that define access to a resource. You can define your own permissions or you can use the predefined permissions in Java. For example, Java has a `SocketPermission` object that can control access to networking resources. The advantage of the Java 2 security mechanism is that a system administrator can define a set of restrictions to place on Java programs. The administrator has fine-grained control of all actions that can possibly be performed in the Java VM. Our focus is not on what all the permissions are or how they are defined, but rather, that a set of permissions have been defined and that we must adhere to these restrictions. For more information about Java security and permissions, see the Java documentation or one of the books recommended in Appendix B.

So how do permissions relate to threads? The simple answer is, "in three ways." Java 2 has defined three permissions that all threads use. They are `modifyThread`, `stopThread`, and `modifyThreadGroup`, all of which are defined in the `RuntimePermission` class. Each of these permissions is used to protect `Thread` resources when certain methods are called.

The following lists the `RuntimePermission` target names that are used in conjunction with Java threads:

- **modifyThread**: This permission is accessed when a calling thread wants to access or modify an unrelated thread in the Java VM.

- **stopThread**: This permission is accessed when a calling thread wants to stop another thread running in the Java VM.

- **modifyThreadGroup**: This permission is accessed when a calling thread wants to access or modify a `ThreadGroup`.

So how does all this work? When a thread resource needs protection, it can make a call into the security mechanism to verify if the requested action should take place. If the security mechanism does not object to the action, the call simply returns. If it does not permit the action, a security exception is thrown. Let's take a look at a simple example (Code Example 10–2). The example simply

```
public class Simple {
   static public void main(String s[]) {

   System.setSecurityManager(new SecurityManager());

   ThreadGroup group = Thread.currentThread().getThreadGroup();

   // This line could generate a security exception
   group.getParent();
   }
}
```

Code Example 10–2 *A Simple Security Exception*

creates a new `SecurityManager` and then calls a few `Thread` and `ThreadGroup` methods. If you execute this program from a command line, you should get a security exception. We say "should" because if you have defined your security permissions to include the "`modifyThreadGroup`" permission, the program will execute without a problem. Also, if you remove the line that sets the `SecurityManager`, the program will also complete without any errors.

The reason that this example throws a security exception is due to the `ThreadGroup.getParent()` method. This method calls the `ThreadGroup.checkAccess()` method, which in turn calls into the `SecurityManager`, which in turn calls into the new Java 2 security mechanism with the "`modify-ThreadGroup`" permission request. If you have not given the security mechanism permission for "`modifyThreadGroup`," it throws an exception. You might wonder why an exception is thrown just for calling the `getParent()` method. The reason is that by calling the `getParent()` method in the example, you are trying to gain a reference a thread group that your program does not control.

In most cases, thread security is controlled by the `checkAccess()` methods in the `Thread` and `ThreadGroup` classes. The `checkAccess()` method in the `Thread` class actually calls into the security mechanism with the "`modifyThread`" permission, and the `checkAccess()` method in the `Thread-Group` class calls in to the security mechanism with the "`modi-fyThreadGroup`" permission. Both of the `checkAccess()` methods are most often called by other methods in the `Thread` and `ThreadGroup` classes.

So how does all of this affect your programs? Well, if you are simply creating and operating with threads and thread groups in your program, you should never have to deal with security in your program. If, however, you are trying to access or modify threads or thread groups that are not under your control, you may run into the security system. If you are not sure if a call you are making is going to run into the security system, the safe thing to do is enclose the section of code you are unsure of with a try/catch block. This will allow you to catch the security exception and then perform some sort of correction to the problem.

To help you understand what methods perform security checks, Table 10–1 lists the `Thread` class methods that may cause a security check to be performed.

Table 10–1   `Thread` *Class Methods That May Cause a Security Check*

Thread class method	RuntimePermission target
`getContextClassLoader()`	`"getClassLoader"`
`setContextClassLoader()`	`"setContextClassLoader"`
`checkAccess()`	`"modifyThread"`
`interrupt()`	`"modifyThread"`
`suspend()`	`"modifyThread"`
`resume()`	`"modifyThread"`
`setPriority()`	`"modifyThread"`
`setName()`	`"modifyThread"`
`setDaemon()`	`"modifyThread"`
`enumerate()`	`"modifyThreadGroup"`
`stop()`	`"modifyThread"`, `"stopThread"`
`Thread()`	`"modifyThreadGroup"`

Table 10–2 lists the `ThreadGroup` class methods that may cause a security check.

In addition to the security permissions provided in Java 2, you could define your own permissions and then add the `checkPermission()` calls in your code. This would force the user or administrator to define your permission in the security file in order for your program to execute. The system security policy file (`java.policy`) is located in the `(jre)/lib/security` directory, where `(jre)` is the path to the location of Java. Take a look at this file and try adding permissions for "`modifyThreadGroup`" and then try running the simple program above. You should find that it now runs without any security exceptions.

Table 10–2   ThreadGroup *Class Methods That May Cause a Security Check*

ThreadGroup class method	RuntimePermission type
ThreadGroup()	"modifyThreadGroup"
checkAccess()	"modifyThreadGroup"
enumerate()	"modifyThreadGroup"
getParent()	"modifyThreadGroup"
setDaemon()	"modifyThreadGroup"
setMaxPriority()	"modifyThreadGroup"
suspend()	"modifyThreadGroup"
resume()	"modifyThreadGroup"
destroy()	"modifyThreadGroup"
interrupt()	"modifyThreadGroup", "modifyThread"
stop()	"modifyThreadGroup", "modifyThread", "stopThread"

Defining your own permission and using it in a program is beyond the scope of this book, but we wanted to point out that you could do this if you really wanted to. For more information on how to do this, as well as other security-related topics, read the Java 2 security documentation.

Real-World Examples

1. The garbage collector thread and the **finalize()** method

A common problem we have seen is when the garbage collector thread becomes deadlocked trying to free up memory. Consider this situation: You have a legacy C-code application that is not thread-safe and you want to call into the C functions from a Java program. This scenario is not all that uncommon. An easy solution would have you synchronize methods that would access the C functions. Defining the methods as synchronized would allow only one Java thread to access the C functions at any given time. This seems like a logical assumption; however, since you are calling into C code, you may also want to define a finalize() method to do some cleanup in the C functions [i.e., calling free() to clean up memory used by the C code].

The problem that can result from a situation like this is a system deadlock. The reason why this can happen is rather simple. Since access to all the non-thread-safe C functions is controlled via synchronized Java methods, only one Java thread can access the C code at any given time. If an object that was using these Java methods goes out of scope, it is eligible for garbage collection. This makes sense, of course; however, when the `finalize()` method is called in the Java class, it will try to call into the C code to perform some cleanup tasks. If a Java thread is already in one of the C functions at the time of garbage collection, the entire system will hang. Why? Well when the garbage collection thread kicks in (begins garbage collection), it suspends all the other threads running in the Java VM. Now when the garbage collection thread calls into the `finalize()` method, it will block waiting for access to the C code. Since the garbage collection thread has suspended all other threads, the thread that is in the C code at the time of garbage collection will never return to free the lock; therefore, the garbage collection thread will block forever and hang the Java VM.

Keep this situation in mind when overriding the `finalize()` method. When `finalize()` is called by the garbage collection thread, all other threads running in the VM become suspended.

2. Performance: Access to synchronized objects

We have seen many situations where the performance of Java code is diminished when accessing synchronized methods or objects. This should not be a surprise, as calling synchronized methods involved locking a monitor before accessing the method. We can't stress this point enough. It seems simple enough, but programmers often fall into it. In one customer situation, a `Hashtable` object was being used to cache results obtained from a database. Using a `Hashtable` for this purpose is not wrong, in fact it is a common technique. However, if the program is to scale up to several concurrent database accesses at any given time, the `Hashtable` becomes a bottleneck to the program's performance. Since access to a `Hashtable` object is synchronized, only one thread is allowed to modify the object at any given time.

A simple solution to a situation like this is to use multiple `Hashtable` objects and then distribute access to the objects so that you can have some level of concurrency. In the case we have outlined, when multiple `Hashtable` objects were used to cache the database data, a hundredfold increase in performance was gained.

3. More problems with the garbage collection thread

Usually, the garbage collector works exactly the way intended and you, the programmer can ignore it completely. In certain cases under certain system requirements, you may wish to change some details of its behavior. Don't even think about this unless you see specific problems.

We have run into a number of issues with the garbage collection thread in the Java VM. Most of the problems revolve around the fact that when the garbage collection thread runs, it suspends all of the other threads in the Java VM. The fact that all the threads in the VM are suspended can be a cause of concern when programming multi-threaded programs in Java, but the simple act of garbage collection can also cause some annoying problems. For example, say you have a Java program that needs a lot of memory for a local cache that you wrote. If the memory heap requirements are large, say 500 MB or more, the simple act of garbage collection can take quite a bit of time to complete. In this example, since the heap requirements are large and system garbage collection does not usually kick in until 75% of the heap is used, it can cause the entire Java VM to halt for quite a bit of time while it cleans up the heap.

A simple solution to a problem like this is to perform garbage collection more often or to define your own garbage collection class. For example, you could have a thread that sleeps for a given amount of time and then wakes up and calls for garbage collection. You may think that this would cause even further program delays, but the simple fact that garbage collection is performed more often means that the amount of heap it needs to clean up is smaller. This means that the delay caused during garbage collection is smaller. In the example where the heap is huge, it is better to have very small delays introduced during program execution than to have a single large halt while the entire heap is collected.

4. Make synchronized code sections as small as possible

A synchronized method invocation is one of the most time-consuming operations in Java. Therefore, you want to avoid its use as much as possible. We realize that when writing threaded programs in Java, you will need to use synchronized code. The synchronized keyword is most commonly used in method signatures. This is a valid use of the keyword, but in many cases the entire method does not have to be synchronized. Why lock an entire method when only a few lines of code in the method have to be locked? A better idea is to synchronize the smallest section of code possible in a method that needs to be protected.

You can do this by using the synchronized keyword in the method code (see Code Example 10–3). Notice that the synchronized keyword is used to protect only the section of code in the method that needs to be protected. This will allow for more concurrency and will also help with the performance of programs.

```
public void aMethod() {
   if (some_condition)
      synchronize (this) {
         // Do synchronized work here
      }
   else {
      // Do unsynchronized work here
      }
   }
```

Code Example 10–3 *Synchronizing Part of a Method*

5. Threaded class downloads

A problem we often see with large Java programs is the time it takes to download all of the class files needed for execution. This problem can be solved by creating a custom class loader, which downloads only the initial class files needed for the program to begin its execution. Then while the program begins its execution, thread(s) can be created to continue the download of other class files in the background. Cyrus InterSoft offers a commercial solution to problems like this. Cyrus offers a number of Java resources that aid in the download and execution of Java programs. For example, they are able to begin the execution of a Java program even before all of it is downloaded, as well as run multiple Java programs inside the same Java VM. Improvements like these can have a dramatic effect on the performance of Java programs.

General Tips and Hints

1. It is very helpful in a thread dump analysis to give the thread a meaningful name. If you spawn many threads without meaningful names, it becomes next to impossible to figure out what is really going on.

2. I'd say the biggest issue I've run into at customer sites is the mismatch between the ease of Java thread syntax and semantics. Everybody talks about how easy threads are to do in Java, and what these people are always referring to is the ease with which someone can write some threaded code, the syntax. What often is overlooked until too late is how complex the thread semantics can be and how difficult these portions of the code will be to debug. Thus, one often ends up with a situation where some fairly novice developers have created code that is too complex for them to debug.

3. Many customers running on Solaris (JDK 1.1) do not realize that by default they are using green threads. They then wonder why their quad processor E4000 runs no better (or worse) than a single-processor NT box, or why the load is not distributed across processors.

Daemon Threads

A daemon[1] thread is normal in every respect save one. When it is time for the JVM to decide if it's time to exit (based on whether there are any active threads), daemons are ignored. Thus if you have ten daemon threads running and your last normal thread exits, the JVM will exit the entire process.

Daemons are used for background tasks that make sense only when there are other threads that are doing the real work. The garbage collector is an excellent example of a proper use of daemons. You can set the daemon flag on or off as your program requires with `thread.setDaemon()`, but you can only do this before you call `start()`. You cannot change the status of a

---

[1] A few years ago, one very conservative (and not very savvy) religious group called for a nationwide prayer meeting to cast out the "demons" that were in UNIX.

running thread. You can also check the status of a thread with isDaemon().

You will probably never use daemons.

Daemon Thread Groups

A daemon thread group is normal in every respect save one. When it becomes empty, it may automatically be destroyed and removed from its parent. There is no relationship between daemon threads and daemon thread groups. You can change the daemon status of a thread group at any time.

Calling Native Code

From Java you can use the JNI (Java Native Interface) library to call C, C++, etc., code from your Java program, or to call Java code from your C, C++, etc., code. If your Java program is multithreaded, calling native code from multiple threads does not change the issues of thread safety at all. If the native code uses data that is shared by multiple threads, that data must be properly protected. By far the simplest and most reliable method of doing this is to have your Java code take care of the locking.

If a Java method calls a native function, which in turn uses some shared data, synchronizing the method properly will ensure that said data is protected properly. Don't worry, be happy!

If for some reason this is not an option (perhaps the native code accesses different bits of data under different circumstances which Java cannot know about, and you want those different bits of data to be accessible concurrently), you have a challenge in front of you. The JNI spec specifies how native threads and locks will interact with Java code. If you're using a native threads library underneath Java, you'll probably be OK using the native locks. If you're using green threads, on the other hand, you're in trouble. Green threads will not interact with native locks in any viable fashion.

If you are running Java with the native threads library, most things work as you would expect, even though they are not necessarily clearly specified. A native method can be declared synchronized just like a non-native method. In addition, within the native method the C code can invoke explicit MonitorEnter() and

`MonitorExit()` operations (Code Example 10–4). [To call `wait()`, `notify()`, etc., it is necessary to make explicit JNI calls back into Java. They are not supported directly as with monitors.] Moreover, `MonitorEnter()` is recursive (as you should expect). However, given that native code (outside the system classes) is usually used for speed or to access system-specific APIs, there is usually little need to do this.

```
(*env)->MonitorEnter(env, obj);
// Critical Section
(*env)->MonitorExit(env, obj);
```

Code Example 10–4   *Locking Monitors from C Code*

Native methods can also use native synchronization objects to coordinate their actions with other native threads. All of this will operate correctly with Java.

Threads originally created outside Java can attach to the JVM using JNI [`AttachCurrentThread()`]. Once a thread is attached to the JVM, it will receive a Java wrapper and appear to the JVM as a normal Java thread, including being entered into a thread group. It will be able to access Java objects and invoke methods on them, including the usual synchronization methods. Any thread, whether originally Java or native, can create additional native threads in the native method. However, any such thread must attach itself to the JVM before it can interact with any Java objects. A native thread that calls in to the JVM can also create and start Java threads.

In Figure 10–1 you can see the basic Java threading design when using the native thread libraries. The Java thread objects are built by and controlled by the JVM, but the threads themselves are actually native threads that are created and controlled by the native library. The actual context switching, locking, etc., are done by the native threads library, which is why things work together.

Within native code all exceptions are synchronous, including those caused by `stop()`. Exceptions are detected either by explicit polling using `ExceptionOccurred()` or in some cases by checking return values. Once an exception is raised it must be dealt with (by clearing or by returning and thus propagating to

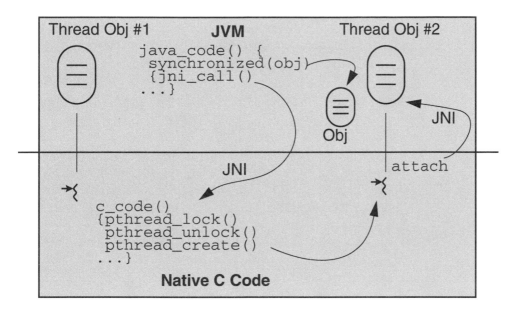

Figure 10–1 *Java Thread Objects Use Native Threads*

Java code). It is not safe to call further JNI methods (other than those for dealing with exceptions) until the exception has been dealt with.

You cannot share local Java objects from one native thread to another, nor should you hold on to references across multiple JNI calls to C code, even from the same thread. Java will pass C an interface pointer (JNIEnv *) which is valid only for that thread on that call. If you wish to share or retain references across calls or threads, you will need to convert those local references into global ones. (By making them global, you are adding a root reference to the objects in question so they won't get garbage collected or moved.)

In short, if your JVM uses the system's native threads library, every combination of threads and synchronization should work correctly. If your JVM uses green threads, you should expect things not to work together.

This is very tricky stuff. Be careful!

A Few Assorted Methods

There are a small number of other methods that provide minor functionality that you probably won't use. You can ask the JVM how many threads there are currently running in a thread's thread group [Thread.activeCount()] and which of them is "alive" [Thread.isAlive()]. You can get a list of them, too [Thread.enumerate()].[2] Unfortunately, by the time you get around to using any of this information, it may have changed. If you need to keep track of the threads in your application, you will need to design an ad hoc mechanism to do so. Just like thread groups, this is not a big deal and is easily accomplished.

Do you need to know how many threads are running? Have them increment a counter upon starting. Need to know if a thread has completed its work? Use a semaphore or a wait/notify. You can also change the print string for a thread [setName()].

Stack Size

The default stack size for Java is implementation dependent. On Solaris the default stack is 500k, which is big enough for 10,000 recursive calls to a method of no arguments and no local variables. This is probably big enough for any program. You can change the stack size by passing a command line argument. This invocation will give you a 1-MB stack for all threads:

```
%java -oss 1000000 Test
```

If a thread overflows its stack, it will hit a guard page that is mapped in nonreadable. This way you will get an immediate SEGV so you can go back and fix your program.

You can find out how deep the current stack is [Thread.countStackFrames()] and even print it out [Thread.dumpStack()].

---

[2]All three of these methods are officially deprecated in Java 1.1 and replaced with the thread group methods threadsCount(), groupCount(), and allThreads().

Deprecated Methods

When a method becomes deprecated (wonderful term, eh?), for how much longer will it be supported? If you have a program written for JDK 1.1 that uses `stop()`, do you need to worry about running it on JDK 1.2?

There's no official answer here. Certainly in other Sun products the guarantee was that a discontinued interface would continue to be supported for five years past the announcement date. So, if you're using any of the deprecated methods, you're probably OK for some time to come, but change your code next time you do a major release.

The Effect of Using a JIT

To maintain complete hardware independence, Java is always compiled to a byte code which is then interpreted. (Yes, we know that there are some companies that write full, native compilers, but that's not "proper" according to the rules for Java. We'll subsume those in the JIT discussion.) Although the performance of the byte interpreters is quite impressive and is sufficient for many I/O-bound programs, it still doesn't hold a candle to native code for computing.

A *Just In Time Compiler* loads the byte code and then compiles that down to native code (possibly at load time, possibly at runtime). The CPU-intensive portions of your program will now run much faster (a factor of 5 or so). The I/O portions won't improve at all (they're either running kernel code or they're blocked, waiting for I/O!). How does this affect your MT programming? Probably not at all. The threads' functions already run almost entirely in the JVM; hence, a JIT will not speed them up at all.

Adaptive Compilers

In the HotSpot compiler only selected portions of code are compiled to native format. As the program runs, HotSpot continues to monitor its progress, compiling other methods as it sees fit. HotSpot has one enormous advantage over JIT compilers: It can compile many things in-line which JIT compilers cannot. To maintain full Java semantics, all programs must allow new subclasses to be loaded at any point during computation. This dynamic loading may invalidate some of the in-line calls that you would like the compiler to make for you. JIT compilers handle this by not compiling in-line. HotSpot gets around this problem by *recompiling* those sections of code affected by the new classes.

HotSpot (or rather the ExactVM, which it is based on) also has a number of optimizations to improve the speed and reduce the memory required for locks. Basically, instead of allocating locks in permanent hashtables or the like, locks are allocated on the stack when first used, and popped from the stack when the owner releases them. Only when another thread blocks on it will the lock be copied off the stack and placed into permanent memory.

The threads functions are mostly in the JVM itself and will not benefit much from the JIT. You should expect the percentage of time that thread overhead takes to increase by a factor of 10 or so (because everything else is getting faster). As long as that can be held to a small percentage of total processing time, you should have no problems.

APIs Used in This Chapter

The Class java.lang.Thread

Thread

```
public Thread(ThreadGroup group, String name)
public Thread(ThreadGroup group, Runnable run)
public Thread(ThreadGroup group, Runnable run,
         String name)
         throws SecurityException,
         IllegalThreadStateException
```

These create a new thread object in the thread group stated.

References: Chapters 4 and 10.

getThreadGroup

```
public final ThreadGroup getThreadGroup()
```

> This returns the thread group for this thread object.

Reference: Chapter 10.

checkAccess

```
public void checkAccess() throws SecurityException
```

> If there is a security manager, its `checkAccess()` method is called with the `Thread` as an argument.

Reference: Chapter 10.

isDaemon setDaemon

```
public boolean isDaemon()
public void setDaemon(boolean on)
        throws SecurityException,
        IllegalThreadStateException
```

> This gets/sets this thread to be a daemon. You cannot change the status of a running thread.

Reference: Chapter 10.

countStackFrames

```
public int countStackFrames()
```

> This returns the depth of the stack.

Reference: Chapter 10.

Comments: Deprecated in Java 2. Not well defined in any case.

dumpStack

```
public static void dumpStack()
```
This prints out the stack.

Reference: Chapter 10.

activeCount

```
public static int activeCount()
```
This returns the number of active threads in the current thread's thread group.

Reference: Chapter 10.

Comments: Deprecated in Java 1.1. See `ThreadGroup.allThreadsCount()`.

enumerate

```
public static int enumerate(Thread tarray[])
```
This fills `tarray` with as many currently active threads as fit, returning that number.

Reference: Chapter 10.

Comments: Deprecated in Java 1.1. See `ThreadGroup.allThreads()`.

The Class java.lang.ThreadGroup

ThreadGroup

```
public ThreadGroup(String name) throws SecurityException
public ThreadGroup(ThreadGroup parent, String name)
     throws SecurityException, Null Pointer Exception
```
These create a new thread group.

Reference: Chapter 10.

toString

```
public String toString()
```

> This returns a printable string.

Reference: Chapter 10.

checkAccess

```
public final void checkAccess() throws SecurityException
```

> If there is a security manager, its `checkAccess()` method is called with the `ThreadGroup` as an argument.

Reference: Chapter 10.

getName

```
public final String getName()
```

> This returns the name that you gave to the group.

Reference: Chapter 10.

getParent

```
public final ThreadGroup getParent()
```

> This returns the parent of this group.

Reference: Chapter 10.

parentOf

```
public final boolean parentOf(ThreadGroup g)
```

> This returns true if this is the parent.

Reference: Chapter 10.

stop

```
public final void stop()throws SecurityException
```

This calls `stop()` on every thread and thread group in this group.

Reference: Chapter 10.

Comments: Deprecated in Java 2.

suspend

```
public final void suspend()
            throws SecurityException
```

This calls `suspend()` on every thread and thread group in this group.

Reference: Chapter 10.

Comments: Deprecated in Java 2.

resume

```
public final void resume()
            throws SecurityException
```

This calls `resume()` on every thread and thread group in this group.

Reference: Chapter 10.

Comments: Deprecated in Java 2.

interrupt

```
public final void interrupt()
            throws SecurityException
```

This calls `interrupt()` on every thread and thread group in this group.

Reference: Chapter 10.

destroy

```
public final void destroy()
            throws SecurityException,
      IllegalThreadStateException
```
This removes the group if it is empty. If the thread group has subgroups, destroy() is called on each of those first. Finally, the newly destroyed thread group is removed from its parent.

Reference: Chapter 10.

getMaxPriority setMaxPriority

```
public final void getMaxPriority()

public final void setMaxPriority(int newMaxPrio)throws
      SecurityException, IllegalArgumentException
```
This gets/sets the maximum priority allowed for any thread in this group.

Reference: Chapter 10.

isDaemon setDaemon

```
public final void isDaemon()

public final void setDaemon(boolean daemon) throws
      SecurityException
```
This gets/sets this group to be a daemon.

Reference: Chapter 10.

threadsCount

```
public int threadsCount()
```
This counts the threads in this group.

Reference: Chapter 10.

allThreadsCount

```
public int allThreadsCount()
```

> This counts the threads in this group and subgroups.

Reference: Chapter 10.

groupsCount

```
public int groupsCount()
```

> This counts the groups in this group.

Reference: Chapter 10.

allGroupsCount

```
public int allGroupsCount()
```

> This counts the groups in this group and subgroups.

Reference: Chapter 10.

threads

```
public Thread[] threads()
```

> This returns an array of all the threads in this group.

Reference: Chapter 10.

allThreads

```
public Thread[] allThreads()
```

> This returns an array of all the threads in this group and subgroups.

Reference: Chapter 10.

groups

```
public ThreadGroup[] groups()
```

> This returns an array of all the groups in this group.

> *Reference:*   Chapter 10.

allGroups

```
public ThreadGroup[] allGroups()
```

> This returns an array of all the groups in this group and subgroups.

> *Reference:*   Chapter 10.

activeCount

```
public int activeCount()
```

> This returns the number of groups in this group.

> *Reference:*   Chapter 10.

> *Comments:*   Deprecated in Java 1.1. Use
> `allThreadsCount()`.

activeGroupCount

```
public int activeGroupCount()
```

> This returns the number of groups in this group.

> *Reference:*   Chapter 10.

> *Comments:*   Deprecated in Java 1.1. Use
> `allGroupsCount()`.

enumerate

```
public int enumerate(ThreadGroup list[])
public final void enumerate(ThreadGroup list[], boolean
        recurse)
```

>   This is deprecated. Use `allThreads()`.

>   ***Reference:***   Chapter 10.

>   ***Comments:***   Deprecated in Java 1.1. Use `allThreads-`
>   `Count()` or `threads()`, `allGroups()`, or
>   `groups()`.

list

```
public final void list()
```

>   This is a debugging utility that prints out a detailed
>   description of this thread group.

>   ***Reference:***   Chapter 10.

uncaughtException

```
public final void uncaughtException(Thread t, Throwable e)
```

>   This is called whenever a thread in this group dies via an
>   uncaught exception.

>   ***Reference:***   Chapter 10.

Summary

We described some of the details of areas of minor interest. You'll
probably never use anything in this section.

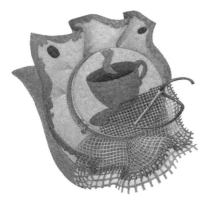

Libraries

In which we explore a variety of operating systems issues that bear heavily upon the usability of threads in actual programs. We examine the status of library functions and the programming issues facing them. We look at some design alternatives for library functions.

Multithreading is a fine and wonderful programming paradigm as we have described it thus far. However, it's not worth too much if it doesn't have the operating system support to make it viable. Most of the major operating systems are in a state of significant flux, so it would be difficult for us to say much about all of them. Instead, we will stick with the issues that need to be considered and describe where the major systems are with respect to them.

The Native Threads Libraries

The native threads library is an integral, bundled part of the operating system for most (Solaris, IRIX, AIX, Digital UNIX, SCO, HP-UX, Win95, NT, OS/2) but not all OSs (Linux). When it is bundled, you can write your program and not worry about whether the dynamic library will be there when you need it. As long as you write your C programs legally, you will be able to move them across different machines and across different versions of the operating system without any problems at all.

JVMs that use green threads are independent of the native threads libraries, so there's no issue here for them. JVMs that do use the native threads library will obviously need that native library in place.

Multithreaded Kernels

Many of the kernels are implemented using threads (Solaris, NT, OS/2, AIX, IRIX, Digital UNIX, HP-UX). The kernels generally use the same C API that you have access to (Solaris kernel threads are very similar, Mach kernel threads are much lower level). There is no inherent connection between the kernel being multithreaded and the existence of a user-level MT library. Kernel programmers could have written the user-level library without the kernel being threaded, and they could have threaded the kernel without supplying a user-level library. They even could have built LWPs, made them realtime, SMP, and preemptable without the use of threads. Theoretically.

In practice, the same things that make MT so attractive to you also make it attractive to the kernel hackers. Because the kernel implements all internal schedulable entities as threads, it is much easier to implement SMP support and realtime scheduling, and make the kernel preemptable. So LWPs are built on top of kernel threads. Interrupts are built with kernel threads. Creation, scheduling, synchronization, etc., of kernel threads work much the same way as for user-level threads.

The OS can be viewed as one gigantic program with many library calls into it [`read()`, `write()`, `time()`, etc.]. Kernels are unusual in that they have always been designed for a type of concurrency. DOS is simple and allows no concurrent calls. If your program blocks while reading from disk, everything waits. Multitasking systems, on the other hand, have always allowed blocking system calls to execute concurrently. The calls would get to a certain point [say, when `read()` actually issues the disk request], save their own state, and then go to sleep on their own. This technique was nonpreemptive, and it did not allow for parallelism. Code paths between context switching points could be very long, so few systems claimed any time of realtime behavior.

In the first case in Figure 11–1 (which is like SunOS 4.1.3 and most early operating systems), only one process can be executing a system call at any one time. Many processes may be blocked in the middle of a system call, but only one may be running. In the second case, locks are put around each major section of code in the kernel, so several processes can be executing system calls, as long as the calls are to different portions of the kernel. In the third case (like most current systems), the granularity of the locks has been reduced to the point that many threads can be executing the same system calls, as long as they don't use exactly the same structures.

Now, if you take these diagrams and substitute *processor* for *process*, you will get a slightly different picture, but the results will be largely the same. If you can execute several things concurrently, with preemptive context switching, you can execute them in parallel. A slightly different but perfectly valid way of looking at this is to consider it in terms of critical sections. In the "no concurrency" case, the critical section is very large—it's the whole kernel. In the "more concurrency" case, there are lots of little critical sections.

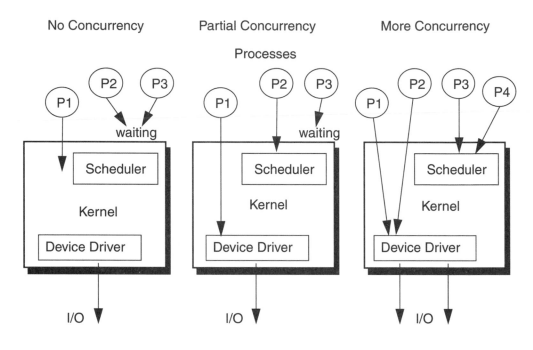

Figure 11–1 *Concurrency within the Kernel*

Symmetric Multiprocessing

SMP merely means that all processors are created equal and endowed by their designers with certain inalienable functionalities. Among these functionalities are shared memory, the ability to run kernel code, and the processing of interrupts. The ability of more than one CPU to run kernel code simultaneously is merely an issue of concurrency—an important issue, of course, but not a defining one.

All of the OSs discussed here were designed to run on uniprocessor systems and tightly coupled, shared memory multiprocessors. The kernel assumes that all processors are equivalent. Processors run kernel threads from the queue of runnable kernel threads (just as in user code). If a particular multiprocessor implementation places an asymmetric load on the processors (e.g., if interrupts are all directed to a single CPU), the kernel will nonetheless schedule threads to processors as if they were equivalent, not taking this asymmetry into account.

Are Libraries Safe?

Just because you write perfectly safe code that will run in a multithreaded environment with no problems doesn't mean that everyone else can. What would happen if you wrote a wonderful MT program, but then called a library routine that used a bunch of global data and didn't lock it? You'd lose. So you must be certain that if you call a routine from multiple threads, it's *MT-safe*, which means that a function must lock any shared data it uses and it in turn must only call other MT-safe functions.

Well, even programmers with the best of intentions find themselves with conflicting goals. "Make it fast" and "Make it MT-safe" don't always agree. Some routines in some libraries will not be MT-safe. It's a fact of life, and you have to deal with it. The documentation for each library call should indicate its level of "MT safeness." It is often quite unclear from the Java spec just which methods are or are not thread-safe.

Libraries and classes themselves are not safe or unsafe, per se. The *methods* in them are (or aren't). Just to confuse things, there are libraries that contain some methods that are safe and some methods that aren't safe. Every time you use a method, you must make sure that it's MT-safe.

The calls `read()` and `write()` are technically MT-safe, inasmuch as you can call them from multiple threads and get correct results. Unfortunately, they both move a pointer associated with the file descriptor. In practice, if you perform concurrent operations from different threads on the same file descriptor, you're likely to get very confused. For this reason, in UNIX98 there is a pair of calls (Figure 11–2): `pread()` and `pwrite()`, which operate exactly the same way as `read()` and `write()`, except that you have to pass an explicit file position pointer along with them.

No such calls exist in Java, so you are forced to open file descriptors for a file if that is the behavior you want. [In our disk performance example (see *Disk Performance with Java* on page 402), this is what we do.]

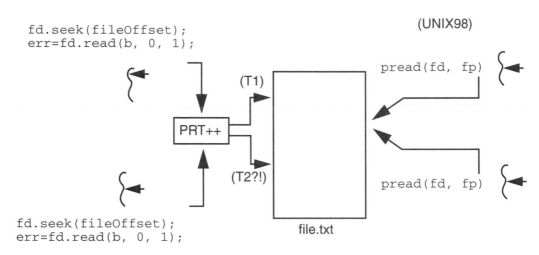

```
fd.seek(fileOffset);
err=fd.read(b, 0, 1);
```

(UNIX98)

pread(fd, fp)

(T1)

PRT++

(T2?!)

pread(fd, fp)

```
fd.seek(fileOffset);
err=fd.read(b, 0, 1);
```

file.txt

Figure 11–2 *Using* pread() *and* pwrite() *to Keep Track of the File Pointer*

Window Systems

All modern window toolkits are designed around the concept of having an *event loop* waiting for window events. Xview, SunView, X11, MS Windows, Motif, CDE, AWT, Swing, etc., are all based on an event loop. Basically, the thread in question will sit in a call to read(), waiting for input. The user may push a button or move the mouse, or a socket or pipe may signal data ready. All of these are encoded as events. (In the different toolkits, different events may be registered with the event loop. Java allows only mouse events and keyboard input events in the AWT and Swing.)

When that event is read by the event loop, the event loop then dispatches the event to the appropriate method. In X11, CDE, etc., the programmer will register specific functions to run when specific events occur. In both Swing and the AWT, events are always dispatched to one of a small number of known methods. If you subclass Applet and create a button, pushing that button will call the Button method actionPerformed(). You (presumably) have specialized that method for your subclass to do what you want.

In a Swing program, the main thread runs main() (as usual) and it typically lays out the components for a window and makes them appear by calling either `show()` or `setVisible()`. As soon as the first Swing window is shown, an event dispatch thread is also created to handle events. All event callbacks run in this thread.

The AWT is *not* thread-safe. This will come as a great surprise to many people (the authors included). There were plenty of indications that it was, and plenty of sample programs in books and manuals that assumed it was, but it isn't.

In a window system that is thread-safe, any method may be called on any object in the toolkit in one thread while any other method is running on any other object (or the same method and object). The results might not always make sense, but it would be legal and would produce the same results as if you had called the methods from the same thread. This is a good thing, because you can call methods from any thread at any time. This is also a bad thing because it will slow down the window system quite a bit.

The future of Java is not in the AWT, so we won't spend much time on it. (A sample AWT program that mimics our Swing example is on the Web.) Swing is the new toolkit that you'll be using to do all of your Java windows work and Swing is most specifically not thread-safe! This is bad because you can't call methods from any thread at random. This is good because you're less likely to make the silly mistakes noted above.

Its one drawback is largely mitigated by the inclusion of two methods, `invokeAndWait()` and `invokeLater()`. These two methods place any operation you want onto a queue that the window thread will run from its read/execute loop. The first function, `invokeAndWait()`, places the event onto the event queue and waits until it completes. The second, `invokeLater()`, places the event onto the queue and returns immediately (Figure 11–3). The event will then get processed some unknown time later. You will probably not use `invokeAndWait()` very often, and obviously you would never call it from the event dispatch thread.

Several other methods are also thread-safe and may be called from any thread, including `JTextComponent.setText()`, `JTextArea.insert()`, `JTextArea.append()`, `JTextArea.replaceRange()`, `JComponent.repaint()`, and `JComponent.revalidate()`. You may also add and remove

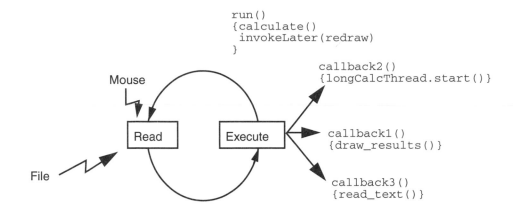

```
run()
{calculate()
  invokeLater(redraw)
}
```

```
callback2()
{longCalcThread.start()}
```

Mouse

```
callback1()
{draw_results()}
```

Read   Execute

File

```
callback3()
{read_text()}
```

Figure 11–3   *Threads Using invokeLater() with the Swing Toolkit*

event listeners from any thread. The listener methods will, of course, run in the event dispatch thread. You may also create components, set their properties, and add them to containers as long as they are not yet realized. Once realized [via `show()`, `setVisible()`, or `pack()`] you cannot manipulate them any longer. You will probably never use any of the latter thread-safe methods, as it is normally possible to do everything from either the main thread or via `invokeLater()`.

The result of this design is that the window thread (the one running the event loop) spends the vast majority of its time blocked in read, waiting for an event. This is good. You want to do your main computing in another thread. The problem that arises is that some button might invoke a long-running method, freezing the GUI until it completes.

So you can have the callback function spawn a new thread to handle the calculation and the callback can return immediately. This way, the GUI is still active and the calculation is performed in the new thread. When the calculation is complete, the thread can then request updates to the windows to be done by calling `invokeLater()` (Figure 11–4).

This is the same technique that is used in the native window toolkits in UNIX. As Motif has no "`invokeLater()`"-style function, C programmers simply send an event directly from the

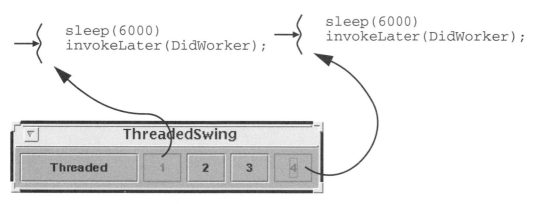

Figure 11–4   *ThreadedSwing Window Example*

thread to the event loop using XCreateEvent(), causing the
event loop to run the callback for that event.

Code Example 11–1 is from the program ThreadedSwing
(see the complete code in *Threads and Windows* on page 366) and
shows the callbacks, the function that runs when you push a button
(which just creates a thread and returns), the work function [which
does its work, then calls invokeLater()] and the display function [which is run by invokeLater()].

```
public class NumericButtonListener implements ActionListener  {


public void actionPerformed(ActionEvent event) {
  ThreadedJButton currentButton = (ThreadedJButton)event.getSource();

  System.out.println("Pressed " + currentButton);
  currentButton.setEnabled(false);
  System.out.println(currentButton + " disabled.");
  DoWorker w = new DoWorker(currentButton);

  if (ThreadedSwing.useThreads)
    new Thread(w).start();
  else
    w.run();
}


}
```

Code Example 11–1   *Using Threads in Swing*

```
class DoWorker implements Runnable {
  ThreadedJButton        button;

public void run() {
  Thread selfName = Thread.currentThread();

  System.out.println(button + " sleeping... " + selfName);
  InterruptibleThread.sleep(6000);
  System.out.println(button + " done. " + selfName);

  // This will run workComplete() in Swing main thread.
  // This is the main point of the whole example.
  SwingUtilities.invokeLater(new DidWorker(button));
}

}


class DidWorker implements Runnable {
  ThreadedJButton        button;

public void run() {     // Run only in Swing main thread.
  Thread selfName = Thread.currentThread();

button.setEnabled(true);
  System.out.println(button + " reenabled. " + selfName);
}

}
```

Code Example 11–1   *Using Threads in Swing (cont.)*

Working with Unsafe Libraries

What do you do if you want to use a class library that contains
unsafe methods? You could use it in locations where it is
already protected (Code Example 11–2). (HashMap is not MT-
safe, but in this code it is used only by methods that are already
safely protected.) You could subclass it and synchronize the
methods (Code Example 11–3). You could use it from only a
single thread.

```
public synchronized Object tweek(Object arg) {
  HashMap.put(arg);
}
```

Code Example 11–2   *Protecting a* HashMap

```
public class MyFoo extends Foo {
...

public synchronized Object frob(Object arg) {
  return foo.super(arg);
}

}
```

Code Example 11–3   *Subclassing an Unsafe Object*

When Should a Class Be Synchronized?

There is a tendency when writing a threaded program to declare all methods synchronized. This would seem a good thing to do, as then they could all be safely called from any thread. But it's not. The vast majority of objects that a program uses are called from code that already contains proper protection. In our producer/consumer examples, there was no need to make workpile.add() and workpile.remove() synchronized because they were only called from producer and consumer.

Synchronized Collections in Java 2

In Java 2 several classes that previously had synchronized methods have gotten replacement classes that don't [e.g., HashTable has synchronized methods, HashMap (new in Java 2) doesn't]. This is a good thing because HashMap runs faster. It is a good thing because it is fairly unlikely that you need it to be synchronized anyway. But sometimes you do.

Java 2 has a clever method of dealing with this situation. Instead of making subclasses of the various collection classes and synchronizing them, Java 2 provides a static factory method for each collection class which will return a synchronized version of the collection. This is known to design pattern folks as a decorator pattern.

So the idea is that you create a class, then call the factory method on it to get back a synchronized version of that same class. Obviously, you must now use only the synchronized version of the class. Each of the core collections has such a factory method:

```
public static Collection synchronizedCollection(Collection c)
public static Set synchronizedSet(Set c)
public static Map synchronizedMap(Map c)
public static List synchronizedList(List c)
public static SortedSet synchronizedSortedSet(SortedSet c)
public static SortedMap synchronizedSortedMap(SortedMap c)
```

So you use these methods to obtain synchronized collections (Code Example 11–4):

```
List syncdList = Collections.synchronizedList(list);
```

Code Example 11–4   *Making Synchronized Collections*

If you use an iterator, you must use it entirely within a synchronized block or else another thread might change the collection while the iterator is using it (Code Example 11–5)

```
synchronized (syncdList) {
    Iterator i = syncdList.iterator();
    while (i.hasNext())
    foo(i.next());
}
```

Code Example 11–5   *Protecting an Iterator*

Java's Multithreaded Garbage Collector

Obviously, Java's garbage collector must work in a threaded environment. There are a number of different algorithms that will do this. They range from simple stop-and-copy garbage collectors to realtime, dynamic, generational collectors. As Java is very specifically not a realtime language, stop-and-copy is perfectly acceptable. The actual algorithm used is not specified by Java, and different implementations use different collectors.

By the very nature of garbage collection, a multithreaded garbage collector is significantly more complex than a single-threaded collector. In a single-threaded collector, the system is able to run freely until it runs out of heap, in which case it can then run a

GC directly. As there is only one thread, that thread is clearly in a known safe state and the GC can proceed immediately. In a multithreaded collector, things are not so simple.

In an MT environment, when a thread discovers that it needs to start a GC, it cannot just begin immediately. There are more threads out there and they must not be allowed to interfere. First, they must not be allowed to use the heap while our GC thread is changing it. Second, they must not be allowed to change any pointers while the GC thread is running. Third, the entire state of the system must be consistent and all internal invariants correct.

This is accomplished by requiring all other threads to arrive at a known safe place in the JVM and stay there. *How* to get all the threads to do this is another matter, and there are plenty of clever schemes used to ensure all threads arrive at one of the GC points as quickly as possible.

Now, can your GC also compact the heap? And do you want it to? Yes, the GC can compact the heap. It's a little bit tricky if you hash on an address, but possible. In some set of programs, compacting will allow you to run in a smaller memory machine. But outside of intentionally mistuned programs, this probably isn't an issue anyway. Memory is plentiful and cheap.

Locks during Finalization

As with all finalization, you never know if or when it is going to happen. Trying to lock locks during finalization can easily get a naively written program into a deadlock. What do you want to use finalization for anyway? There is almost certainly a better way to do whatever you're thinking about.

Summary

Many library functions are not MT-safe, and several different techniques are used in dealing with this, some by the JVM, some by individual vendors. In most cases you will find that you want MT safety at a higher level than Java base classes anyway. It is often unclear from the documentation exactly how some of the Java classes have been defined.

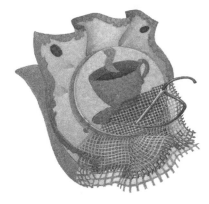

Design

In which we explore some designs for programs and library functions. Making both programs and individual functions more concurrent is a major issue in the design of these functions. We look at a variety of code examples and the trade-offs between them.

Making Libraries Safe and Hot

Now that we've discussed the grand generalities of what is possible, let's move to the other extreme and take a look at some of the specific programming issues that MT programs come up against and how they can be dealt with. We'll look at the issues of designing and working with libraries—the vendor's libraries, third-party libraries, and your own libraries—how they can be written to be both correct and efficient. *By far the most important design issue is simplicity.* Debugging multithreaded programs is difficult and the current tools are not that good (because none of us have figured out how to build better tools!), so this is a major issue.

Often, there are simple, obvious methods of making functions MT-safe. Sometimes these methods work perfectly, but sometimes they introduce contention between different threads calling those functions. The job of the library writer is to analyze those situations and make things fast.

We're going to look first at some functions in C because (1) these are good examples of the issues involved, (2) they are real examples from productions systems, and (3) we had this section left over from the last book and wanted to use it. We can divide functions into a number of categories.

Trivial Library Functions

Many functions are trivially safe. Functions like `sin()` have no need to write any shared data and can be used exactly as first implemented thirty years ago.

Another set of functions has very little shared state and can be made thread-safe simply by surrounding the use of global data with a lock. The pseudo-random number generator, `rand()`, is a very small, fast function that takes about 1 μs on an SS10/40. It uses a seed value that it changes on each call. By protecting that seed, the function can be made safe (Code Example 12–1). This new version of `rand()` is safe and now runs about 1 μs slower due to the mutex. For most programs, this is fine.

```
rand_1()
{static unsigned int seed;
 static pthread_mutex_t m = PTHREAD_MUTEX_INITIALIZER;
 int value;

 pthread_mutex_lock(&m);
 value = _rand(&seed);      /* Calculate new value, update seed */
 pthread_mutex_unlock(&m);
 return(value);
}
```

Code Example 12–1 *Simple MT-Safe Implementation of* rand(),
Version 1

Functions That Maintain State across Invocations

There are cases where you might wish to use a function to set values in one invocation and use those same values in another invocation but don't want those values shared by different threads. When you call strtok(), for example, you first pass it a string to be parsed, and it returns the pointer to the start of the first token in that string. When you call it a second time (with a NULL argument), it returns a pointer to the start of the second token, etc. It is highly unlikely that you would want thread 1 to get the first token in a string and thread 2 to get the second, although this is exactly what strtok() will do.

There are two possible solutions. One is to write a new function, strtok_r(), which takes an extra argument that the programmer uses to maintain state explicitly. (This is what POSIX does.) This is a good technique because the programmer can explicitly choose how to use the arguments to the best advantage. But at the same time, it puts an additional burden on the programmer, who must keep track of those arguments, passing them from function to function as required.

The second solution is to use thread-specific data and have strtok() maintain separate state for each thread (this is what Win32 does). The advantages to this solution are consistency (no code changes required) and simplicity at the cost of some efficiency.

We'll use `rand()` again to illustrate these points (Code Example 12–2). Normally, a function like `rand()` will be used only occasionally in a program , and there will be very little contention for its critical section (which is very short anyway). However, should your program happen to call `rand()` a great deal, such as in a Monte Carlo simulation, you may experience extensive contention. By keeping the seed as thread-specific data, this limitation can be avoided.

```
int rand_2()
{unsigned int *seedp;
 int value;

 seedp = (int *) pthread_getspecific(rand_key);
 value = _rand(seedp);      /* Calculate new value, update seed */
 return(value);
}
```

Code Example 12–2   *Implementing `rand()` with TSD, Version 2*

With the `rand_2()` definition, there is no contention for a critical section (as there is none). However, even `rand_2()` is two times slower than `rand()`. One advantage of `rand_1()` and `rand_2()` is that they don't change the interface of `rand()`, and existing libraries that use `rand()` don't need to be changed.[1]

Well, that's interesting, but is it really relevant to Java? Most of the issues above are subsumed by the use of objects. In Java the object `Random` contains its own state and is (potentially) just as fast as `rand()` in POSIX. So no, these are not terribly relevant to Java, but it's good to know how the lower-level libraries deal with these issues.

---

[1] The semantics of `rand_2()` are different than those of `rand()`, inasmuch as pseudo-random number generators *are* deterministic, and their results *are* repeatable when a known seed value is used. Both `rand()` and `rand_1()` would be nondeterministic, as thread scheduling is nondeterministic. This is unlikely ever to be a problem.

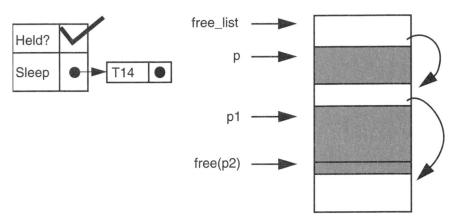

Figure 12–1 *Current Solaris Implementation of* malloc()

Making malloc() More Concurrent

The implementation of malloc() on Solaris 2.5 is quite simple (Figure 12–1). There's one global lock that protects the entire heap. When a thread calls either malloc() or free(), it must hold that lock before doing the work. It's a simple, effective design that works fine in most programs. When you have numerous threads calling malloc() often, you can get into a performance problem. These two functions take some time to execute and you can experience contention for that one lock. Let's consider other possible designs. Keep in mind that we are not going to be changing the definition of malloc(), nor will we change the API. We are only going to change the implementation underneath.

Using Thread-Specific Data to Make malloc() More Concurrent

When used sparingly, a simple mutex works fine. But when called very often, this can suffer from excessive contention. The TSD solution is a possibility, but it introduces some problems of its own.

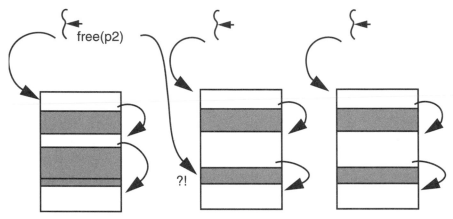

Figure 12–2   *Threads with Individual TSD* `malloc()` *areas*

What if T2 mallocs some storage and T1 frees it? How does T1 arrange to return that memory to the correct free list? [Because `free()` will glue adjacent pieces of freed memory together into a single large piece, the `free()` must be called with the original malloc area; see Figure 12–2.] If T2 exits, who takes care of its malloc area? If an application creates large numbers of threads but seldom uses `malloc()`, it will be creating excessive numbers of malloc areas.

So this is possible, but not very attractive. One of the fellows in our group actually implemented this for a customer with a very specific problem. It worked well, but it was not at all generalizable.

Using Other Methods to Make **malloc()** *More Concurrent*

It is possible to assign a mutex to protect each piece of free storage and have threads skip over those areas when locked. Although possible, this technique suffers from excessive complexity. It also suffers from excessively fine-grained locking. [If `malloc()` has to lock a mutex for every single node in the free list, it could easily spend more time doing the locking than looking for the memory. We do exactly this in *One Local Lock* on page 276.]

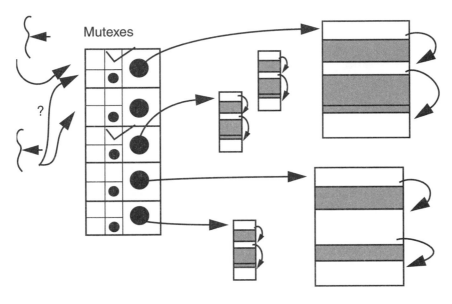

Figure 12–3 *Threads Using an Array of* malloc() *Areas.*

A different approach to this problem is to build a static array of malloc areas to be shared by all threads (Figure 12–3). Now a thread calling malloc() can check for an unlocked malloc area by calling pthread_mutex_trylock() on the area's mutex. If held, the thread will simply check the next area. The probability of more than a few malloc areas being locked is vanishingly small for any vaguely normal program. This version of malloc() would be safe, fairly fast, and relatively simple.

Storage being freed must still be replaced into its area of origin, but this is a manageable problem. The freeing thread could simply block. It could place the pointer to be freed onto a list for that area and let the thread holding the lock take care of doing the freeing on its way out. We could dedicate a special thread to the task of returning freed storage to its proper location. A variation on a theme for this design involves using a small hashtable that maps the TID to a specific malloc area, reducing the amount of searching involved.

These are a few of the most common problems that we have seen. There are two points worthy of note: (1) There are many viable solutions to every problem; and (2) no one solution is optimal for all aspects of a problem. Each of the three versions of `mal-loc()` is fastest in some situation.

Although Java does not have `trylock` methods, virtually the same effect may be accomplished by locking the array of pointers and including an "in use" bit. As of the writing of this book, several people were working on different variations of this last solution. We will probably see them in later operating system releases by the different vendors.

Manipulating Lists

Now we are going to take a look at some designs for a program that adds, removes, and searches for entries on a singly linked list (Figure 12–4). The program creates a list of people with their salaries. One set of threads is going to search down that list looking for friends of Bil's, and give those people raises. Another set of threads is going to search down the list looking for people whom Dan detests and remove those people from the list. There may be some overlap of Bil's friends and Dan's enemies.

To make the program a bit more interesting (and emphasize certain issues), we will associate a delay time with each raise and liquidation. These delays may represent the time to write to disk or to do additional computation. For this purpose we'll make a call to `sleep()`. On Solaris, the minimum sleep time is 10 ms (it's based on the system clock), which is typical for most OSs. The main question we'll be asking is: "For a given configuration of CPUs, delay times, list length, and number of threads giving raises and performing deletions, which design is best?" For different configurations we'll get different answers.

Basic Design

The complete code for all examples is available on the Web (see *Code Examples* on page 410).

A few notes about the program. The function `findPer-son(name)` is to be used by both the friends and enemies threads; hence, it will return a pointer to the *previous* element of

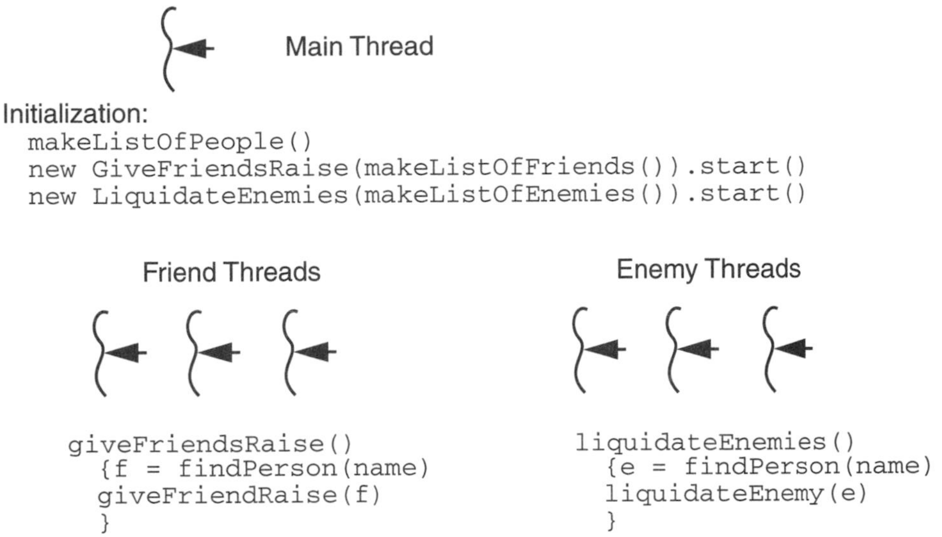

Main Thread

Initialization:
```
 makeListOfPeople()
 new GiveFriendsRaise(makeListOfFriends()).start()
 new LiquidateEnemies(makeListOfEnemies()).start()
```

Friend Threads

Enemy Threads

```
 giveFriendsRaise()              liquidateEnemies()
   {f = findPerson(name)           {e = findPerson(name)
   giveFriendRaise(f)              liquidateEnemy(e)
   }                               }
```

Figure 12–4 *Friends/Enemies: Basic Design*

the people list (the liquidate function needs access to the previous person to remove a person from the list). The appropriate element of the list must remain locked when findPerson() returns, and which lock is appropriate will change with the different designs. It is possible to search for someone who has been liquidated, so null is a possible return value. We'll have to be careful.

Single, Global Mutex

Single, global mutex is by far the simplest design (Code Example 12–3). All that is necessary is to lock the mutex before starting a search and release it after the thread is finished with liquidation or giving raises (Figure 12–5). This is the extreme case of *coarse grain locking*. It has very little overhead and has the best performance when there is only one thread or when the delay times are zero. Once the delay times go up and more threads are added, the wall-clock performance of this design goes to pot. It will not get any advantage from using multiple CPUs either.

There are a couple of things worth noting. The mutex protects the entire list—every element on it, all the pointers, and

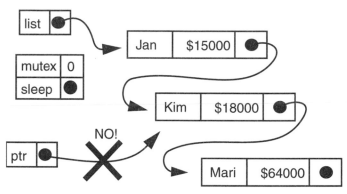

Figure 12–5   *Friends/Enemies: Global Mutex Lock*

the data inside (name and salary). It is not legal for a thread to use a pointer to any element of the list if it does not hold the mutex.

One other thing that you may notice if you run this code is an odd tendency for one thread to get the mutex and then keep it. Typically, one thread will get the lock and execute a dozen or more iterations of its loop before another thread ever runs its loop at all. Often, one thread will run to completion before any other thread even starts! Why? Because there is no work being done outside the synchronized loop and as soon as the running thread releases the synchronized section, the very next thing it does is reacquire it. A call to `Thread.yield()` in the code forces it to behave more the way we'd expect. In a "real" program, this would not be an issue because it would be doing real work outside the loop.

In Code Example 12–3 we see the central function that runs down a list of friends, looking them up and giving them raises. It locks the mutex, does all its work, then unlocks the mutex. It gets the next friend off the list of friends and starts all over again. There are no more than a few dozen instructions between the time it unlocks the mutex and locks it again! The probability of another thread getting in there fast enough to get the mutex is quite low. Using a FIFO mutex in this code would make it much fairer. And slightly slower.

```
public void run() {

  while (friends != null) {
    synchronized(test.people) {
      Person p = Person.findPerson(friends, test.people);
      if (p != null) {
          p.next.giveRaise();
      }
      friends = friends.next;
    }
    Thread.yield();// If running Green Threads
  }
}
```

Code Example 12–3   *Giving Friends Raises (from FriendThread.java)*

Global RWLock with Global Mutex to Protect Salaries

Version two of the program uses a readers/writer lock to protect the list and a mutex to protect the salaries. This way, any number of threads can run down the list, at the same time searching for people to receive raises. Once found, we need to protect the salary data while we update it. We add the `SalaryLock` for this purpose. Clearly, we could not update the salary if we only held a read lock. When a thread wishes to remove one of Dan's enemies from the list, that thread must hold a writer lock while it searches down the list and removes the offending element (see Figure 12–6).

It's important for us to think very carefully about what each lock is protecting. The RWlock protects the list structures and the pointers. It does not protect the salaries. Surprisingly, the performance of this code is not much better than that of the previous code! Inspecting the code closely, you should realize that very little time is spent actually searching down the list (about 1 μs per element). It is the contention for the salary lock when the delay is non-zero that takes all the time.

Once again, no thread may hold a pointer to any portion of the list unless it owns one of the locks.

Code Example 12–4 is the code that updates the salary of Bil's friends. The delay is inside the critical section; thus, while one

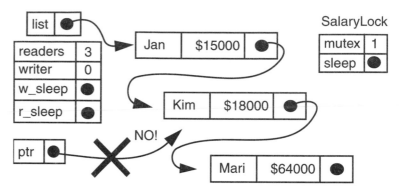

Figure 12–6 *Friends/Enemies: Global RWlock and Salary Lock*

thread is sleeping here, all the other threads must wait outside. Moving the delay outside would vastly increase the performance of the program. It wouldn't be terribly realistic to do so. As the delay represents a write to disk or some other operation on the salary, it really must be inside the critical section.

```
public synchronized void giveRaise() {
 rwlock.unlock();
 salary++;
 delay(raiseDelay);
}
```

Code Example 12–4*:   giveRaise() (listGlobaRW.java)*

Note that we release the RWlock as soon as we obtain the salary lock, allowing liquidator threads to begin their searches. The liquidator threads are allowed to run while we're updating the salary! To make this work correctly, the function `liquidatePerson()` must also lock the salary lock before it changes anything in the object (Code Example 12–5). Also notice how we are mixing our RWlocks with Java's synchronized sections.

```
public synchronized void liquidate() {
 next = next.next;
 rwlock.unlock();
 delay(liquidateDelay);
}
```

Code Example 12–5   *Removing an Element from the List*
(ListGlobalRW2.java)

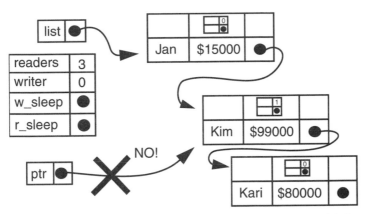

Figure 12–7 *Friends/Enemies: Global RWlock and Local Salary Lock*

Global RWLock with Local Mutex to Protect Salaries

Version three of the program (Figure 12–7) uses a readers/writer lock to protect the list and a local mutex to protect individual salaries. This way, any number of threads can run down the list searching for people to give raises to at the same time. Once found, we need to protect the individual salary data while we update it. Now we have overcome the major bottleneck of this program. Many threads may now update different salaries at the same time.

Once again, no thread may hold a pointer to any portion of the list unless it owns one of the locks. If it only holds a local salary lock, it may not do anything except access that one data item. As soon as the element is removed from the list (see Code Example 12–5), we can release the RWlock (no one else will ever be able to access our item).

In this code, the only points of contention are:

- Only one liquidator at a time may search.
- Only one thread at a time may give a raise to a given individual.

Something that you might consider at this point is: Why not allow multiple liquidators to search at the same time, then once they've found the object, convert the read lock into a write lock? We could modify the definition of RWlocks to allow this possibility; however, it wouldn't work. We would have to ensure that only one thread ever wanted to make the conversion at a time, and as soon as it made that request, every other thread with a read lock would eventually have to release that lock without making a conversion request. In other words, it's possible to do, but it's so limited in functionality as to be nearly worthless.

For pretty much any program of this nature, design 3 will turn out to be the best. However, there are other possibilities.

One Local Lock

What if we allocated one mutex per element to protect only one element? In Figure 12–8, each mutex protects a pointer and the structure to which the pointer points. (The global mutex protects only the global pointer and first structure.) With this design, multiple threads may search down the list at the same time, either to update a salary or to remove an element. Now, multiple liquidator threads may search and destroy simultaneously! Unfortunately, as soon as one thread finds the element it is searching for, it will continue to hold the lock while it finishes its work. Other threads will quickly pile up behind it,[2] waiting to acquire that mutex. This design yields abysmal results for every combination of CPUs, threads, list length, delay times, etc.

It is illegal for a thread to hold a pointer to an element unless it holds the appropriate mutex. In this case, the appropriate mutex is local, so numerous threads may hold pointers to different elements. Note that the mutex in Jan's structure protects the "next" pointer and the following structure (Kim's).

To update Kim's salary, a thread will need to hold the mutex in Jan's structure, not the one in Kim's. To remove Kim from the list, once again the thread must hold the mutex in Jan's structure. As soon as it has been removed from the list, Jan's mutex may be

---

[2]Ever drive 101 at rush hour?

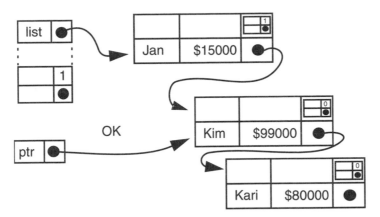

Figure 12–8 *Friends/Enemies with Only One Local Mutex Lock*

released. It will be impossible for any other thread to get a pointer to Kim.

Let's look at the searching routine (used by both liquidators and raisers; Code Example 12–6). The basic loop is simple: Look at each element, compare the name strings, return the previous pointer if found. What is interesting about this function is the order in which locks are acquired and released.

```java
public static Person findPerson(Person p, Person people) {
  Person previous;

  people.mutex.lock();

  while (people.next != null) {
    if (p.name.equals(people.next.name))
      return(people);                    // Previous person (holding lock!)
    people.next.mutex.lock();
    previous = people;
    people = people.next;
    previous.mutex.unlock();
  }
  people.mutex.unlock();
  return(null);
}
```

Code Example 12–6 *Searching Code (`ListLocalLock.java`)*

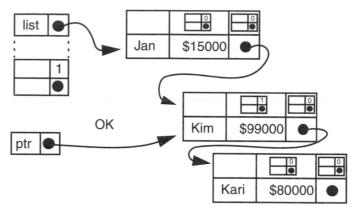

Figure 12–9 *Friends/Enemies: Two Local Locks*

First we lock the global lock and compare our name to the first element (Jan). If this isn't it, we lock Jan's lock, release the global lock, and compare again. The locking/unlocking is being done in an overlapping fashion! (It's often called *chain locking*.) This makes it somewhat challenging to ensure that the correct locks are locked and unlocked in the correct order in all the different functions.

Two Local Locks

A superior version of the local lock design may be had by providing two local locks, one to protect the element and one to protect the salary. Now we have the advantage of allowing multiple liquidator threads to search down the list while not causing bottlenecks. The only points of contention occur when two threads wish to operate on the same element. There's nothing we can do about that.

That's the good news. The bad news is that it takes time to lock mutexes. It may well take more time to lock and unlock each mutex than it takes to do the comparison! In this code, it does. This version of the program, shown in Figure 12–9, is significantly slower than the RWlock version. Only if the list were short and the time to execute a comparison were long would this design give superior results.

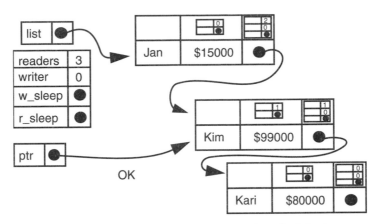

Figure 12–10 *Friends/Enemies: Local Lock and RWlock*

Local RWLock with Local Mutex to Protect Salaries

Just for the sake of completeness, we'll consider one more design (Figure 12–10). By making the local lock an RWlock, we can allow multiple threads to do comparisons on the same element at the same time. If comparisons took significant amounts of time, this could be a viable design. For our program, which does a simple string compare, this design proves to be the worst yet. It takes up much more space, adds more complexity, and is slower by a very significant amount.

We've now completed the journey from very coarse-grained locking to very fine-grained locking and come to the obvious conclusion. The best results are usually found in the middle, but the only way to know is to try.

Program Design

A small number of high-level design strategies have been discussed in several books (see *The Authors on the Net* on page 412). These names are not used completely uniformly. They are:

- **Master/Slave:** One thread does the main work of the program, creating other threads to help in some portion of the work.
- **Client/Server (Thread per Request)**: One thread listens for requests, then creates a new thread to handle each request.
- **Producer/Consumer (a.k.a. Work Queue or Workpile or Thread Pool)**: Some threads create work requests and put them on a queue. Other threads take the work requests off the queue and execute them.
- **Pipeline**: Each thread does some work on a task, then passes the partially completed task to the next thread.
- **Client/Server (Thread per Client):** One thread listens for new clients to attach, then creates a new thread to handle each client. The thread is dedicated to its client, doing work only for that client.

In the discussion below we will elaborate on each of the designs and include some sample code. All the code will be based on a client/server program that takes in requests from a socket, processes them, and sends replies back out over the same socket file descriptor. The complete code for three versions of the program (thread per request, producer/consumer, and nonthreaded) is on the Web site.

Master/Slave

The master/slave design is the most obvious for many kinds of tasks. In its most elemental form, it will be implemented by a library, and the programmer will not even be aware of there being multiple threads. A matrix multiply routine may well spawn a set of threads to do the work, but all the programmer knows is that she called `matrix_multiply()`.

Client/Server (Thread per Request)

This is really just a master/slave design for client/server programs. The master thread will do the listening. In the fragment of the socket program shown in Code Example 12–7, each time a new request comes in from a client, the main thread spawns off a thread to handle that request. The main thread then returns to its `accept()` loop while the thread works on the request independently, exiting when it's done.

```
public void runServer() throws Exception { // Executes in main thread

  for (int i = 1; true; i++) {
    socket = serverSocket.accept();
    Thread t = new Thread(new ProcessRequest(socket));
    t.start();
  }
}

public void process() {

    int n = csocket.is.read(request);// request = "Request ..."
    reply=getReply(request);
    csocket.os.write(reply);// reply = "Reply ..."
}
```

Code Example 12–7 *Master/Slave Socket Design*

Although this design has some positive aspects (e.g., simplicity and directness), it also admits to some drawbacks. The cost of thread creation is not going to be significant unless the task itself is very short (<10 ms). Of more significance is that the programmer has no simple control over the number of threads running at any one time. Should there be a sudden spike in the number of requests, there will be an equal spike in the number of threads, causing performance degradation due to the excessive number of threads competing for the same locks, CPUs, virtual memory, and other resources. (Running this program on a fast 32-bit machine will crash the program when it runs out of virtual memory.)

Rewriting the program to limit the number of threads would be somewhat ugly, and there are better ways of handling the problem. This is probably not a good design for any program!

Producer/Consumer

In the producer/consumer model (Code Example 12–8), the programmer can exert full control over the number of threads with very little effort. The threads may be created at startup time and then be left to wait for work to appear on the queue. Should some of the threads never run at all, there will be no great cost—probably immeasurable. Should there be too many incoming requests, they can be placed on the queue and handled when convenient.

```
public void startUp() throws Exception { // Executes in main thread

   for (int i = 1; i < nConsumers; i++) {
     Thread t = new Thread(new Consumer(workpile));
     t.start();
   }

     socket = serverSocket.accept();
     Thread t = new Thread(new Producer(workpile, socket));
     t.start();
     System.out.println("Server[" + t.getName()
               + "]\tStarted new socket server: " + socket);

}

public static Request read(Socket socket) {
   int n = csocket.is.read(b);
   return new Request(csocket, b);
}
```

Code Example 12–8 *Producer/Consumer Socket Design*

An important aspect of the work queue is that you can allow the queue to grow to any length you deem appropriate. If your clients block, waiting for the results of query 1 before issuing query 2, then allowing the length of the queue to grow to the number of clients will assure you that requests will never be lost, and you can maintain peak efficiency.

If clients are able to issue unlimited overlapping requests, you have no choice. At some point you must begin rejecting requests. However, as long as the average rate of incoming requests is below what your server can handle, then by allowing the queue to grow up to some modest limit, you can effectively buffer burst traffic while retaining peak efficiency. This is a popular design and is the general design of NFS.

Pipeline

The pipeline model is based directly on the same work model that is used in CPUs and on factory floors. Each processing element will do a certain amount of the job and then pass the partially completed task on to the next element (Code Example 12–9). Here the processing elements are threads, of course, and each thread is going to do a portion of the task, then pass the partial results on to the next thread.

```
processRequest_A()
{
  ...
 while(true) {
    is.read(data, LENGTH);
    resultA = processDataA(data);
    addQueueA(resultA);
  }
}

processRequest_B()
{
  ...
 while(true) {
    resultA = getFromQueueA();
    resultB = processDataB(resultA);
    os.write(resultB, LENGTH);
  }
}
```

Code Example 12–9 *Pipeline Design*

We can certainly see that this model would be valuable for simulations in which what you're simulating is a pipeline. For other situations, it's not so clear. In silicon and on factory floors, specialization is important. One section of a chip can execute only a single task (the instruction fetch unit can only fetch instructions, never decode them), and it takes time for a worker to put down a wrench and pick up a paintbrush.

This is not so for threads. It is actually easier and faster and the programming simpler for one thread to execute an entire operation than to do a little work, package up the partial result, and queue it for another thread. Although a number of programs that use this paradigm have been suggested, it is not clear to us that any of them are superior to using one of the other designs.

Client/Server (Thread per Client)

The final model is also somewhat questionable to us. In this model, each client will have a thread devoted to it, and that thread will remain inactive the vast majority of the time (Code Example 12–10). The advantage of having a thread devoted to an individual client is that the thread can maintain state for that client implicitly by what's on the stack and in thread-specific data. Although this does save the programmer the effort of encapsulating that data, it's unclear that it's worth it because of the large number of threads required. In POSIX we avoid doing this by having one producer thread call `select()` on hundreds of sockets. In Java, this is not an option [there is nothing similar to `select()` in Java; see *Dealing with Many Open Sockets* on page 335], so you are pretty much forced to use this design.

```
public void startUp() throws Exception { // Executes in main thread

   for (int i = 1; i < nConsumers; i++) {

     Thread t = new Thread(new Consumer(workpile));
     t.start();
   }

   for (int i = 1; true; i++) {
     socket = serverSocket.accept();
     Thread t = new Thread(new Producer(workpile, socket));
     t.start();
     System.out.println("Server[" + t.getName()
             + "]\tStarted new socket server: " + socket);
   }
}
```

Code Example 12–10   *Thread per Client Design*

We'll consider these last two as interesting possible designs that need some practical fleshing out.

Design Patterns

Design patterns are an excellent tool for conceiving of and constructing programs. This is especially relevant to threaded programs, where the interactions between the threads may become complex. A pattern describes a design form consisting of the interfaces, classes, and objects that make up a program and their interactions. As such, they are a more formal way of stating what we have just described.

There are a series of well-thought-out patterns that are used in multithreaded programs. The use of design patterns lies just above the focus of this book, so we will not attempt to cover it at all. Doug Lea's excellent book *Concurrent Programming in Java* is devoted to describing how such patterns are designed and used (see *Threads Books* on page 414). We recommend it highly.

Summary

Numerous trade-offs exist in the creation of MT-safe and MT-hot libraries. No single locking design works best for all programs. How different threads will interact and how they will be created and exit are open questions. We offer a few insights and some examples. *The most important design issue is simplicity.*

Chapter 13

RMI

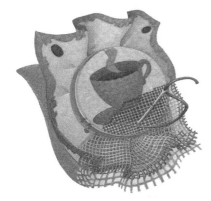

▼ REMOTE METHOD INVOCATION

In which we examine RMI and see what it provides in terms of a distributed object programming model. We look at how threading interacts with it and how it uses threads.

287

RMI is not a thread topic per se, but it does often play a significant role in threaded programs because of its use by threaded programs. The prototypical MT program is a client/server system where the server is threaded to provide greater throughput. In our previous examples, we implemented client/server programs using simple byte streams to communicate across raw sockets. This was good because it was simple and fast, but it was bad because encoding any level of complexity (integers, symbols, objects, etc.) into the byte stream required complicated, ad hoc byte stream formats for those more complex objects.

RMI provides us a simple method of encoding and transmitting arbitrarily complex objects, making it a natural replacement for our raw socket code. Thus we expect a great deal of threaded code to use RMI and therefore include a section on it.

Remote Method Invocation

The basic idea of remote objects is very simple. A server program creates an object and makes a reference to that object remotely available. Client programs find that reference and use it remotely to perform work. The client code treats that reference as if it were a normal, local object, calling methods on it and getting results back. For the most part, the client is unaware that there is anything special about the object. The underlying RMI system takes care of packaging up method invocations and arguments, transmitting them across the wire and returning results. This is a good thing.

In Figure 13–1 we see a typical, simple RMI application. The `rmiregistry` is started first. (The registry is a "poor man's" name server. It can be started directly from the command line or it can be started by the server when that first starts up. We'll use the command line method.) Next the server program is started. At (1) the server program instantiates a new `ServerImpl` object (this is just a regular class that implements `java.rmi.Remote`; we'll subclass `UnicastRemoteObject`). At (2) it calls the RMI `bind()` method, which first finds the registry (by default it looks on port 1099 on the current host), then tells the registry to associate the string supplied ("`frobber`") with the object (`f`). Now the main thread is done, exporting that object. We'll let it exit, although you could keep it around if you wanted. The server startup code has done its work and is done. Behind the scenes,

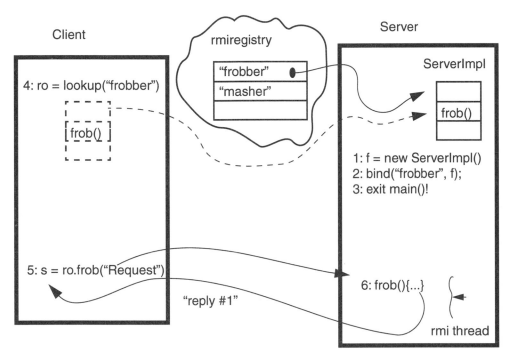

Figure 13–1 *A Simple RMI Call Sending and Receiving a String*

RMI has started up a new thread of its own [while executing the `bind()` call] which will now handle all requests for the object `f`. (Lots of details here; we'll discuss them in a bit.)

Next the client is started up. It calls the RMI function `lookup()` to ask the registry for any object associated with the supplied string. The registry returns the reference to the server object `f`. This object is returned as a remote object, meaning that the client basically has a "fake" local copy (a stub) of that object which it can use normally. When the client calls one of the remotely callable methods [e.g., `frob()`], the arguments are passed to the stub, which uses RMI to "package up" the arguments (known as *serializing an object*) and send them across the wire to the actual object in the server along with the method being invoked. That method runs in the server (6), doing whatever it wants, and returns the result, which RMI serializes and ships back across the wire to the client. We can now implement the same client/server program

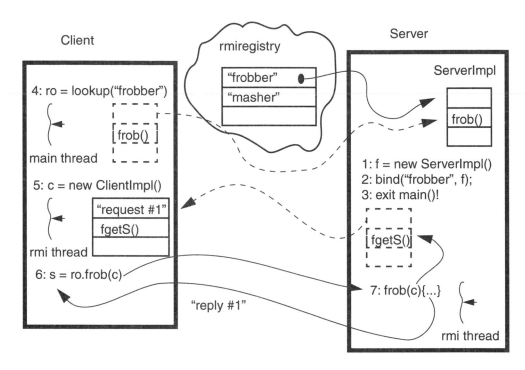

Figure 13–2 *A More Complex RMI Call Sending a Remote Object Reference*

as before without bothering with the details of working with raw sockets. This is a good thing.

Sending Remote References

It is also possible for the client to ship remote references to objects over to the server. In Figure 13–2 we expand upon the previous example by declaring a class in the client which subclasses UnicastRemoteObject. In (5) we create an instance of that object and in (6) we cause RMI to send a reference to it over the wire by passing it as an argument to frob(). Now the server has a remote reference to an object in the client, and the client has one to an object in the server. The server can call remote methods on this object and get arbitrary data from the client.

Note that as soon as a remote reference is exported from the client, the client starts up an RMI thread of its own to handle remote calls on any exported object. Thus when the server calls the remote method `fgetS()` on `c` at (7), that remote call will run in the client's new RMI thread, not the main thread which made the initial call to `frob()`.

The basic idea is that an object can (a) implement `Remote`, in which case passing it as an argument will cause RMI to ship a remote object reference to the server. An object can (b) implement the `Serializable` interface instead (or subclass `Remote-Stub`), in which case passing it as an argument will cause RMI to ship a complete copy of that object to the server. (Strings are serializable.) Finally, (c) an object can do neither, in which case passing it as an argument is not legal and the compiler will complain.

In the code for this program (Code Example 13–1), we see the declaration of the interface for the `ServerImpl` object (`ServerOp`), where the remote method `frob()` is declared. Next we see the `ServerImpl` object itself,[1] where the actual method `frob()` is defined. The `ClientOp` interface and `ClientImpl` class look very similar.

```
//              ServerRMI/Server.java

/*
  A simple RMI server program.  It sets up a registry name for the client
  program to connect to. It creates an unknown number of threads FOR you,
  exiting them when it feels like it.

*/


import java.rmi.*;
import java.rmi.server.*;
import Extensions.*;
```

Code Example 13–1   *Simple RMI Server and Client*

---

[1]The use of the postfixes "Op" for the interface and "Impl" for the object are a general RMI naming convention that we use for convenience and uniformity. You may choose any names you like, but we recommend sticking with the convention.

```
public class Server {
  static int                   serverDelay = 0;
  static boolean               DEBUG = false;
  static boolean               KILL = false;


public static void main(String[] argv) throws Exception {
  Thread                       t;

  if (System.getSecurityManager() == null)
     System.setSecurityManager(new RMISecurityManager());
  if (argv.length > 0) serverDelay = Integer.parseInt(argv[0]);
  if (System.getProperty("DEBUG") != null) DEBUG = true;
  if (System.getProperty("KILL") != null) KILL = true;
  System.out.println("Server(serverDelay: " + serverDelay + ")");

  if (KILL) new Thread(new Killer(120)).start();

  Naming.rebind("Frobber", new ServerImpl());
  System.out.println("Server: 'Frobber' now registered with rmiregistry.");
}

}



//                 ServerRMI/Client.java

import Extensions.*;
import java.rmi.*;
import java.rmi.server.*;


public class Client implements Runnable {
  static boolean               DEBUG = false;
  String                       name;
  static int                   nCalls = 100;
  static int                   nThreads = 2;
  static int                   clientDelay = 10;
  static SingleBarrier         barrier;
  static boolean               KILL = false;


public static void main(String[] argv) {

  if (System.getSecurityManager() == null)
```

Code Example 13–1 *Simple RMI Server and Client (cont.)*

```
      System.setSecurityManager(new RMISecurityManager());
  if (argv.length > 0) nCalls = Integer.parseInt(argv[0]);
  if (argv.length > 1) nThreads = Integer.parseInt(argv[1]);
  if (argv.length > 2) clientDelay = Integer.parseInt(argv[2]);
  if (System.getProperty("DEBUG") != null) DEBUG = true;
  if (System.getProperty("KILL") != null) KILL = true;
  System.out.println("Client(nCalls: " + nCalls + " nThreads: "
                     + nThreads + " clientDelay: " + clientDelay
                     + ")");

  barrier = new SingleBarrier(nThreads);

  for (int i=0; i<nThreads; i++) {
    Thread t = new Thread(new Client());
    t.start();
  }

  if (KILL) new Thread(new Killer(120)).start();
  barrier.barrierWait();
  System.exit(0);
}


public void run() {
  String                selfName = Thread.currentThread().getName();

  try {
    System.out.println("Client[" + selfName + "]\tStarted new thread.");

    ServerOp ro = (ServerOp)Naming.lookup("Frobber");

    for (int i=0; i<nCalls; i++) {
      String msg = "[Client " + selfName + "] Request: " + i;
      ClientImpl ci = new ClientImpl(msg);

      if (DEBUG) System.out.println("Client[" +  selfName
                                    + "] \tSent: '" + msg + "'");
      String reply = ro.frob(ci);
      if (DEBUG) System.out.println("Client[" +  selfName
                                    + "] \tGot:  '" + reply + "'");
      InterruptibleThread.sleep(clientDelay);
    }
  }
  catch (Exception x) {
    x.printStackTrace();
    System.exit(1);
```

Code Example 13–1 *Simple RMI Server and Client (cont.)*

```
  }
  barrier.barrierPost();
}

}


//              ServerRMI/ClientImpl.java

import java.rmi.*;
import java.rmi.server.*;
import Extensions.*;


public class ClientImpl extends UnicastRemoteObject implements ClientOp {
  static int                     delay = 0;
  String                         message;

public String getString() {
  return(message);
}

public ClientImpl() throws RemoteException {
  message = "No Message";
}

public ClientImpl(String msg) throws RemoteException {
  message = msg;
}

}




//              ServerRMI/ClientOp.java

import java.rmi.*;

// A remote interface for an object that supports the "call"
// operation.

public interface ClientOp extends Remote {
```

Code Example 13–1 *Simple RMI Server and Client (cont.)*

```
public String getString() throws RemoteException;
}


//                ServerRMI/ServerImpl.java

import java.rmi.*;
import java.rmi.server.*;
import Extensions.*;


public class ServerImpl extends UnicastRemoteObject implements ServerOp {
  int nCalls = 0;


public ServerImpl() throws RemoteException {}


public String frob(ClientOp o) throws RemoteException {
  int               localCalls;
  ClientOp          ci = (ClientOp) o;
  String            request = ci.getString();
  String            selfName = Thread.currentThread().getName();
  String            reply;

  synchronized (this) { localCalls = nCalls++; }

  if (Server.DEBUG)
    System.out.println("Server[" + selfName + "]\t Starting:  '"
                    + request + "'");
  InterruptibleThread.sleep(Server.serverDelay);
  reply = "[Server" + selfName + "] Reply: " + localCalls
    + " to: " + request;
  if (Server.DEBUG)
    System.out.println("Server[" + selfName + "]\t Processed: '"
                    + reply + "'");
  if ((localCalls%100) == 0)
    System.out.println("Server[" + selfName + "]\t Processed: "
                    + localCalls + " requests.");
  return(reply);
}


public String getName() throws RemoteException {
  return("<ServerImpl: " + nCalls + ">");
```

Code Example 13–1   *Simple RMI Server and Client (cont.)*

```
}

}


//                  ServerRMI/ServerOp.java

import java.rmi.*;

// A remote interface for an object that supports the "call"
// operation.

public interface ServerOp extends Remote {

public String getName() throws RemoteException;
public String frob(ClientOp o) throws RemoteException;

}
```

Code Example 13–1   *Simple RMI Server and Client (cont.)*

In the server, `main()` establishes a security manager (this is required—we use `RMISecurityManager`, but any security manager will do) and then calls `Naming.rebind()` to register with the `rmiregistry`. That's all. [The method `rebind()` will overwrite previous registration of an object, whereas `bind()` will throw an error if there is a previous registration.]

The client establishes a security manager and then calls `Naming.lookup()` to ask the `rmiregistry` for a remote object reference. When it gets the reference, it then creates a pile of `ClientImpl` objects and passes them as arguments to `ro.frob()`. And that's pretty much it.

The full source code for this program includes a lot of debugging statements that will print out information about which thread is where and doing what. It is informative to examine the code in more detail and watch its output. Compiling the program currently requires you to call a special compiler, `rmic`, to build the stub code for the remote objects. (This may change.)

To run the program, you start the registry (Code Example 13–2), then the server, and finally, the client. The registry needs to know the details of the class, so you must set `CLASSPATH` for it. We'll simply start the registry from the code directory (as `CLASSPATH` includes ".").

```
bil@cloudbase[259]: rmic ServerImpl ClientImpl

bil@cloudbase[260]: rmiregistry &

bil@cloudbase[261]: java -DDEBUG Server &
Server: 'Frobber' now registered with rmiregistry.

bil@cloudbase[262]: java -DDEBUG Client &
```

Code Example 13–2 *Running ServerRMI*

RMI's Use of Threads

RMI starts up one thread to listen for remote invocations on the exported object. RMI's threading behavior is not specified beyond this. All RMI says is that it will run your request in some thread other than the ones you created. If you trace this program on Solaris 2.6, you will notice that the server will run a bunch of remote requests in RMI thread 1, a few more in RMI thread 2, etc. It will probably run multiple requests simultaneously in different threads. This is officially hidden from you, and the only way to discover this is to print out the thread's name from `frob()`.

The good part of this is that it doesn't matter. It's not part of your contract with RMI, so who cares? The bad part is that if you mean to use RMI for high-performance programs, you have lost control over the creation and number of threads that your server is running.

Exactly how and in which threads RMI executes remote requests is not specified, nor should it be. All you care about is that your client made a remote invocation on an object and that methods were run on the object in the server on some thread that you did not create.

In the reference implementation of Java 2, a single "accept" thread (`TPC-Accept`) is started when the first object is exported [either via `bind()` or when you pass it as an argument to another process]. This thread will listen on a dynamically allocated port for any and all incoming requests. When a client connects and sends a request, the accept thread arranges for that request to run in a `TPC-Connection` thread. If no connection threads exist, the accept thread will create one. If there is an idle connection thread, the accept thread will use that. Idle connection threads eventually exit.

There are no guarantees about which connection thread a request will run in or about how many connection threads RMI will create. If your application needs absolute control over server threads, you may have to build a consumer/producer model on top of RMI. In this case, the initial remote method would place a request object on a queue and return a "working" message to the client. When the consumer thread completes its work, it can return the desired results via a remote invocation on a remote client-side object.

The Deadlock Problem with RMI

What would happen if you locked a synchronized section on an object c, made a remote call, passing c to the server, and then the server made a synchronized remote callback on c? The server's callback would run in the client's RMI thread. It would try to get the lock, fail (because the main thread owns that lock), and go to sleep, waiting for the main thread to release it. Unfortunately, the main thread is waiting for frob() to return. Deadlock (Figure 13–3).

What can you do about it? Nothing. In the best of situations you can simply ensure that a locking hierarchy is maintained, recognizing that remote callbacks run in different threads. This has the potential of becoming quite complex in more elaborate applications where hundreds of different programs on different machines may all hold references to different remote objects scattered across the network. In the very best of situations, you write your code so that this never comes up.

Another minor note: You can synchronize on the local object stub for the remote object. This will lock the lock on the *stub*, not the actual object. This is probably not what you want to do.

Running synchronized remote methods on remote objects could get quite complicated. Don't do that.

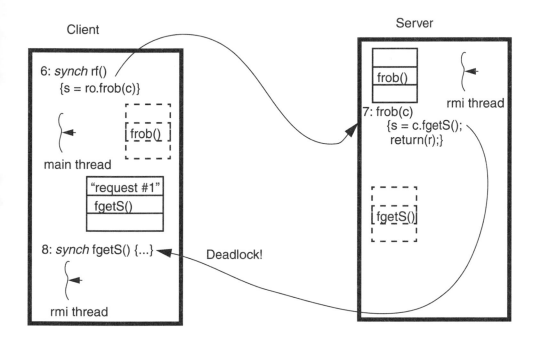

Figure 13–3 *Deadlock by Remote Callback*

Remote Garbage Collection

A reasonable question at this point is: How does RMI handle garbage collection? Clearly, an object that is not referenced locally could still have remote references to it which our local process wouldn't know about. RMI has a clever, optimistic distributed garbage collector (DGC). Basically, each RMI process has a DGC client that periodically sends messages to other processes telling them that it has references to objects there (this is called *lease renewal*).

The DGC does its level best, collecting all objects to which it can't find references. Should a reference to one of these objects later turn up in some client process that didn't renew the lease, too bad. The object is gone, and any remote method invocations on it will throw `RemoteException`, and it will be up to the programmer to deal with the problem. Presumably the program will catch that exception and go back to the server it got it from and request a new object. This is a good research area for Ph.D. students.

Summary

RMI creates its own threads to handle remote method invocations. The details are implementation specific, but this is not a problem. The one challenge is avoiding cross-process deadlocks.

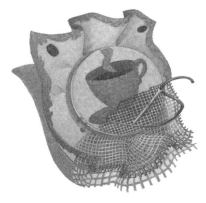

Chapter 14

Tools

- ▼ STATIC LOCK ANALYZER
- ▼ USING A THREAD-AWARE, GRAPHICAL DEBUGGER
- ▼ PROCTOOL
- ▼ TNFVIEW

In which we consider the kinds of new tools
that a reader would want when writing a
threaded program. An overview of the Solaris
tool set is given, as representative of what
should be looked for.

Programming with threads adds new challenges to the development tools that you use. "Normal" toolsets, in most cases, will not work well with threaded programs, because they were designed with single-threaded programs in mind. All the vendors have some set of products to be used with multithreaded programs—debuggers, code analyzers, and performance analysis programs.

This chapter focuses on some of the current tools that Sun Microsystems provides for the development of multithreaded programs. Tool offerings from Symantec, IBM, etc., are fairly similar.

Static Lock Analyzer

For C programs there is a tool called LockLint, which is a lint-type program for locks. It verifies consistent use of mutexes and RWlocks in multithreaded ANSI C programs. LockLint performs a static analysis of the program and looks for inconsistent or incorrect use of these locking techniques. It can tell you definitively if your program is subject to deadlock as long as the calling structure of your program is predictable. Unfortunately, there is no similar tool for Java.

Using a Thread-Aware, Graphical Debugger

All of the different vendors have some version of a graphical debugger, all of which have the same basic functionality. We'll look at a few screen shots from Sun's Java Workshop Debugger. To say the least, the value of a graphical debugger for multithreaded programs is enormous.

Figure 14–1 uses the debugger to take a look at the code in *An Example: Create and Join* on page 59. We started by loading the program into the debugger and then setting a breakpoint in `main()`. Then we started the program and let it hit the breakpoint.

When *any* thread hits a breakpoint, *all* threads will stop. (This is a good thing, because you *want* things to stop while you try to figure them out.) Notice that the Sun's Java implementation creates several threads for its own use in the `main` thread group. All of our threads are by default located in the `Multi.main` thread

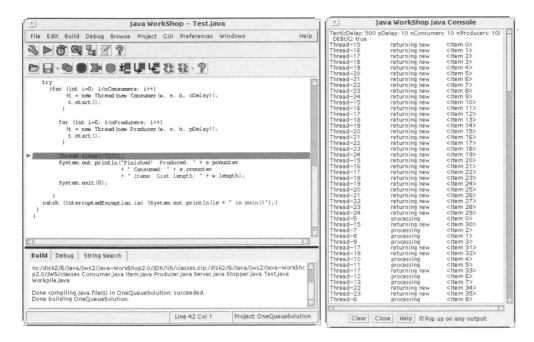

Figure 14–1 *Sun's Debugger [Program Stopped in* `sleep()`*]*

group. The JDK's threads are managed by the JDK and have no effect on your programing.

Also notice that the main thread is always "`Main.`" You can see from the thread pane that `Main` is stopped in `sleep()`. The stack pane will show the entire call stack for the selected thread.

The tiny folders are thread groups, the double lines are threads. The dark double lines indicate threads that have been suspended, hence "Main" and "C" were running at the time of interruption, whereas "A," "B," and "D" have arrows, hence were all blocked in a call to `wait()` or `sleep()`. These three blocks piled on top of each other—"[1]," "[2]," and "[3]"—indicate calls on the stack (those blocks are stacks, get it?). You can see the stack frame (and details thereof) for any thread you choose. The graphics and interface are a bit awkward, but they are quite functional.

It is possible to single step an individual thread, or to continue all threads. No other options exist. You can let a program run and then interrupt it. This allows you to look at deadlocked programs and figure out the problem.

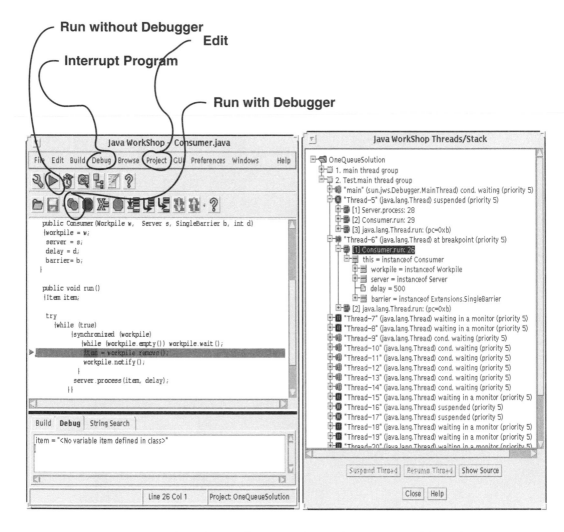

Figure 14–1   *Sun's Debugger [Program Stopped in* `sleep()`*] (cont.)*

Some caution must be exercised, as the first option can get you into confusion. If you step into a call to a synchronized section, and that lock is locked, the thread will not be able to enter that section and JWS will allow all the other threads to run. And you may get confused.

Even in the best designed programs, it is common to have problems getting critical sections to work exactly the way you want. When you do run into problems, it can be extremely time consuming to find the information you need to fix them. Java locks do not appear in the debugger at all and there is no way for you to find out which thread owns them.

Proctool

For Solaris 2 systems, there is a very nice system status display tool (Figure 14–2), which is freely available via FTP (see *Freeware Tools* on page 411). It will show you all the system statistics on your program, including the details for each individual LWP. This tool can be useful when you want to know how your threads are behaving with respect to system calls.

In the main display window you see the complete status line for each process (you get to select what to display). This is data that is derived from the /proc file system. Selecting one of those, you can look at detailed information about that process. In Figure 14–3 you see the detailed statistics for each LWP. (This is

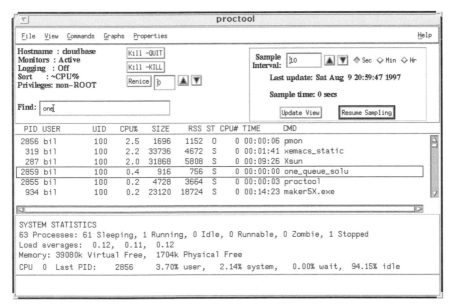

Figure 14–2   *Proctool, Main Display Window*

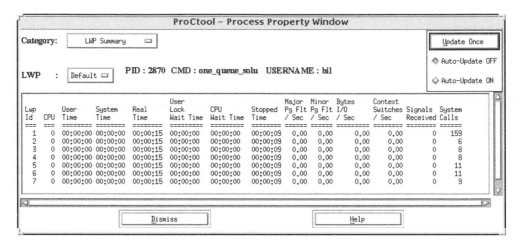

Figure 14–3 *Proctool, LWP Display Window*

one of the places where it's nice to have bound threads, because you get to see what each individual thread is doing.)

TNFview

Many of the new, multithreaded kernels have internal instrumentation in both the kernel and standard libraries. In Solaris, this instrumentation takes the form of a *TNF* (trace normal form) probe. The basic idea for all these types of instrumentation is that probes are included in various important routines. These probes write their names into the file and, optionally, details of the current program state (i.e., some variable values) into a file, along with the exact time of the call. The probes are normally turned off but can be enabled when timing data is desired.

In Figure 14–4 we see calls to TNF_PROBE_N() (N is the number of data values that the probe will write out) in the Pthread library code, in the UNIX kernel, and even calls that we included in our own code. When we run the program with tracing enabled, the probes will write their information out into a file.[1] The timing

---

[1]Actually, it's a bit more complicated than we show, as there is an intermediate, binary format between the probe and the human-readable file. Kernel probes write out to an internal buffer instead of a file, so that must be merged into the final output.

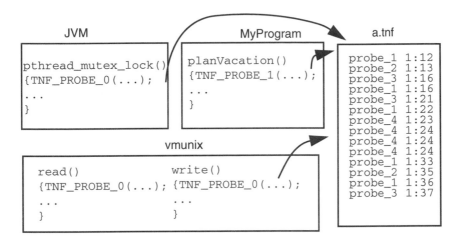

Figure 14–4 *Data Collection for TNF*

---

information is based on the high-resolution clock, which is part of all new Sun hardware. That clock can be read directly (no system call required) with a resolution of 10 μs.

To use TNF probes from Java, it is necessary to write the probes themselves in C and then use JNI to call those probes from your Java code. This is more than a little bit awkward and totally nonportable, but it does give you a great deal of very detailed performance information. We have an example of this in the code on the Web page (TNFExample.java).

Once that data is collected, all that's left is to make sense of it. While you could simply read the file itself, that would probably prove to be rather difficult—there's just too much data to read from a printout.

```
bil@cloudbase[89]: tnfdump /tmp/trace-45132
probe tnf_name: "give_friend_raise_middle" tnf_string: "keys
lgl;file tnf_list_global_lock.c;line 157;"

probe tnf_name: "give_friend_raise_end" tnf_string: "keys
lgl;file tnf_list_global_lock.c;line 159;"

probe tnf_name: "liquidate_enemies_start" tnf_string: "keys
lgl;file tnf_list_global_lock.c;line 186;"

probe tnf_name: "liquidate_enemies_end" tnf_string: "keys
lgl;file tnf_list_global_lock.c;line 198;"

probe tnf_name: "give_friends_raise_end" tnf_string: "keys
lgl;file tnf_list_global_lock.c;line 164;"

Elapsed (ms)    Delta (ms)   ...    Probe Name
-----------     ----------          ----------
```

0.000000	0.000000	give_friends_raise_start
0.695500	0.695500	give_friend_raise_start
0.955000	0.259500	give_friend_raise_middle
1.447000	0.492000	give_friends_raise_start
16.150000	14.703000	give_friend_raise_end
16.703000	0.553000	give_friend_raise_start
17.311000	0.608000	give_friend_raise_middle
36.163000	18.852000	give_friend_raise_end

A better method is to use a special viewer, TNFview (also available via FTP), which condenses that data into graphical form and produces a series of histograms and plots.

In Figure 14–5 we see the details of one run of our program (Code Example 14–1). The different threads are shown as hori-

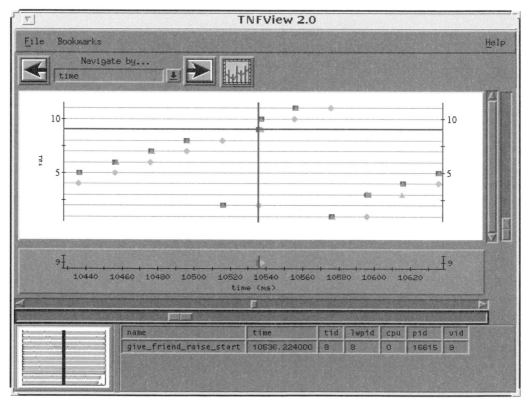

Figure 14–5 *Main Data Display Window for TNF*

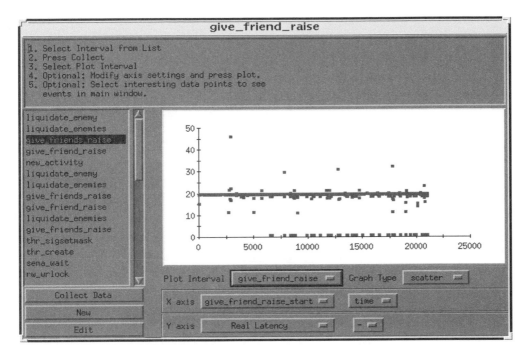

Figure 14–6   *Histogram Display Window for TNF*

zontal lines and specific probes are shown as different colored shapes, squares, triangles, circles, etc. The time line can be scaled and individual events examined.

In Figure 14–6 we see a histogram of method latencies. TNF-view assumes that pairs of probes ending in the words "start" and "end" are related and will produce graphs of latencies between the time the "start" probe fires and when the "end" probe fires. In this example we see that the vast majority of calls to `give_friends_raise()` took 20 ms (in this example the delay time was 20 ms), a few took zero seconds (these are the friends we couldn't find), and a few more took 10 or 30 ms (due to the 10 ms granularity of the system clock), and one last one took 50 ms (wonder why!).

To insert TNF probes into Java code, you need to make calls outside the JVM. It's a bit awkward to do, but not particularly difficult, as we show in Code Example 14–1.

```
//              TNFExample

/*
  Show how to use TNF from Java.   (Only a bit messy.)
  */


import java.io.*;
import java.util.*;
import Extensions.*;

class ProbedObject {
  public native void objectCreateStart();
  public native void objectCreateEnd();


  static {System.loadLibrary("javaProbe");}

}



class TNFExample implements Runnable {
  static SingleBarrier barrier = new SingleBarrier(1);

public static void main (String[] arg) throws Throwable {
  long startTime = System.currentTimeMillis();
  long endTime;

  if (arg.length == 0) {
    System.out.println("Running single-threaded");
    new TNFExample().run();      // Non-threaded
  }
  else {
    System.out.println("Running multi-threaded");
    for (int i=0; i<1; i++) {
      new Thread(new TNFExample()).start();
    }
    barrier.barrierWait();
  }
  endTime = System.currentTimeMillis();
  System.out.println("Done after " + (endTime - startTime) + "ms");
  System.exit(0);
}
```

Code Example 14–1 *Using TNF Probes in Java*

```
public void run() {
  ProbedObject obj = new ProbedObject();

  for (int i=0; i<100; i++) {
    obj.objectCreateStart();
    obj = new ProbedObject();
    obj.objectCreateEnd();
  }
  barrier.barrierPost();
}


}


/*                    javaProbe.c              */

/* cc -G -I/usr/java/include -I/usr/java/include/solaris javaProbe.c -o
   libjavaProbe.so */


#include <jni.h>
#include <tnf/probe.h>
#include "ProbedObject.h"


JNIEXPORT void JNICALL
  Java_ProbedObject_objectCreateStart(JNIEnv *env, jobject obj) {

  TNF_PROBE_0(object_create_start, "object creation", "");
}



JNIEXPORT void JNICALL
  Java_ProbedObject_objectCreateEnd(JNIEnv *env, jobject obj) {

  TNF_PROBE_0(object_create_end, "object creation", "");
}


#              run.csh

# Show how to compile, link, and run a program to get TNF information
```

Code Example 14–1 *Using TNF Probes in Java (cont.)*

```
echo "Compiling java code..."
javac -O TNFExample.java
javah -jni ProbedObject

echo "Compiling C code..."
cc -G -I/usr/java/include -I/usr/java/include/solaris javaProbe.c -o
libjavaProbe.so

echo "Running program under prex..."
prex -o /tmp/tnf.tmp java TNFExample < cmds

echo "Dumping results (or view with tnfview)..."
tnfdump /tmp/tnf.tmp | head

echo "Viewing results with tnfview..."
tnfmerge -o /tmp/tnfview.tmp /tmp/tnf.tmp
$TNFHOME/bin/tnfview2 /tmp/tnfview.tmp
```

Code Example 14–1   *Using TNF Probes in Java (cont.)*

Summary

Using the Solaris toolset as an example, a brief overview of what you can expect from MT tools was given, along with a few hints about what to look for and what to look out for.

Performance

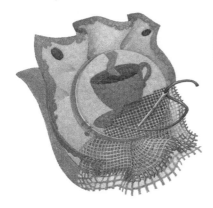

▼ OPTIMIZATION: OBJECTIVES AND OBJECTIONS

▼ CPU TIME, I/O TIME, CONTENTION, ETC.

▼ LIMITS ON SPEEDUP

▼ BENCHMARKS AND REPEATABLE TESTING

▼ THE LESSONS OF NFS

In which we make things faster, look at general performance issues, political performance issues, and thread specific performance issues. We conclude with a discussion of the actual performance of multithreaded NFS.

Optimization: Objectives and Objections

Performance is an incredibly wide topic that means different things to different people. It is often referred to broadly and vaguely as an obvious requirement for all programs, without ever defining exactly what it is. We are not aware of any truly good and comprehensive texts on the subject.[1] In one short chapter, about all we can do is point out the things you probably already know.

Before you begin optimizing your program, you must answer the fundamental question: What do you really want? We're not being silly. This is not an easy question. Major factors surrounding performance tuning include:

- Time to market
- Available human resources and programming costs
- Portability
- User perception
- Competition
- Targeted machine configuration
- Algorithm
- CPU time, I/O time, contention, etc.

In general, your customers' only objective is going to be: "Do my work for the least cost." They really do not (well, should not) care about any of the details. They have their job to do and that's the sole value of your software to them. Many of us engineering types have a tendency to skip over all this touchy-feely stuff and jump straight into the code. Let us resist for a moment and consider these details that affect our paychecks so much. We may not like this, but it really is vitally important.

---

[1]There are a number of books discussing kernel tuning, many discussing algorithmic issues for general programs, and numerous texts and papers do detailed analyses of theoretical limits.These are all fundamental and important places to start, but they are all weak on many important aspects of actual implementation.

Time to Market

Most optimization issues are ultimately marketing issues. These marketing aspects are important and have to be hashed out with management. It's no use having a program that runs twice as fast if your company's out of business. We'll get to the techniques in a moment, but we wish to emphasize this point. The amount of optimization to do on a program is a marketing issue.

Related to this is correctness. Correctness is more important than either performance or time to market. Minor bugs and occasional crashes can be traded off against time to market, but fundamental correctness is essential. Unfortunately, this is a major battle between engineering and marketing all the time.

Available Human Resources and Programming Costs

If you can speed your program up by 50 percent, but it takes 60 programmers two years to do it, is it worth it? Maybe yes, maybe no. It's up to you and you should be thinking in these terms when you begin the optimization efforts.

Portability

Some of the techniques we're going to discuss will require customizing to a particular platform or even to a particular configuration. Is such specialization worthwhile to you? Maybe yes, maybe no. Sunsoft does a PSR (*Platform Specific Release*) of Solaris for each different machine (one for the SS1, another for the SS2, a third for the SS10, etc.). Ninety-nine percent of the code will be shared, but things like byte copy will be optimized for the exact CPU, memory bus, and cache configuration.

It is highly unlikely you would ever go as far in your own code. The normal thing is to optimize for a specific configuration (typically, the highest-performance one) and admit that the others will be a bit suboptimal. Would you want to write and maintain upward of 20 PSRs just for Sun machines? And another 20 for SGI, DEC, etc.?

User Perception

Yes, you might be able to optimize an editor to process keystrokes twice as fast. The user wouldn't care, because the user can't tell the difference between 1-ms and 2-ms response time anyway. Don't waste your time on useless optimization.

Easier said than done, of course. Especially as the world is rife with inappropriate benchmarks upon which people do base their buying decisions. Sorry.

Competition

Being 10% faster means nothing to the user. It looks great on the data sheets, but that's about it.[2] Your program is not a commodity; don't sell it as if it were. Of course, if your program runs 50% slower than the competition, you may need to speed it up significantly. Make sure that you get the time and support you need.

Targeted Machine Configuration

You have to select your primary target machine and you have to declare some configurations inadequate. If you can't get your desired performance on a x286, don't sell on a x286.[3] Next year's machines will be twice as fast anyway. Sometimes, "throwing money at the problem" is the right answer.

Algorithm

There are three vitally important aspects of performance optimization: algorithm, algorithm, and algorithm. Seriously. Forget all of this other stuff until you have settled on the very

---

[2]Yes, performance numbers on data sheets are important because people do make decisions based upon a 1% difference in a published benchmark (dumb, but real). Nonetheless, given a choice between releasing 5% slower than the competition today and 5% faster next year, we'd opt for today.

[3]At one of Bil's first software division meetings (back when everyone fit into the cafeteria!), there was a big debate concerning the poor performance of SunOS on a 4-MB machine. Some of management wanted to restrict all developers to 4-MB machines so we would be more motivated to control code inflation. The final resolution was to make 8 MB the minimum shippable configuration.

best possible algorithm. We can show you programs that will run faster on a uniprocessor VAX 780 than on a 64-way, 500-MHz Alpha Server, simply due to algorithm choice.

You *can* multithread bubblesort, and it *will* run twice as fast, but...

CPU Time, I/O Time, Contention, Etc.

That should be enough moralizing on the practicalities of dealing with the real world. Now let's get serious—you're an ISV and you really want to get the best performance you can (for some "reasonable" programming cost). First let's look at the overall system design and define our true objectives.

The primary components are the CPU, the cache, the main memory bus, main memory, the I/O bus, and the peripherals (disks, tapes, possibly displays, networks, etc.), all of which can be viewed generically as resources. There is a tendency to view the CPU as unique, and we often speak of maximizing CPU usage before considering any other subsystems. However, that's not really what we want. We really want our program to run in minimal wall-clock time. Let's consider these subsystems.

CPU

Some programs are completely CPU-bound. They don't make great demands upon the peripherals and have a small enough working set to be largely cache resident. A huge number of programs are partially CPU-bound. To optimize such programs, our primary technique will be to reduce the number of instructions executed, and our primary method of doing so will be by choosing the best algorithms.

Our secondary method will be to examine our code very carefully to see if there are places where loops can be made tighter. Sometimes we will even examine assembly code to verify the tightness of the complied code. In all cases, we will first analyze our program, then focus our efforts on those sections that consume the most time.

We will leave clever use of registers, optimal instruction scheduling, and the like to the compiler. Only in the rarest of circumstances will we ever "bum" code (write assembly code). *Byte copy* can be written in a single line of C code. On Sun machines, the actual library call occupies roughly 500 lines of carefully hand-optimized assembly code. It is specialized for each of the different byte alignments, and a different version is written for each PSR. The programmer counts the instructions, spreads data across numerous registers to maximize pipelining and multiple instruction issues, etc. It runs upward of ten times as fast as the one line of C.

The chances of you doing anything similar is quite small. It takes a lot of effort, and it is valuable for only a few very tight, very intensively used loops. The hassle of maintaining "bummed" code is also quite significant. Don't do this at home!

Memory Latency

The speed at which the main memory system can fill cache requests is a major factor on the CPU side of performance. It is not at all unusual for memory latency to occupy 50% of total CPU time. Memory latency is difficult to identify as separate from CPU time because there are no standard tools for measuring the amount of time it takes. As far as the OS is concerned, the entire CPU/cache system is a single entity and is lumped into a single number—CPU time.

No measurements of cache activity are recorded, so the only means of distinguishing cache from CPU are (1) counting instructions, (2) comparing target code to known code, and (3) using simulators. Simulators are not generally available.[4] We'll focus on (1) and (2). Once we determine the cache behavior of our program, we may be able to reorganize data access to improve performance (see *Reducing Cache Misses* on page 359).

Memory Bandwidth

No single CPU can come vaguely close to saturating a main memory bus. At the insane rate of one memory access per cycle, a

---

[4]They're too complex to use easily, so there's no reasonable way for vendors to market them. If you are willing to go through a lot of pain and spend big bucks for one, tell your vendor. Vendors will do anything for money.

200-MHz Ultra could demand nearly 100 MB/s—one-twelfth of the UPA bus's bandwidth. Of course, the CPU wouldn't have any time to do anything. Realistic programs demand data rates closer to 50 MB/s, and 95% or more of that is serviced by the cache. Main memory bus rates of 5 MB/sec per CPU are normal for actual programs. A UPA bus can sustain data rates of over 1 GB/s.

It is true that a maximally configured ES10000 with 64 CPUs can easily saturate the 100-MHz UPA crossbar switch. We don't have any clever techniques for minimizing it.

I/O Latency

Making a disk request takes a long time, about 20 ms. During this time a thread will typically go to sleep, letting others run. Depending upon the details of the access pattern, there are a couple of things we can do either to reduce the number of requests or to pipeline them. When the working set is just a bit larger than main memory, we can simply buy more memory.

When the working set is enormous, we can duplicate the techniques that we'll use for optimizing memory access (see *Reducing Cache Misses* on page 359). Disk accesses are easier to deal with than cache misses because the OS does collect statistics on them and because the CPU is able to run other threads while waiting.

Other types of I/O must simply be endured. There really is no way to optimize for asynchronous network requests.

Contention

Sometimes one CPU will hold a lock that another CPU needs. This is normal and unavoidable, but it may be possible to reduce the frequency. In some programs, contention can be a major factor in reducing the amount of parallelism achieved. Contention is only an issue for multithreaded (or multiprocess) programs, and primarily only on MP machines. Although threaded programs on uniprocessors do experience contention, the most important cause of the contention is the speed of other components of the system (e.g., you're holding a lock, waiting for the disk to spin). Reducing contention is always a good thing, and is often worth a lot of extra work.

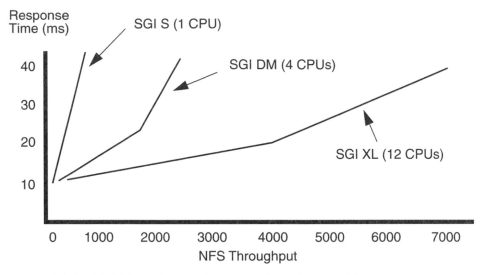

Figure 15–1 *NFS Throughput vs. Latency on Some SGI Machines*

Throughput vs. Latency

Given these resources, we next must refine our definition of performance—do we want to minimize latency for individual subsystems, such as having an NFS server respond to individual requests as fast as possible, or do we want to maximize the number of requests per second that the server can handle? This is a serious consideration and we cannot blithely answer "both."

Consider Figure 15–1.[5] We get to select the point on the graph where we wish to operate. For some programs (e.g., numerical calculations), this latency vs. throughput issue is nonexistent; for others (e.g., NFS) it is paramount. The answer to the question is almost always, "Maximize throughput with 'reasonable' latency." For NFS this means that everyone designs their servers to give maximum throughput at 40-ms average latency.[6] The question

---

[5]Program data and graphs from Hennessy and Patterson, *Computer Architecture,* 2nd edition (San Francisco: Morgan Kauffmann, 1996).

[6]Forty milliseconds is also the limit chosen for the maximum allowable latency for the SPEC Laddis benchmark.

now becomes: "For my individual application, which of these subsystems is the limiting factor, and how much can I accelerate that before another subsystem becomes saturated?"

Limits on Speedup

A naive view of multiprocessing says that we should expect a two-CPU machine to do twice as much work as a one-CPU machine. Empirically, this is not at all the case. Indeed, it is not unusual to hear reports of people who see very little improvement at all. The truth is that it all depends upon what you are doing. We can cite examples of programs that get near-linear speedup, a few that show superlinear speedups, a large majority that show some speed up, and even a few that slow down.

One basic fact should be acknowledged up front: There is always a limit. For every program or system load that you can imagine, there is an optional number of CPUs to run it on. Adding more CPUs to the machine will slow it down.

You could, if you wanted, build a 1-million-CPU SMP machine. It just wouldn't be very efficient. And while we can invent programs that would make good use of all 1 million CPUs (e.g., analyze all 20 move chess games), they would be highly contrived. Most "normal" programs can make use of only a small number of CPUs (typically, 2–20).

Let's start by looking at some data from some simple programs (Figure 15–2). These are numerically intensive programs that run entirely in memory. Because there is no I/O involved, and because the amount of shared data is often quite limited, all of these programs show a superb scaling up to 16 CPUs.

Fast Fourier transforms are performed by a set of matrix manipulations. It is characterized by largely independent operations with significant interthread communication in only one section. The next three programs all have largely constant amounts of interthread communications. *LU factorization* is dense matrix factorization, and also performed by a set of matrix manipulations. *Barnes-Hut* is an *N*-body simulation for solving a problem in galaxy evolution. *Ocean* simulates the effects of certain currents on large-scale flow in the ocean.

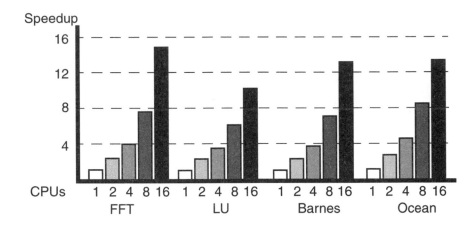

Figure 15–2   *Parallel Speedup on Several Numerical Programs*

Notice that all of these programs do show a falloff in performance for each additional CPU. At some point, that falloff will drop below zero and begin to slow the total throughput. Why? Well, let's take a look at where these programs are spending their time. As you can see from Figure 15–3, the amount of time that the CPUs actually spend working on the problem drops as the number of CPUs increases. Notice that memory overhead can easily occupy 50% for total CPU time. On database-style programs, it can exceed 50%. The requirement for synchronization takes up more and more of the time. Extrapolating out to just 128 CPUs, we can infer that performance would be dismal indeed.

Superlinear Speedup

In a very small number of programs, such as Ocean on two and four CPUs (Figure 15–2), it is possible to see speedups slightly better than linear. This is a result of having more cache and possibly reducing overhead because of fewer context switches. It's nice if you get it, but don't expect it.

Timing Threaded and Nonthreaded Programs

In our measurements, we compare the runtime of identical code that creates different numbers of threads, appropriate to the

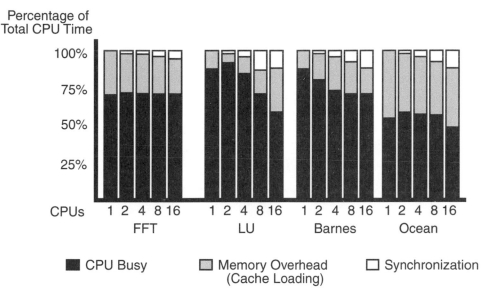

Figure 15–3 *Program Behavior for Parallelized Benchmarks*

available CPUs. This isn't really fair, because we're including the synchronization overhead (and possibly a less efficient algorithm) for the one-CPU case, which doesn't need that synchronization.

Unfortunately, for any real program, it's far too complex to implement, optimize, and maintain two different programs (the PSR argument again). Most ISVs ship a single binary and simply run suboptimally on uniprocessors. You may console yourself (and your marketing department) by noting that you can probably find more performance improvement in the techniques mentioned above than you can in writing a uniprocessor-only version.

Amdahl's Law

Amdahl's law (Figure 15–4) states: If a program has one section that is parallelizable, and another section that must run serially, the program execution time will asymptotically approach the time for the serial section as more CPUs are added.

Although obviously true, this fact is of no interest to many programs. Most programs with which we have worked (client/ server, and I/O intensive) see other limitations long before they

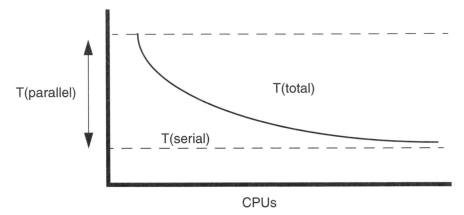

Figure 15–4   *Amdahl's Law: Time(total) = Time(serial) + Time(parallel) / Number_of_CPUs*

ever hit this one. Even numerically intensive programs often come up against limited memory bandwidth sooner than they hit Amdahl's limit. Very large numeric programs with little synchronization will approach it. So don't hold Amdahl's law up as the expected goal. It might not be possible.

Client/server programs often show a lot of contention for shared data and make great demands upon the I/O subsystem. Consider the TCP-C numbers in Figure 15–5. Irrespective of how representative you think TPC-C is of actual database activity (there's lots of debate here), it is very definitely a benchmark into whose optimization vendors put enormous effort. So it is notable that on a benchmark as important as this, the limit of system size is down around 20 CPUs.

So what does this mean for you? That there are limitations. The primary limiting factor might be synchronization overhead, it may be main memory access, it might be the I/O subsystem. As you design and write your system, you should analyze the nature of your program and put your optimization efforts toward these limits. And you should be testing your programs along the way.

Performance Bottlenecks

Wherever your program spends its time, that's the bottleneck. We can expect that the bottleneck for a typical program will vary

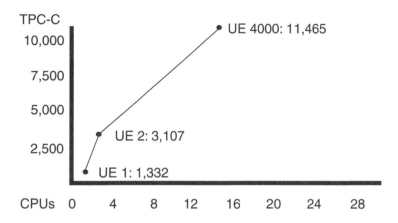

Figure 15–5 *TPC-C Performance of a Sun UE6000*

from subsystem to subsystem quite often during the life of the program. *Bottleneck* is a somewhat pejorative term that isn't really fair. After all, whichever subsystem is the bottleneck is the one that's doing your work! There is also a general tendency to want to "balance out" the work across the different subsystems, keeping them all busy all the time. Once again, that's a bit inaccurate. Balancing the work is useful only if it helps your program run faster.

In Figure 15–6 we show a representation of where a program is spending its time and where the bottleneck is with respect to CPU, cache latency, and I/O latency. Each block represents how busy that subsystem is during some period of time (say, 10 μs).

Black indicates a subsystem used at full capacity, white indicates zero usage. A black CPU is never stalled for anything; the other subsystems are waiting for it to make requests. A black cache indicates that the CPU is stalled, waiting for data at least some of the time, and the same for I/O. Depending upon system design, it may or may not actually be possible for CPU and cache to be busy simultaneously. (We show a system where there is overlap.) The solid white sections for CPU 1 and 2 indicate that they are suffering contention, waiting for CPU 0 to release a lock.

Typically, we expect CPU and cache to take turns being the bottleneck, alternating very rapidly. When I/O is the bottleneck,

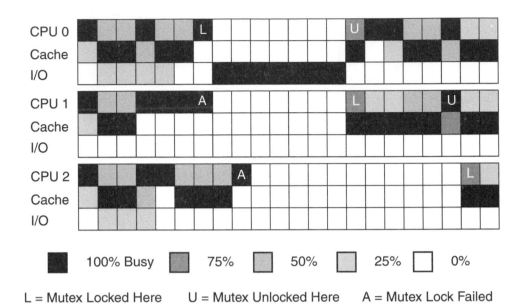

Figure 15–6 *Performance Bottlenecks and Capacities of Programs*

it will be so for extended periods of time (the latency on a disk read runs on the order of 20 ms).

By definition, there must be a line of solid black from one end of our graph to the other. In some sense, the more solid black in the CPU section, the more work is getting done. A typical subgoal will be to maximize the amount of time that all the CPUs actually work. (The primary goal is to make the program run fast. Normally, you expect that making more CPUs do more work will have that effect.) Eliminating contention is a major factor in doing so.

Benchmarks and Repeatable Testing

Before you get into the details of optimizing your code, you need to be very clear on what your starting point is and what your objective is. Your overall objective is to make the entire system run faster. Perhaps you have a specific target (you need 13.5% improvement to beat the competition); perhaps you just want to spend six months and get as much improvement as you can. Your starting point will be a specific release of your program, a specific machine to run it on, and a very well-defined set of input data. You absolutely must have an unambiguous, repeatable test case for which you know the statistics.

Things you may have to control for include other activity on the test machine, unanticipated network traffic, file layout on your disk(!), etc. Once you have all of that, you will generally find that most of your time is used by a few small loops. Once you're convinced that these loops really are the right ones, you'll separate them out into their own little testbeds and verify that you can produce the same behavior there. Finally, you will apply your efforts to these testbeds, investigating them in great detail and experimenting with the different techniques below.

When you feel confident that you've done your best with them, you'll compare the before and after statistics in the testbeds, then integrate the changes and repeat the tests in the original system. It is vitally important that you repeat the test in both original version and in the new version. Far, far too many times people have discovered that "something changed," that the original program now completes the test faster than before, and that the extensive optimizations they performed didn't actually make any improvement at all.

Is It *Really* Faster?

Even "simple, deterministic programs" show variation in their runtimes. External interrupts, CPU selection, VM page placement, file layout on disks, etc., can cause wide variation in runtimes. A difference of 20% between two runs of the same "deterministic" CPU-bound program is not unusual. Consider the runtimes listed in Table 15–1. A program was run four times, giving the first set of results. It was changed, recompiled, and gave the second set of results.

Table 15–1   *Runtimes for Four Trials*

Run 1	Run 2
rate: 27.665667/s	rate: 28.560094/s
rate: 23.503779/s	rate: 28.000473/s
rate: 20.414748/s	rate: 25.274012/s
rate: 20.653608/s	rate: 35.249477/s

Table 15–1 *Runtimes for Four Trials (cont.)*

Run 1	Run 2
Mean rate: 23.05/s	Mean rate: 28.27/s
Standard deviation: 3.34	Standard deviation: 4.20

The question is: How sure are we that the difference we measured is the difference between the actual means? The answer requires a tiny bit of statistics which you can take straight from a book or even "eyeball" the data. You just have to know what you're looking for. We want to know this: $\mu_1 - \mu_2 =$? $x_1 - x_2$ given the data in Table 15–1.

$$x_1 = 23.05 \qquad\qquad s_1 = 3.34$$
$$x_2 = 28.27 \qquad\qquad s_2 = 4.20$$

The answer is that for four measurements (which isn't very many), looking for the usual 95% confidence level:

$$\mu_1 - \mu_2 = x_1 - x_2 \pm 1.96 \; SE(X_1 - X_2) \quad \textit{(1.96 for 95\% confidence)}$$

$$
\begin{aligned}
SE(X_1 - X_2) \quad &= \quad (s_1^2 / n_1 + s_2^2/n_2)^{1/2} \\
&= \quad (3.34^2 / 4 + 4.20^2 / 4)^{1/2} \\
&= \quad 2.7
\end{aligned}
$$

Thus
$$\mu_1 - \mu_2 = 5.22 \pm 5.4$$

The interval includes zero. We are less than 95% certain that the two sets of measurements are different! And indeed, this is taken from a set of runs that were done incorrectly. After modifying the program, it was recompiled to a.out by mistake. The two sets of measurements actually come from exactly the same binary!

If you run only four measurements, the difference between the measured means must be greater than (1.96 × std. error), or roughly twice the measured standard deviation. By running it ten times (see Table 15–2) the 95% confidence level is obtained when the difference is greater than the standard error. When the numbers are reasonably close together, you can eyeball the mean and standard error fairly easily.

Table 15–2 *Runtimes for Ten Trials*

Run 1	Run 2
N_PROD = 1 N_CONS = 4	N_PROD = 1 N_CONS = 5
rate: 85.965975/s	rate: 89.984372/s
rate: 86.802915/s	rate: 91.710778/s
rate: 88.528658/s	rate: 91.075302/s
rate: 85.411582/s	rate: 91.741185/s
rate: 85.957945/s	rate: 87.995095/s
rate: 84.514983/s	rate: 93.661803/s
rate: 86.732842/s	rate: 89.505427/s
rate: 84.284994/s	rate: 89.262953/s
rate: 85.024726/s	rate: 89.611914/s
rate: 85.602694/s	rate: 91.972079/s
Mean rate: 85.88/s	Mean rate: 90.65/s
Standard deviation: 1.25	Standard deviation: 1.67

The difference between the means is about 5 and the standard deviation is about 1.5. The difference, 5 – 1.5, is much greater than zero, so we can conclude with confidence that run 2 is indeed superior to run 1. Doing this stuff well is not at all obvious, and doing it wrong is all too common. We're not expecting you to do this carefully on every test, but you do have to be aware of it.

General Performance Optimizations

By far the most important optimizations will not be specific to threaded programs, but rather, the general optimizations you do for nonthread programs. We'll mention these optimizations but leave the specifics to you. First, you choose the best algorithm. Second, you select the correct compiler optimization. Third, you buy enough RAM to avoid excessive paging. Fourth, you minimize I/O. Fifth, you minimize cache misses. Sixth, you do any other loop optimizations that the compiler was unable to do. Finally, you can do the thread specific optimizations.

Best Algorithm

That's your problem.

Compiler Optimization

This is not necessarily obvious and is highly dependent upon the individual compiler. If you just use the usual byte code compiler, there are no particular issues—your program will run at a nominal speed on any platform. With a JIT compiler or an adaptive compiler such as HotSpot, the compiler is able to take advantage of specific instructions on individual machines and you should expect much better performance and you should not have to do anything extra to obtain it.

C Compiler Optimization   By contrast, let's consider what you need to do for optimal performance of a C program. You need to select the individual machine to compile for. For example, Sun supports SS1s and SS2 (both SPARC version 7 machines, which trap to the kernel to handle the integer multiply instruction), SS10s, SS20, SS1000s, and SC2000s (all SPARC version 8 machines, which have hardware integer multiply); and Ultras (SPARC version 9 machines, which have 64-bit registers and 64-bit operations). Optimizing for an Ultra might produce lousy code for an SS1. Optimizing for an SS1 will produce OK code for an SS10 or Ultra. (This is a marketing decision, of course.)

You need to choose the optimization level for your program. You may choose different levels for different modules! Sun compilers, for example, provide five levels of optimization. Level –xO2 is the normal good optimization level, producing fairly tight code, highly reliable and highly correct. Levels 3, 4, and 5 produce extremely fast code (it may be larger), which is much faster than –xO2 in some cases and possibly *slower* in others. They are much more likely to fail (i.e., not compile at all).

Thus, expect to compile and test your program at –xO2 (default). Compile and profile it at –xO2. Separate out the high time functions and recompile them at higher levels. If they work and are faster, great. If not, too bad.

Java Compiler Optimization   Java compilers do not in general have anything similar to the switches in C, and you often have no options at all.

Buy Enough RAM

Test the program with different amounts of memory and select the best price/performance level.

Minimize I/O

Organize your data so that when you do read a disk block, you make maximum use of it and you don't have to read it again. One obvious thing is to use the `mmap()` calls to map files into the address space instead of calling `read()`. This eliminates an extra kernel memory copy and allows you to give access pattern hints to the OS.

Again, Java does not have any such options. The only way to get data into the program is to call `read()`. Unfortunately, system calls are particularly expensive in Java because Java must do a lot of setup before calling the native code, so I/O in Java is significantly slower than even regular I/O in C.

Minimize Cache Misses

Organize your data so that when you do load a cache line, you make maximum use of it and you don't have to load it again (see *Reducing Cache Misses* on page 359).

Any Other Loop Optimizations

There are all sorts of things you might be able to do to assist the compiler in performing optimizations that it can't do by itself for some reason: inlining functions, loop unrolling, loop interchange, loop fusion, etc. Generally, these things are done by the optimizer. We will look at the assembly code for very tight loops just to verify our expectations. Your vendor documentation will help here.

Thread-Specific Performance Optimizations

Now that we have wildly emphasized the importance of doing all the normal performance work first, let's take a look at the stuff that's specific to multithreaded programs. There are just a couple of performance areas specific to MT: reducing contention, minimizing overhead, and creating the right number of threads.

Reducing Contention

Clearly, we do not want to have lots of CPUs waiting around idle because they can't get a mutex they need. Equally obviously, we cannot neglect proper locking to avoid this contention. Your options for dealing with this situation are limited by what you're doing.

In some circumstances, you will be able to divide your global data into smaller groups, with more locks. Then a thread that needs to use item 1 will not block other threads that need item 2. This will work only if the two items are not used together all the time. This is fine-grained locking. There is a trade-off between grain size and overhead. Other times, you'll be able to substitute readers/writer locks for mutexes.

Minimizing MT Overhead

There are a few different threads functions that you might call often enough to make a significant impact upon performance. The first case is the fine-grained vs. course-grained locking trade-off. In cases where different data items are used together, making the locking finer-grained will increase the overhead due to locking, slowing the total performance even though contention may be reduced. In the friends/enemies program (*Manipulating Lists* on page 270), it is possible for us to lock every single list node individually. This will increase the parallelism of the program over the global mutex design, but total runtime will be many times worse.

What is the right granularity? It will be obvious in most cases, but sometimes the only solution is to experiment.

Reducing Paging

In most operating systems, overlapping I/O and computation can be accomplished without threads. Most operating systems have some sort of asynchronous I/O that allows you to issue an I/O request, then go back to what you were doing without waiting for it to complete. When it does complete, a signal will be sent to your process and you will then ask the operating system which request it was that completed and deal with it as you please. (Obviously, this is not a direct issue for Java, which has nothing similar.)

This asynchronous I/O can be awkward to deal with, but it will do the job. Using threads instead of asynchronous I/O is much easier to program and equally fast (Figure 15–7). The one place where async I/O will not work is with page faults. When a nonthreaded program takes a page fault, it waits. Threaded programs can finesse this, because there is no problem with thread 4 continuing to run while thread 1 is waiting for a page fault. The finesse yields a nice performance improvement for many programs, even on uniprocessor machines.

Communications Bandwidth

Sometimes the amount of data that needs to be exchanged between threads for a program is very low compared to the total computing time. For example, a chess position can be encoded into a dozen or so bytes, whereas the time to compute the best move might be hours. Such a problem, which also requires only a tiny amount of synchronization, can be productively spread across thousands of very distant processors that don't even share memory.[7] Distributed parallel systems such as PVM are well suited to such problems.

When the data/computation ratio is higher, or when more synchronization is required, distributing across a network is not feasible, as the communications costs would exceed the CPU time to execute the entire computation locally. Most image processing programs fit into this category. Dithering a 1000 × 1000 image

---

[7]In one of the big computer chess tournaments back in the late 1980s, one of the contestants managed to convince several thousand of us to run a networked chess program over the weekend.

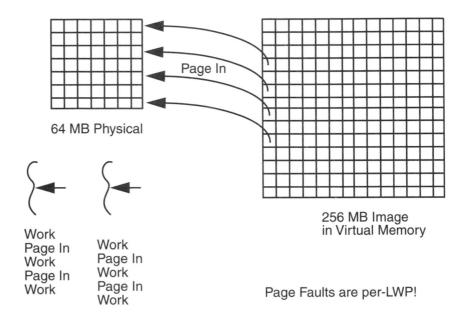

64 MB Physical

256 MB Image
in Virtual Memory

Work
Page In
Work
Page In
Work

Work
Page In
Work
Page In
Work

Page Faults are per-LWP!

Figure 15–7   *Using Threads to Optimize Paging*

might take 1 second on one CPU and require very little synchronization. Executing this program on 1000 CPUs would take only 1 ms of computation time, yet moving that 1-meg image out and back across a network would take far longer. Executing it on a 10-CPU shared memory multiprocessor would make far more sense, taking more like 100 ms total.

Right Number of Threads

You want to have enough threads to keep all the CPUs busy all the time (if possible), but not so many that the CPUs are doing unnecessary context switching. Determining exactly the right number is ultimately an empirical experiment. We give rough estimates in *How Many LWPs?* on page 87.

Short-Lived Threads

Thread creation and synchronization time is quite low (about 1.5 ms on an 110-MHz SS4), making it reasonable to dispatch relatively small tasks to different threads. How small can that task be? Obviously, it must be significantly larger than the thread overhead.

Something like a 10×10 matrix multiply (requiring about 2000 FP ops @ 100 Mflops = 20 μs) would be much too small to thread. By contrast, a 100×100 matrix multiply (2M FP ops @ 100 Mflops = 20 ms) can be threaded very effectively. If you were writing a matrix routine, your code would check the size of the matrices and run the threaded code for larger multiplies, and run the simple multiply in the calling thread for smaller multiplies. The exact dividing point will be about 3 ms. You can determine this empirically, and it is not terribly important to hit exactly.

One ISV we worked with was doing an EDA simulation, containing millions of 10-μs tasks. To say the least, threading this code did not produce favorable results (it ran much slower!). They later figured out a way of grouping the microtasks into larger tasks and threading those. The opposite case is something like NFS, which contains hundreds of 40-ms tasks. Threading NFS works quite well.

Dealing with Many Open Sockets

In C, C++, etc., when you want to have a large number of clients connected to your server at the same time, you use a `select()`[8] call [in Win32 it's `waitForMultipleObjects()`]. This function takes a list of file descriptors as an argument and returns when there is data ready on one of them. This allows a single thread to wait on 1000 sockets. This is a good thing because the overhead of having 1000 threads, each waiting on a single socket (as we've done in our programs), would be prohibitive.

Unfortunately, Java does not have anything similar, putting an extra constraint on the size and scalability of your server. In Java you must have one thread devoted to each client, rendering the producer/consumer version of a server awkward. Many of the major Java server programs actually use JNI calls into C to

---

[8]Or `poll()`, which is actually more common now, due to its ability to handle very large numbers of open connections.

make use of the `select()` there. There is pressure for Java to implement `select()`.

The Lessons of NFS

One practical problem in evaluating the performance of threaded programs is the lack of available data. There are simply no good analyses of real threaded programs that we can look at. (There are analyses of strictly computational parallel programs but not of mixed usage programs, client/server, etc.) Nobody's done it yet! Probably the best data we have comes from NFS, which we shall look at now.

The standard metric for evaluating NFS performance is the SPEC LADDIS benchmark, which uses a predefined mix of file operations intended to reflect realistic usage (lots of small file information requests, some file reads, and a few file writes). As the NFS performance goes up, LADDIS spreads the file operations over a larger number of files on more disks to eliminate trivial, single-disk bottlenecks.

An NFS server is very demanding on all subsystems, and as the hardware in one area improves, NFS performance will edge up until it hits a bottleneck in another. Figure 15–8 shows configurations and performance results for a variety of systems. Notably, all of these systems are configured below their maximum size. Adding disks, controllers, or CPUs will not improve the performance. They do not use the maximum throughput of either I/O or memory buses.

In all of these maximum performance configurations, the bottleneck is contention and memory latency. One CPU will be working on some portion of a file system and will have locked inodes, allocation tables, etc., that another CPU requires. Once these locks are released, the other CPUs may have to context switch to the appropriate thread. It will certainly have to take a lot of cache misses to load those newly changed tables. Additional CPUs will not improve the situation, but higher-performance CPUs will. This is because one CPU can now do more work, hence the data in cache will be used more, reducing both the number of misses and the amount of contention.

NFS is not a "typical" client/server application in one particular aspect: NFS is started as a typical user-level process, but all that process does is to make a single call into the kernel. For the

NFS Throughput

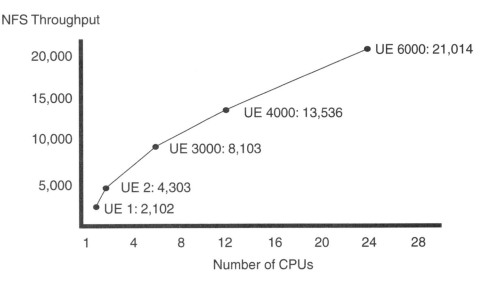

Figure 15–8 *NFS Throughput on a Series of Sun UE Machines (The performance improvement is somewhat exaggerated, as a two-way UE6000 will outperform a two-way UE 2.)*

rest of its lifetime, NFS remains in the kernel, spawning threads there as it deems necessary. Thus, NFS does not have to do any context switching for I/O as normal user-level programs must do, and it can avoid the extra step of copying data from kernel buffer to user space.[9] NFS could have been written as a user-level program, but the context switching would have killed performance. It was never tried.[10]

A 24-way ES6000 can sustain about 21,000 NFS operations/ second (about 900 ops/CPU) with a latency of about 40 ms. A one-

---

[9]Most programs would not benefit from the "optimization" of executing entirely in the kernel. Outside the horrible complexity of trying to build and maintain a patched kernel using constantly changing internal kernel interfaces, very few programs spend so much time in system calls and so little time in their own code. NFS spends about 45% of its time in the transport layer, 45% in the file system, and 10% in actual NFS code. Even DBMSs which are known for their enormous I/O demands pale in comparison to NFS. The distinction is that DBMSs are going to use much of the data they load, as opposed to just pushing it across the network like NFS.

[10]There is one example of precisely this being done, but it was never optimized to any degree, so we can't validly compare the (abysmal) results.

way machine gets about 2000 ops. This implies a requirement of 500 μs on the CPU per NFS op and thus 80 outstanding requests (waiting for the disks) at any one time. The limiting factor is CPU power plus locking contention. There is plenty of room for more or faster disks, and more network cards, but they wouldn't help.

Actual data transfers are accomplished via DMA from/to disks and the network. The data is brought into the CPU only to perform checksums; it is never written by the CPU. Checksums have horrible data locality—they load lots of data, but use that data only once, and only for a single addition. This means that the CPU will spend an inordinate amount of time stalled, waiting for cache loads, but that it will do virtually no writes. (Some folks are building checksumming hardware for exactly this purpose.) Normal programs spend more time using the data once loaded into cache, do more writes, and generally spend less time stalled on cache misses.

NFS is constructed as a producer/consumer program. The master/slave design was rejected as being inappropriate because of the nature of interrupt handling. When a network card gets a packet, it issues an interrupt to one of the CPUs (interrupts are distributed in a round-robin fashion on Sun's UE series). That CPU then runs its interrupt handler thread.

For an NFS request, the interrupt handler thread acts as the producer, building an NFS request structure and putting that onto a list. It is important for the interrupt handler thread to complete very quickly (as other interrupts will be blocked while it's running); thus it is not possible for that thread to do any appreciable amount of work (such as processing the request or creating a new thread). The consumers pull requests off the queue (exactly like our P/C example) and process them as appropriate. Sometimes the required information will be in memory, but usually a disk request will be required. This means that most requests will require a context switch.

Many of the original algorithms used in single-threaded NFS proved to be inappropriate for a threaded program. They worked correctly, but suffered from excessive contention when appropriate locking was added. A major amount of the work on multithreaded NFS was spent on writing new algorithms that would be less contentious.

The results? An implementation that scales extremely well on upward of 24 CPUs.

Summary

Performance tuning is a very complex issue that has numerous trade-offs to be considered. Once a performance objective and level of effort has been established, you can start looking at the computer science issues. Even then the major issues will not be threading issues. Only after you've done a great deal of normal optimization work will you turn your eyes toward threads. We give a cursory overview of the areas you need to consider, and wish you the best of luck.

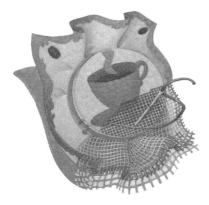

Hardware

- ▼ TYPES OF MULTIPROCESSORS
- ▼ BUS ARCHITECTURES
- ▼ MEMORY SYSTEMS

In which we look at the various designs for SMP machines (cache architectures, interconnect topologies, atomic instructions, invalidation techniques) and consider how those designs affect our programming decisions. Some optimization possibilities are looked at.

Types of Multiprocessors

In dealing with MT as we have described it here, we are also making some assumptions about the hardware we are going to be using. Everything we discussed is based on our using shared memory symmetric multiprocessor (SMP) machines. There are several other types of multiprocessor machines, such as distributed shared memory multiprocessors (Cray T3D, etc.) and massively parallel multiprocessors (CM-1, etc.), but these require very different programming techniques.

Shared Memory Symmetric Multiprocessors

The fundamental design of this machine requires that all processors see all of main memory in an identical fashion. Even though a memory bank might be physically closer to one CPU than another, there is no programming-level distinction in how that memory is accessed. (Hardware designers can do all sorts of clever things to optimize memory access behind our backs, as long as we are never aware of them.)

The other distinguishing aspect of this machine is that all CPUs have full access to all resources (kernel, disks, networks, interrupts, etc.) and are treated as peers by the operating system. Any CPU can run kernel code at any time (respecting locked regions, of course) to do anything. Any CPU can write out to any disk, network device, etc., at any time. Hardware interrupts may be delivered to any CPU, although this is a weaker requirement and is not always followed.[1]

All of the multiprocessors in the PC, workstation, and server realms are shared memory symmetric multiprocessors: the two-way Compaq machines and all of the Sun, SGI, HP, DEC, HAL, and IBM RISC machines. (IBM also builds the SP-2, a large, distributed memory machine—basically, a cluster of PowerServers.) Obviously, all manufacturers have their own internal designs and optimizations, but for our purposes, they have essentially the same architecture.

---

[1] In practice, interrupts are generally distributed to CPUs in a round-robin fashion.

The CPU

All of the CPUs have the same basic design. There's the CPU proper (registers, instruction set, fetch, decode, execution units, etc.), and there's the interface to the memory system. Two components of the memory interface are of particular interest to us. First there's an *internal cache* (*I$*[2]—typically 20–32 kB), then an *external cache* (*E$*—typically, 0.5–16 MB),[3] and finally, there's a *store buffer.* The I$ holds all of the most recently accessed words and provides single-cycle access for the CPU. Should the I$ in CPU 0 contain a word that CPU 1 changes, there has to be some way for CPU 0 to beware of this change. E$ access is about 5 cycles, with the same coherency issue. This is problem 1.

The store buffer is a small, specialized cache that holds words the CPU is writing out to memory. The idea is that instead of requiring the CPU to stall while a write is going on (it takes 30–100 cycles), the word will be placed into the store buffer, which will then arrange to write the word out to main memory when it sees fit. This way the CPU can run at full speed, not worrying about exactly when a word arrives in main memory.

Of course, the store buffer must be closely coupled with the I$ and memory fetch unit to ensure that the CPU has a coherent view of memory. It wouldn't do for CPU 0 to write x1234545F into location x00000010, then load x00000010 and not see x1234545F. Hardware architects take care of that, so we don't have to bother. The other issue with using a store buffer is that of determining when writes arrive in main memory. CPU 0 might write out dozens of words, placing them in the store buffer, while CPU 1, which then accesses those words, wouldn't see the changes, because the store buffer hasn't written them out yet. This is problem 2.

Just to further complicate the hardware picture, it is possible for the hardware designers to give the store buffer more latitude in its choice of which words to write out when. *Total store order* re-

---

[2]"$" stands for U.S. dollars (i.e., money). Another word for paper money is *cash*, which sounds just like the way Americans pronounce *cache*. Aren't hardware designers funny?

[3]The distinction between unified caches and divided caches (one section for instructions, a different section for data) is not particularly interesting for what we're doing.

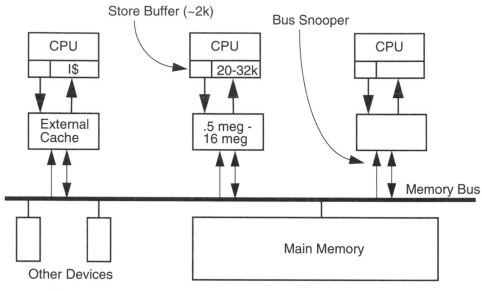

Figure 16–1 *SMP System Architecture*

fers to a design that requires the store buffer to write words to main memory in the same order as the instruction stream. It can be more efficient for the store buffer to write words out in a different order (perhaps it can write a series of contiguous words out together; perhaps it can write a word to memory bank 1, then memory bank 2). There are a variety of schemes for this out-of-order writing (*partial store order, weak order*, etc.). The importance to us is that we must not rely on write order! This is problem 3.

One more complication is that CPUs might do out-of-order execution, too. If a CPU has to wait for a cache fill before executing instruction 1, it is allowed to look at instruction 2. If there is no dependency on 1, the CPU may proceed to execute 2 first. This is a wonderful thing for hardware architects, as it gives them enormous leeway in their designs, allowing the CPU to run at maximum possible speeds. It also complicates CPU design, ensuring full employment for hardware designers. For us software types, it means that we cannot rely on order of execution.[4] Also problem 3.

---

[4]There are some fancy algorithms, such as Decker's algorithm, which avoid using mutexes by depending upon the write order of CPUs. These techniques will not work on modern SMP machines.

The System

Figure 16–1 shows a typical SMP system. Each CPU has its own on-chip "I$" and store buffer. It also has a much larger, off-chip E$. All external communication is done over a single memory bus. Part of the memory bus protocol for all these machines is that each CPU will do *bus snooping*. Every memory transaction will be observed by every bus snooper, and every time that CPU 0 writes a word out to main memory, every other bus snooper will see it and invalidate[5] that entry in its own caches (both "E$" and "I$"). The next time that CPU 1 wants to use that word, it will look in its own cache, see that the entry has been marked invalid, and go out to main memory to get the correct value.

What if CPU 1 also wants to write out the same word? What if CPU 1's store buffer is waiting to write it out? No answer. It would never happen, because that would mean that two different threads were manipulating the same data at the same time without a mutex and that's not proper. (If you did this anyway, the value would just get overwritten.) Problem 1 solved.

What if a global variable is in a register so the CPU doesn't see the invalidated word in cache? This also won't happen because the compiler is not allowed to keep nonlocal data in registers across function calls [e.g., `pthread_mutex_lock()`!].

Store Barriers

Problems 2 and 3 are solved with the same mechanism—*store barriers*. A store barrier is a machine instruction which says[6], effectively, "flush the store buffer." The CPU will then stall until the store buffer has been written out to main memory. On a SPARC machine, there are two instructions, `stbar` and `membar`.

---

[5]There are other schemes for dealing with this problem, such as cache broadcast, which simply sends out the updated value immediately, but this won't change our programming decisions.

[6]In reality it says, "Place a token here in the output buffer and prevent any future writes from crossing this boundary." This is actually more efficient than flushing the store buffer, but harder to explain.

Now then, when should we flush the store buffer? Whenever a CPU has changed some data that it wants other CPUs to see. This would be shared data, of course, and shared data may be used by other CPUs only after the first CPU has released the lock protecting it. And that's when `stbar` is called—when a mutex is being released. This is done by all the synchronization variable functions, so you will never call it yourself.

Thus, the short answer to all the problems above is, "Protect shared data with a mutex."

Bus Architectures

The design of the main memory bus does not have much effect on how we write MT programs specifically, but it does have enormous influence over how fast our programs run, and for high-performance programs we must pay it respect. Depending on the specific program, anywhere from 25% to 90% of the runtime will be devoted to waiting for the memory bus. (You can find programs that run entirely in cache and have zero percent bus waits, but they are the exceptions.)

There are two primary bus designs in use in SMP machines. There is the simple, *direct-switched bus* such as the MBus, which was used in Sun's early SMP machines and the SPARCstation 10 s and 20 s. Then there is the more expensive, more complex, *packet-switched bus* (a.k.a. *split-transaction bus*) such as is used in all the server machines from all the manufacturers (Sun's SPARCservers, Sun's Ultra series, SGI's Challenge series, HP's PA-RISC, IBM's POWERservers, DEC's Alpha servers, HAL's Mercury series, Cray's S6400 series, etc.). In addition to these, there are also *cross-bar switches* that allow several CPUs to access several different memory banks simultaneously (Sun's Ultra servers and SGI's Origin servers).

Direct-Switched Buses

In a direct-switched bus (Figure 16–2), memory access is very simple. When CPU 0 wants to read a word from main memory, it asserts bus ownership, makes the request, and waits until the data is loaded. The sequence is:

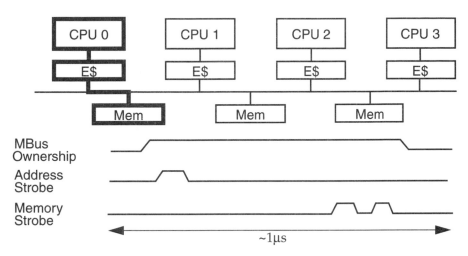

Figure 16–2 *Direct-Switched Memory Bus*

1. CPU 0 takes a cache miss. E$ must now go out to main memory to load an entire cache line (typically, 8 words).

2. CPU 0 asserts bus ownership (perhaps waiting for a current owner to release).

3. CPU 0 loads the desired address onto the bus address lines, then strobes out that address on the address strobe line.

4. Memory sees the strobe, looks at the address, finds the proper memory bank, and then starts looking for the data. DRAM is fairly slow and takes roughly a microsecond[7] to find the desired data.

5. Once found, memory puts the first set of words onto the bus's data lines and strobes it into the E$. It then loads the next set of words, strobes that out, and continues until the entire cache-line request has been satisfied.

---

[7]Depending on when you're reading this book!

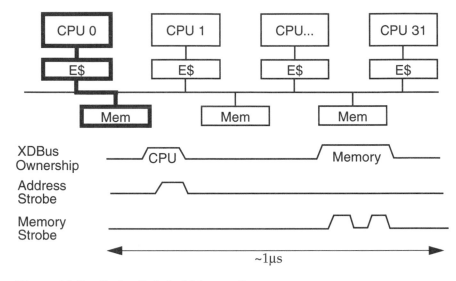

Figure 16–3 *Packet-Switched Memory Bus*

The total bus transaction latency, from initial request to final transfer, is on the order of 1 µs for all machines. It simply takes DRAM that long to find the data. Once found, DRAM can deliver the data quite rapidly, upward of 60 ns per access, but the initial lookup is quite slow.

On a direct-switched bus, the total memory bandwidth is quite small, not because of limited bus speeds, but because each transaction occupies the bus for so long, most of the time just waiting. Obviously, this is not an optimal situation. Sun's MBus was designed to accommodate up to four CPUs. In practice, it was found that four CPUs generated too much bus traffic in most programs, and the vast majority of MBus machines were shipped with just two CPUs.

Packet-Switched Buses

In a packet-switched (a.k.a. *split-transaction*) bus (Figure 16–3), the transaction is split between the CPU's request and the memory's reply. The objective of this design is to overcome the enormous periods of dead time that the direct-switched buses suffer. In this design the CPU will release bus ownership while memory is busy looking up the address, hence freeing it for use by other CPUs. The sequence is:

1. CPU 0 takes a cache miss. E$ must now go out to main memory to load an entire cache line (typically, 8 words).
2. CPU 0 asserts bus ownership (perhaps waiting for a current owner to release).
3. It loads the desired address onto the bus address lines, then strobes out that address on an address strobe line.
4. Memory sees the strobe, looks at the address, finds the proper memory bank, and then starts looking for the data.
5. At this point, CPU 0 releases bus ownership.
6. Once found, memory reasserts bus ownership.
7. Memory then strobes the data into CPU 0's E$.

Total latency for a packet-switched bus is no shorter than for a direct-switched bus, but because the bus is now free for use by other CPUs, the total throughput is much, much higher. Sun's UE10000 can run productively with upward of 64 CPUs on a single bus.

Crossbar Switches

A crossbar is a routing switch that allows any one element on one axis to communicate directly with any one element on the other axis. This does not affect the ability of other elements on the first axis to communicate with other elements on the second. Contention occurs only when two elements on one axis want to communicate with the same element on the second. Crossbar switches are much faster than buses—and more expensive.

The practical limit on crossbar switches right now (1999) seems to be about 4×4 (Figure 16–4), the size of both the Sun and SGI designs. To build machines larger than four CPUs, some additional interconnect is required. On the larger Sun Ultra machines, a centerplane bus is used that can accommodate up to 16 quad CPU boards. On the larger SGI machines, an entirely different approach is used.

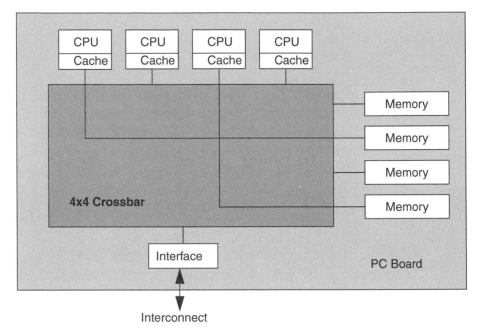

Figure 16–4   *Cluster Using a Crossbar Switch*

Hierarchical Interconnects

The practical (and legal[8]) limit to bus length is approximately 16 boards. Beyond that you have horrendous problems with signal propagation. The "obvious" solution to this limit is to build a hierarchical machine with clusters of buses communicating with other clusters of buses, ad infinitum. In its simplest form, this is no big deal. Want some more CPUs? Just add a new cluster! Sure, you'll see longer communication latencies as you access more distant clusters, but that's just the way things are.

There is one aspect of SMP design that makes a mess of this simple model—cache memory. We need to use caches to avoid saturating the interconnect, but at the same time caches need to be kept coherent, and *that's* tricky. If the cache for CPU 169 contains

---

[8]186,000 miles/second. It's not just a good idea, it's the law!

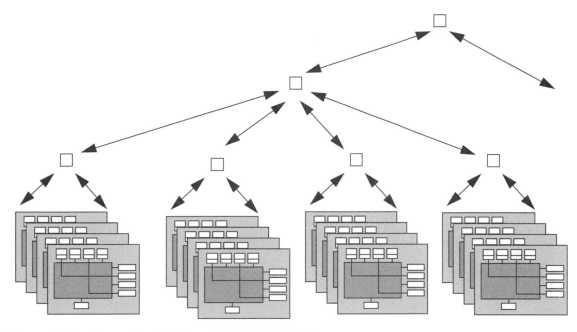

Figure 16–5 *Hierarchical Design of the SGI Origin Series*

an entry for address x31415926, and CPU 0 writes into that address, how is cache 169 going to get invalidated? Propagating every invalidate across the entire interconnect would saturate it quickly. The object now becomes finding a method to propagate invalidations only to those caches that need them.

Built along the designs of Stanford's DASH project, the SGI Origin (Figure 16–5) uses a small crossbar for its clusters and an expandable, hierarchical lattice instead of a bus. Embedded in each cluster is an invalidation directory, which keeps track of which other clusters have cached copies of its local memory. When main memory is written to, the directory knows to which clusters to send invalidations. The result is that the basic machine can be expanded well past the 16-board limit of bus-based machines, at a cost of about 150 ns extra latency for each hop across the lattice. The Origin is spec'd to expand out to 4096 CPUs. Now the only problem is writing programs that can use 4096 CPUs.

Multithreaded Programming with Java Technology

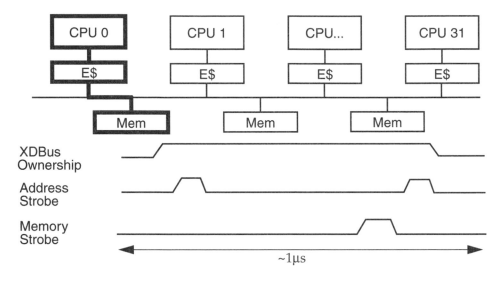

Figure 16–6 *Packet-Switched Memory Bus Running* `ldstub`

ccNUMA

Cache coherent nonuniform memory architecture is what the Origin does. The Origin clearly supports a coherent cache via its elaborate scheme for directly cache invalidates. It also supports nonuniform (speed) memory access, as on-board memory access is much faster than off-board access. There are also strict bus-based systems that are CCNUMA. Sun's machines are not among these, as they all define access memory to run at the same speed on-board and off-board.

Packet-Switched Buses and `ldstub`

There is one place we care about the bus design very directly (see Figure 16–6). Remember `ldstub`, the mutex instruction? Well, the definition of `ldstub` says that it must perform its work atomically. For a packet-switched bus, this means that it must retain bus ownership throughout the entire operation, first fetching the byte in question, then writing all ones out to it. In other words, using `ldstub` completely defeats the packet-switched nature of a packet-switched bus!

There is no way around the fundamental problem, as `ldstub` must be atomic. It *must* occupy the bus for the duration. What we can do is simply not call it too often. In particular, this means modifying our definition of spin locks. Whereas our first definition of spin locks resulted in our calling `ldstub` on every iteration of the loop (thus flooding the bus), our better definition (Code Example 16–1) will avoid calling `ldstub` unless we're fairly sure that it will succeed. What we'll do is spin in a loop, looking at the value of the ownership byte. As long as it's owned, we'll just keep spinning, looking at the value in cache, not generating any bus traffic at all.

```
/* Implementation dependent. This is valid only for Solaris 2.5 */
void spin_lock(mutex_t *m)
{int i;

  for (i = 0; i < SPIN_COUNT; i++)
     {if (m->lock.owner64 == 0)                  /* Check w/o ldstub */
             if (pthread_mutex_trylock(m) != EBUSY)
                        return;                   /* Got it! */
        /* Didn't get it, continue the loop */
     }

 pthread_mutex_lock(m);                           /* Give up and block
*/
}
```

Code Example 16–1 *Spin Locks Done Better*

When the lock is released, the owner CPU will write out zero, which our bus snooper will see, invalidating our copy of the byte. On our next iteration we'll get a cache miss, reload from main memory, and see the new value. We'll call trylock (hence `ldstub`), and if we're lucky, it will succeed and we'll get lock ownership. On the off chance that some other CPU sneaks in there at exactly the right nanosecond, our `ldstub` will fail, and we'll go back to spinning. Generally, you should expect spin locks to be provided by your vendor.

The Thundering Herds

This is as far as we're going to go with spin locks. This covers 99.9% of all programs that need spin locks. For that final 0.1%, where there is enormous contention for a single spin lock, even this scheme will suffer. If there are 10 CPUs all spinning on this lock, the moment it's released, all ten of them will take cache misses, flooding the bus first with cache load requests, then `ldstub` requests. This is known as the *thundering herds problem* and is discussed in more detail by Hennessy and Patterson (see Appendix B). Suffice it to say, if you're suffering from this problem, you have real problems. The best thing you can do is to find another algorithm with less contention.

LoadLocked/StoreConditional and Compare and Swap

We mentioned that there are other types of atomic instructions that are a bit more versatile. On SPARC v9, there is the *Compare and Swap if Equal* instruction. On the Alpha, there is a different approach to the same issue, using two instructions, known as *Load Locked* and *Store Conditional* (Code Example 16–2).

```
try_again:LoadLocked address_1 -> register_1
         add register_1, 1 -> register_2
         StoreConditional register_2 -> address_1
         Compare register_2, 0
         branch_not_equal try_again
```

Code Example 16–2   *Atomic Increment Using* `LoadLocked` *and* `StoreConditional`

The Alpha instructions require a tiny bit more hardware but reward the designer with an atomic instruction that *doesn't* lock the memory bus. Alongside the bus snooper hardware is one more register (Figure 16–7). When a `LoadLocked` instruction is issued, the data is fetched directly from main memory, and that address is recorded in the register. Should some other CPU write to that address, the register notices it. Later the program will issue a `StoreConditional` instruction. This instruction looks at the register before doing the store. If the register says that the address is unchanged, the store proceeds. If the address has been written to already, the store doesn't take place. After `StoreConditional` is finished, the programmer must

LockedLoad Register

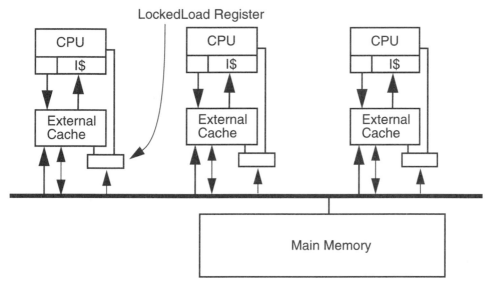

Figure 16–7 *SMP System Architecture*

check to see if the store took place. If so, all is well. If not, go back and repeat.

Building a mutex with these instructions is simple. Of more interest are the other types of synchronization we can do, such as atomic increment/decrement, and atomic list insertion. In effect we will be implicitly locking the word in question, updating it, and releasing the implicit lock. The important distinction is that we can now execute these operations with no possibility of the lock owner going to sleep.

In Code Example 16–2 we assume that memory location `address_1` will not change between the time we read it and the time we execute the `StoreConditional`. If it does change, we simply loop back and try it again. This operation is equivalent to acquiring a lock, incrementing the word, and releasing the lock, with the exception that it is impossible to go to sleep while holding the lock. We cannot mix use of these instructions and normal mutex locks.

The advantage to these instructions is that they run roughly twice as fast as mutex-protected code and there is no danger of being context switched in the middle of execution. The disadvantage is that the operations you can perform are very simple and may not be sufficient to our purposes. Inserting an element onto the front of a list is simple, but inserting elsewhere in the list is impossible. (Yes, we can correctly change the next pointer of item_n, but item_n might have been removed from the list while we were reading the next pointer!) For more general use we need mutex locks.

The tricky part is that you can use these instructions to increment or decrement a variable automatically, but you can't make any decisions based on "current" value because the variable's value may change before you make your decision. In normal code you would make a decision based on the value of a variable while in a critical section, so that the variable couldn't change. You will sometimes see the use of these instructions referred to as *lock-free synchronization*.

All of this is quite interesting of course, but it is not applicable to Java, as you have no ability to access such low-level instructions without going through JNI. Going through JNI would both break the program's portability (it would not be a pure Java program anymore) and it would be slow (going through JNI is expensive).

Lock-Free Semaphores and Reference Counting

Semaphores need to know if a decrement attempt succeeded or not. If successful, there is nothing else for the semaphore to do. It's done (this will be our "fast path"—the most common case). Should the semaphore value already be zero, a bit of careful programming will allow the thread to go to sleep confident that the next sem_post() will wake it up. This means that sem_wait() can execute in a single instruction (we don't even have to block out signals because no lock is being held)! Calls to sem_post() will be somewhat more complex (they have to look for sleepers) but still *very* fast.

Reference counting is one of the few other things that you can use such atomic instructions for, because the only decision you make in reference counting occurs when the count hits zero. Once zero, the reference count cannot be changed (there are no pointers left to the item to copy), hence you can rely on this value.

Volatile: The Rest of the Story

At last we have the background we need to discuss `volatile`. As in C, `volatile` ensures that a variable will not be cached in either registers or memory cache. Every read of that variable will go out to the main memory bus, and every write will result in a write on the main memory bus. Moreover, `volatile` will insert a store barrier after every write. This means that things like Dekker's algorithm will work, even on an out-of-order execution machine.

Now, what does this give you? Very, very little. You can write something like Dekker's algorithm[9] to do locking instead of using locks. You can write data atomically and in order, but for the same reasons as above, it's unlikely to give you want you want. Consider that every use of a `volatile` variable requires a main memory read. Every main memory read costs upward of 100 cycles, whereas a simple direct nonvolatile use of the same variable would execute in one cycle.

The definition of `volatile` does imply that 64-bit data (e.g., doubles and longs) will be treated atomically. On a machine that does 64-bit writes (UltraSPARC, Alpha, etc.), this is straightforward to implement. On a machine that only does 32-bit writes (SPARC v7, x86, etc.) this is a bit more difficult. To meet the definition of `volatile`, it is actually necessary for 32-bit machines to maintain a lock specifically for 64-bit `volatile` data.

It is unlikely that you will ever use `volatile` at all.[10] Be careful!

Atomic Reads and Writes

Most writes on most systems are either 32 or 64 bits wide, aligned on the appropriate word boundary. Such writes are

---

[9]Dekker's algorithm is basically a clever way of building locks for a known number of threads based on the assumption that writes to main memory arrive in order. Without a volatile declaration, it is not possible to implement on an out-of-order machine.

[10]In the 2nd edition of his book, Doug Lea (see Appendix B) is including a simple example of using volatile to manage a list. The code is amazingly complex for such a simple problem. I figure that if it's that difficult for Doug to get it right, I don't want to be doing it at all!

atomic—you never have to be concerned that the first 16 bits have been written before the second 16 bits. What good does this do you? Very little. You cannot test a value because it may change. You cannot increment a value because someone else might be using it at the same time. You may be able to figure out a tricky way of combining this fact with a `volatile` declaration to allow you to avoid using a lock, but it probably won't make your program go any faster.

Interlocked Instructions

In Win32 there are a set of interlocked functions [`Inter-lockedIncrement()`, `InterlockedDecrement()`, and `InterlockedExchange()`] which call the respective inter-locked instructions on x86 machines. These instructions provide equivalent functionality to the fancy synchronization instructions we just looked at. Although some Win32 programmers will gladly attest to their glory, they don't actually provide the C program with much value, and they cannot be called from Java. Use locks!

Memory Systems

The memory system in modern SMP machines is designed to be ignored. You shouldn't have to spend any time thinking about it—it should just work. And it succeeds in this, to a degree. As long as you are writing a program that is reasonably well behaved and that doesn't have overwhelming needs for absolute maximum performance, you can skip over this section. Probably 95% of all programs fit into this category. As for the other 5% percent...

In 1980, memory speeds were about the same as CPU speeds, and a machine could access main memory in a single cycle. Since then, DRAM speeds have improved by an order of magnitude and CPU speeds by almost four. Direct main memory access now costs between 30 and 100 CPU cycles. It is not at all unusual for a CPU to spend over half its time stalled, waiting for memory. To the degree that you can reduce the number of main memory ac-cesses (i.e., cache misses), you will be handsomely paid in program performance. (N.B.: There is nothing unique to MP machines or MT programs here.)

Reducing Cache Misses

So how to reduce cache misses? There are a couple of generalities that we can point to, but not much more. Happily, these generalities do cover a lot of programs.

1. Write your program so that you never have to load a cache line more times than is absolutely necessary.
2. Organize your data so that when you do load a cache line, you are able to make use of all the data.
3. Keep data used regularly by different threads out of the same cache line.

Depending upon your particular program, it may or may not be reasonable to apply the above. For well-behaved programs that reuse the data in cache many times, a great deal can be done just covering these three rules. We can show a factor of 10 difference between a naive matrix multiply and the most highly optimized implementation, all due to better cache management. For programs with very poor data locality, such as NFS or databases, which spend a lot of time bringing in new data and looking at it only once, it is almost impossible to do anything at all.

Two SPECfp95 benchmarks were submitted by Sun for almost the identical machine. The first was a 400-MHz, 8-way UE 3500 with 4-MB E$. The second was the same, but with an 8-MB E$. We show (in Table 16–1) the three most affected benchmarks along with the geometric average for SPECfp.

Table 16–1 *Selected SPEC Benchmarks for Two UE 3500s*

	4-MB E$	8-MB E$
101.tomcat	105	122
102.swim	278	671
107.mgrid	108	147
SPECfp95	50.1	57.7

Cache Blocking

For something like matrix manipulation or image processing, a naive algorithm might load and reload a cache line numerous times. The same operation can be performed much faster in a more clever algorithm that does *cache blocking*—arranging to load a subset of the data and use it many times before loading a new block.

A naive multiply algorithm would multiply all of row 1 by column 1. Then row 1 by column 2, column 3, etc. Next, row 2 would be multiplied with each column, etc. For a 1024 × 1024 matrix, each row would be loaded only once, but the columns would be reloaded 1024 times! Assuming 64-bit floats and 64-byte cache lines, that adds up to a total of 128k cache loads.

A cache-blocked program would multiply rows 1–64 with columns 1–64, then columns 65–128, then 129–192, etc. Each of those sets will fit completely in a 2-MB E$, so the total number of cache loads will be reduced to a mere 16k column load plus 1k row loads.

That's the basics of cache blocking. There's plenty more that can be done. For example, you can optimize I$ blocking on top of the E$ blocking. You can take into account the writing scheme (does the CPU write back via the cache, write through the cache, or write around it?). You can recall that E$ is physically mapped, hence it requires a TLB translation. (The *translation lookaside buffer* performs high-speed virtual-to-physical mappings.) Of course, TLBs are very small. The Sun TLB for the large SC2000 server holds a translation for only 0.5 MB, so if you can avoid referencing data in cache beyond the current contents of the TLB, you can avoid extraneous TLB misses. Then you may also wish to consider which data is coming from which memory bank.

We really don't expect you to deal with these fine-grained optimizations. We don't. They involve a lot of careful estimation and painstaking verification, and they have to be tailored to individual machines. But this kind of thing is possible, it does yield impressive improvements for some programs, and the truly high-performance obsessive types do it. (Dakota Scientific's numerical libraries take all of these parameters into account and get impressive results.)

Data Reorganization

What if you had a large number of records about people—names, ages, salaries, addresses, favorite programming languages, etc.? To calculate the average salary for these folks, you would have to bring in the cache block with the first person's salary in it (along with seven other words), add that to the total, then bring in the next person's salary, etc. Each cache miss would bring in exactly one piece of useful data, and every salary would require a cache miss.

If you organized the data differently, placing all of the salaries into one array, all of the names in another, etc., you would be able to make much better use of each cache load. Instead of one salary being loaded with each miss, you'd get eight, significantly reducing cache wait times.

This is not something you'd do for a casual program. When you have this kind of program design and data usage, and you are desperate for optimal performance, that's when you do this kind of thing (see *Portability* on page 315).

Word Tearing

What is the minimum-size data item that you can write to memory? On most modern machines it's 8 bits. On some it's 32. It's possible that on some machines it could be 64!

Now, what would happen if you used one lock to protect the first bit in a word, and another lock to protect the second? It wouldn't work. Every time you wrote out bit 1, you would over-write bit 2, and if someone else was using bit 2, . . . Too bad.

Don't do that. Happily, it is easy to avoid word tearing and it would be a pretty odd program indeed that actually violated this restriction.

False Sharing

A cache memory is divided up into cache lines (typically, eight words) which are loaded and tracked as a unit. If one word in the line is required, all eight are loaded. If one word is written out by another CPU, the entire line is invalidated. Cache lines are based on the idea that if one word is accessed, it's very likely that the next word will be also. Normally, this works quite well and yields excellent performance. Sometimes it can work against you.

If eight integers happened to be located contiguously at a line boundary, and if eight different threads on eight different CPUs happened to use those (unshared) integers extensively, we could run into a problem. CPU 0 would write a[0]. This would, of course, cause the a[0] cache line to be invalidated on all the other CPUs. CPU 1 now wishes to read a[1]. Even though it actually has a valid copy of a[1] in cache, the line has been marked invalid, so CPU 1 must reload that cache line. And when CPU 1 writes a[1], CPU 0 will invalidate its cache line, etc., etc.

This is what is called *false sharing*. On an 8-way, 244-MHz UE4000, the program shown in Code Example 16–3 runs in 100 s when the integers are adjacent (SEPARATION == 1), and in 10 s when the integers are distant (SEPARATION == 16). It is an unlikely problem (it can happen, however), one that you wouldn't even look for unless you did some careful performance tuning and noticed extensive CPU stalls. Without specialized memory tools, the only way you could find this out is by counting instructions and dividing by CPU speed. If there is a large discrepancy, you can infer memory system stalls (see *Memory Latency* on page 318).

```
int a[128];
public class FalseSharing {
    int index;

public void run()
{
 while (MANY_INTERATIONS)
  a[index]++;
}


...
for (i=0; i<8 ;i++)
   new FalseSharing(i * SEPARATION).start();
...
```

Code Example 16–3   *False Sharing*

Summary

There are numerous machine designs, most of which will not affect our programming decisions. There are a lot of issues concerning memory coherency, all of which are solved by using proper locking. For very high performance programs, clever, semiportable cache blocking schemes and data organization can have an enormous impact.

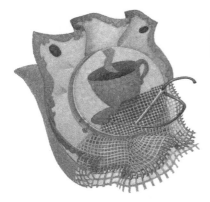

Examples

In which several complete programs are presented. The details and issues surrounding the way they use threads are discussed, and references to other programs on the Net are made.

This chapter contains several example programs that use Java threads. The examples use threads to demonstrate different concepts from previous chapters. All the example code (except for the JNI example) has been compiled and run on Solaris, IRIX, Digital UNIX, and Windows NT.

Use this code in whatever manner you choose; many of the concepts demonstrated in the examples can be reworked to be used in your applications. Of course, there are some bugs in the code somewhere. All the source code used in this book is available on the Web (see *Code Examples* on page 410).

Threads and Windows

This example (Code Example 17–1) uses threads to speed up the operation of a GUI program which has long running operations. Without threads, this program would have to wait for each long-running operation to complete before the next button could be pushed.

```
//              ThreadedSwing/ThreadedSwing.java

/*
  When the user pushes a button, disable it and sleep for 6 seconds.
  If "Threaded," do the sleeping in a new thread, allowing the
  other buttons to remain active. If "Non-Threaded," do the sleeping
  in the SWING thread, effectively disabling the other buttons.

  After sleeping, reenable the button by calling invokeLater().
  (Swing is NOT thread-safe.)

  CF: Same program in AWT: ThreadedAWT and in PThreads: ThreadWin.c

*/


import java.applet.*;
import java.awt.*;
import java.awt.event.*;
import com.sun.java.swing.*;
import Extensions.*;
```

Code Example 17–1 *ThreadedSwing Program*

```
public class ThreadedSwing extends JFrame {
  static boolean          useThreads = false;
  static boolean          KILL = false;



public ThreadedSwing() {
  ThreadedJButton         button;

  if (System.getProperty("KILL") != null) KILL = true;
  setTitle("ThreadedSwing");
  JPanel topPanel = new JPanel();
  getContentPane().add(topPanel);

  ThreadButtonListener tbl = new ThreadButtonListener();
  NumericButtonListener nbl = new NumericButtonListener();

  button = new ThreadedJButton("Non-Threaded");
  topPanel.add(button);
  button.addActionListener(tbl);

  for (int i=1; i<5; i++) {
    button = new ThreadedJButton(""+i);
    topPanel.add(button);
    button.addActionListener(nbl);
  }
}


public static void main(String args[]) {
  ThreadedSwing           mainFrame = new ThreadedSwing();

  mainFrame.pack();
  mainFrame.setVisible(true);
  // Killer MUST be in another thread.
  if (KILL) new Thread(new Killer(120)).start();
}

}


//            ThreadedSwing/NumericButtonListener.java

/*
  This classes listens only for button pushes on the numbered buttons.
*/
```

Code Example 17–1 *ThreadedSwing Program (cont.)*

```java
import java.applet.*;
import java.awt.*;
import java.awt.event.*;
import com.sun.java.swing.*;
import Extensions.*;


public class NumericButtonListener implements ActionListener  {


public void actionPerformed(ActionEvent event) {
  ThreadedJButton currentButton = (ThreadedJButton)event.getSource();

  System.out.println("Pressed " + currentButton);
  currentButton.setEnabled(false);
  System.out.println(currentButton + " disabled.");
  DoWorker w = new DoWorker(currentButton);

  if (ThreadedSwing.useThreads)
    new Thread(w).start();
  else
    w.run();
}

}



class DoWorker implements Runnable {
  ThreadedJButton        button;


public DoWorker(ThreadedJButton b) {
  button = b;
}



public void run() {
  Thread selfName = Thread.currentThread();

  System.out.println(button + " sleeping... " + selfName);
```

Code Example 17–1 *ThreadedSwing Program (cont.)*

```
  InterruptibleThread.sleep(6000);
  System.out.println(button + " done. " + selfName);

  // This will run workComplete() in Swing main thread.
  // This is the main point of the whole example.
  SwingUtilities.invokeLater(new DidWorker(button));
}

}


class DidWorker implements Runnable {
  ThreadedJButton         button;


public DidWorker(ThreadedJButton b) {
  button = b;
}

public void run() {     // Run only in Swing main thread.
  Thread selfName = Thread.currentThread();

  button.setEnabled(true);
  System.out.println(button + " reenabled. " + selfName);
}
}


//              ThreadedSwing/ThreadButtonListener.java

/*
  This classes listens only for button pushes on the
  "Threaded" / "Non-Threaded" button.

*/

import java.applet.*;
import java.awt.*;
import java.awt.event.*;
import com.sun.java.swing.*;
import Extensions.*;



public class ThreadButtonListener implements ActionListener  {
```

Code Example 17–1   *ThreadedSwing Program (cont.)*

```java
public void actionPerformed(ActionEvent event) {
  ThreadedJButton currentButton = (ThreadedJButton)event.getSource();

  System.out.println("Pressed " + currentButton);
  ThreadedSwing.useThreads = !ThreadedSwing.useThreads;
  if (ThreadedSwing.useThreads)
    currentButton.setText("Threaded");
  else
    currentButton.setText("Non-Threaded");
}

}


//              ThreadedSwing/ThreadedJButton.java

/*
  Once upon a time this was an interesting class.  Now it
  provides a nice print string.
*/


import java.applet.*;
import java.awt.*;
import com.sun.java.swing.*;
import Extensions.*;



public class ThreadedJButton extends JButton {


public ThreadedJButton(String s) {
  super(s);
}


public String toString() {
  return("ThreadedJButton_" + getText());
}

}
```

Code Example 17–1 *ThreadedSwing Program (cont.)*

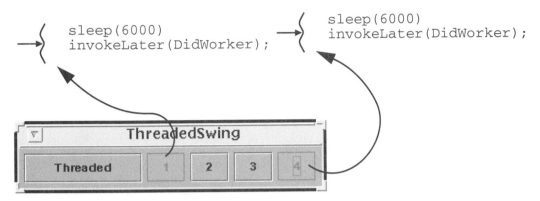

Figure 17–1   *ThreadedSwing Window Example*

In a "normal" windowing application, when a button is pressed, some task is executed and then control in the program is returned to the window. This is fine if the time required to execute the task is minimal. If the time required for the task is not minimal, the window *freezes* or the clock icon is displayed while the task is executing. This behavior is not desirable in most cases, because the graphical interface should always be active for the user to select other actions.

This example demonstrates how we can get around the *freezing* problem. A simple window is created and filled with pushbutton widgets. When a button is pushed, the program simulates some processing [i.e., `sleep(6000)`] that would normally cause the interface to freeze. In this example the work is performed in separate threads. This way, when a button is pressed, a thread is created to do the work, and the window can return to its event processing for the user (Figure 17–1).

When you run this example, you will see that when a button is pressed, it changes colors and is deactivated while the work is being done. However, you can press as many buttons as you like, one right after the other without waiting for the first to complete.

This program is exactly what was described in *Are Libraries Safe?* on page 253. The main thread builds a window. This starts up an event thread that then enters the event loop and waits for input. When you push a button, the callback `ThreadButton-Listner.actionPerformed()` runs, deactivates the button, changes its colors, and (optionally) creates a new thread (T2) to run the work function [`DoWorker.run()`].

The event thread then returns to the event loop. You press another button and the cycle repeats. In the meantime (back at the ranch), the new thread has started up and begun running. With our second push, a third thread (T3) has started up, just like T2. After a few seconds, T2 completes its work and calls `invokeLater[new DidWorker()]` and exits.

The event thread sees the `invokeLater` request and runs the method `DidWorker.run()`. That function sets the button back to the original colors and reactivates the button. Now only T3 is running. Soon it will complete and repeat the actions of T2. In this fashion, the event loop is always active and the Swing calls are made only from the event thread.

If you push the "Threaded" button, the program will not use threads, but rather, it will do all the work directly in the event thread. And the program will slow down a lot.

Notice that we are using a runnable as the item of work to be performed and we are going to allow it to be run either in a new thread or in the event thread itself. This is one of the reasons that runnables are good.

Displaying Things for a Moment (`Memory.java`)

Sometimes you would like an applet (or any windowing program) to display something for the user to see for a short time, then continue on to do other things. In their excellent book *Java by Example* (see Appendix B), Jackson and McClellan show a little program that tests human memory. We wrote an abbreviated version of it. It shows four colored boxes: red, blue, green, yellow (Figure 17–2). When the game starts, it makes one of those boxes brighter for a couple seconds, then dims it again. Next it chooses another (at random) and brightens that for a couple seconds.

After the pattern has been displayed, the player must now take the mouse and duplicate the sequence. If the game flashed blue, green, red, green, the player must mouse blue, green, red, green. Pretty simple.

The question comes up: How can we arrange for the flashing colors to be displayed to the player? If we ran this game entirely

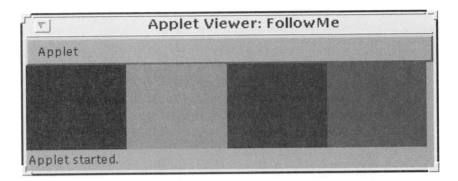

Figure 17–2 *The Memory Game*

in the main applet thread, it wouldn't work. All painting happens in the main applet thread, so if you made a box bright blue, you could then request a repaint, but that repaint would not occur until your function returned. If you tried to have your function sleep, the repainting would have to wait.

So running the snippet of code shown in Code Example 17–2 in the main applet thread would brighten a box, request a repaint, sleep, then dim the box, etc. After you were all done with this, your method would return and then the repaints would happen all at once. Not very useful.

```
private void reset() {

  for (int i = 0; i < patternLength; i++) {

    // Select random cell

    int randomX = (int)((Math.random() * 10) % numCellsOnSide);
    pattern[i] = Cell.cells[randomX];

    // Display the pattern square by redrawing it briefly in a
    // brighter version of its current color.

    chosenCell = Cell.cells[randomX];
    chosenCell.brighten();
    repaint();
```

Code Example 17–2 *How to Display Something for a Short Time*

```
    // Sleep so the user can see the bright color before we
    // darken it again.

    InterruptibleThread.sleep(sleepTime);

    // Redraw the square in its original color before going to
    // the next square.

    chosenCell.darken();
    repaint();

    // Sleep between squares.

    InterruptibleThread.sleep(sleepTime);
  }
}
```

Code Example 17–2 *How to Display Something for a Short Time (cont.)*

The right way to do this is to run your method in a separate thread. This way, when you run the method, the applet thread is idle. You request a repaint, you go to sleep, and now the repaint can occur in the applet thread!

Socket Server (Master/Slave Version)

The socket server example uses threads to implement a "standard" socket port server. A standard socket server listens on a socket port and when a message arrives, forks a process to service the request. The server program first sets up all the needed socket information. The server then enters a loop, waiting to service a socket port. When a connect request is sent to the socket port, the server creates a new thread to handle the requests on this socket file descriptor.

The newly created listener thread then receives requests on this socket in the function `producer()` until the string "End" comes across. For each request, the listener thread creates a new thread to handle it. That worker thread processes the request in `process-Request()`, which sleeps for a bit (simulating disk I/O) and then sends a reply back across the file descriptor.

The client side of the example (not shown) sends 1000 requests to the server for each file descriptor you request on the command line (default 1). It waits for each reply and exits when the server returns `"End."` This client code can also be run from different machines by multiple users.

The code is a little bit artificial because we wrote it to look as much as possible like our producer/consumer example. We also added some instrumentation to it, so it will count the number of threads created and running. One notable artifice is that we accept 1000 requests from each socket rather than one request from each of 1000 sockets, as you might expect. Our design gives the program a two-level structure, with the main thread waiting for new socket requests [in the `accept()` call]. The main thread creates a new thread to handle each new socket, and that new thread then waits for the 1000 requests, spawning 1000 additional threads, one per request.

Socket Server (Producer/Consumer Version)

Run the master/slave code on a fast enough machine and you will discover that it creates so many threads that it runs out of memory! This is not a good thing. One solution is to keep careful track of how many threads you have created and how many have exited. A better solution would be to redesign the program to be a producer/consumer model. This way you will be able to control the number of threads with no problem and you will be able to use the list of outstanding requests as a buffer for when the number of requests exceeds the ability of the program to handle them.

Of course, if the rate of incoming requests exceeds the ability to reply for too long, you will eventually have to simply reject the requests. You could have the producer thread send explicit rejections to the client programs, or it could simply refuse to call `accept()` until there is room on the list. In this case, the kernel will queue up a few requests, then simply refuse to acknowledge any more requests.

Most of the code for the producer/consumer version (Code Example 17–3) is identical to that in the master/slave version. You will notice that most of the code is stolen directly from Code Example 6–12 on page 113. Both the `producer()` and consumer() functions are identical. Really, all that we're doing is redirecting the producer, from creating new threads for each request, to placing those requests onto a queue and letting the consumers worry about them.

```
//              ServerProducerConsumer/Server.java

/*
  A simple server program.  It sets up a TCP port for the client
  program to connect to. Then it accepts connections, spawning a
  new producer thread for each. [Java has no "select()" function.]

  It starts up nConsumers consumer threads to pull requests off the
  list and process them, sending a reply string back to the client.

  Any IO failures are handled by printing out an error message, closing
  the socket in question, then ignoring it.  Check out the location of
  the exception handlers and which methods throw exceptions. This is
  carefully designed and *should* be fully robust.

  This version is really just a producer/consumer program that happens
  to run across a socket.

*/

import java.io.*;
import java.net.*;
import Extensions.*;



public class Server {
    ServerSocket          serverSocket;
    static int            port = 6500;
    static int            delay = 10;
    static int            spin = 10;
    static boolean        DEBUG = false;
    static int            nConsumers = 10;
    static int            MAX_LENGTH = 10;
    static boolean        KILL = false;



public static void main(String[] args) {
```

Code Example 17–3 *Producer/Consumer Socket Program*

```
Server               server = new Server();
Thread               t;
int                  stopperTimeout = 10; // 10s

if (args.length > 0) port  =           Integer.parseInt(args[0]);
if (args.length > 1) delay =           Integer.parseInt(args[1]);
if (args.length > 2) spin =            Integer.parseInt(args[2]);
if (args.length > 3) nConsumers =      Integer.parseInt(args[3]);
if (args.length > 4) stopperTimeout = Integer.parseInt(args[4]);
if (System.getProperty("DEBUG") != null) DEBUG = true;
if (System.getProperty("KILL") != null) KILL = true;

System.out.println("Server(port: " + port + " delay: " + delay
                + "ms spin: " + spin + "us nConsumers: "
                + nConsumers + " stopperTimeout " + stopperTimeout
                + "s)");

if (KILL) new Thread(new Killer(120)).start();
server.runServer();
}



public void runServer() { // Executes in main thread
  Socket               socket;
  Workpile             workpile = new Workpile(MAX_LENGTH);

  try {
    serverSocket = new ServerSocket(port);
    System.out.println("Server now listening on port " + port);

    for (int i = 1; i < nConsumers; i++) {
      Thread t = new Thread(new Consumer(workpile));
      t.start();
    }

    while (true) {
      socket = serverSocket.accept();
      Client client = new Client(socket);
      Thread t = new Thread(new Producer(workpile, client));
      t.start();
      System.out.println("Server[" + t.getName()
                     + "]\tStarted new client: " + client);
    }
  }
```

Code Example 17–3 *Producer/Consumer Socket Program (cont.)*

```
    catch (IOException e) {         // Log failure, then ignore it.
      System.out.println("Cannot get I/O streams in new Client()" + e);
    }
  }
}


public Server() {
}

}


//                ServerProducerConsumer/Client.java

import java.io.*;
import java.net.*;

public class Client {
  int                     outstandingRequests = 0;
  Socket                  socket;
  InputStream             is;
  OutputStream            os;
  int                     delay = 10;
  int                     count = 0;
  static int              total = 0;
  int                     MessageLength = 70;



public String toString() {
  return("<Client: " + count + ">");
}


public Client(Socket s) throws IOException {
  socket = s;
  is = socket.getInputStream();
  os = socket.getOutputStream();
  synchronized (getClass()) {
    total++;
    count = total;
  }
```

Code Example 17–3   *Producer/Consumer Socket Program (cont.)*

```
}


public Request read() throws IOException {
  byte[] b = new byte[MessageLength];

  int n = is.read(b);
  if (n != MessageLength)
    throw new IOException(this + "Read too few characters " + n);
  incrementOutstandingRequests();
  return new Request(this, b);
}


  // Methods something like these might be useful...  :-)

public synchronized void incrementOutstandingRequests() {
  outstandingRequests++;
}



public synchronized void decrementOutstandingRequests() {
  outstandingRequests--;
  if (outstandingRequests == 0)
    notifyAll();                   // In case someday there's more than 1.
}


public synchronized void waitForOutstandingRequests() {
  boolean interrupted=false;

  while (outstandingRequests != 0) {
    try {wait();}
    catch (InterruptedException e) {interrupted = true;}
  }
  if (interrupted) Thread.currentThread().interrupt();
}

}


//               ServerProducerConsumer/Consumer.java

import java.io.*;
```

Code Example 17–3 *Producer/Consumer Socket Program (cont.)*

```
import Extensions.*;



public class Consumer implements Runnable {
  Workpile                        workpile;



public Consumer(Workpile w) {
  workpile = w;
}



public void run() {
  while (true) {
    workpile.mutex.lock();
    while (workpile.empty()) {
      workpile.consumerCV.condWait(workpile.mutex);
    }
    Request request = workpile.remove();
    workpile.mutex.unlock();
    workpile.producerCV.condSignal();
    request.process();
  }
}

}


//              ServerProducerConsumer/Producer.java

import java.io.*;
import Extensions.*;


public class Producer implements Runnable {
  Workpile                        workpile;
  Client                          client;



public Producer(Workpile w, Client c) {
  workpile = w;
```

Code Example 17–3 *Producer/Consumer Socket Program (cont.)*

```
    client = c;
  }



public void run() {
  String selfName = Thread.currentThread().getName();

  try {
    for (int i = 0; true; i++) {
      Request request = client.read();
      if (request.string.startsWith("End")) {
        client.decrementOutstandingRequests();
        client.waitForOutstandingRequests();

        // Send "End" right back to client.  We're done!
        client.os.write(request.bytes);
        client.socket.close();
        System.out.println("Server[" + selfName
                                    + "]\tCompleted processing.");
        InterruptibleThread.exit();
      }

      workpile.mutex.lock();
      while (workpile.full()) {
        workpile.producerCV.condWait(workpile.mutex);
      }
      workpile.add(request);
      workpile.mutex.unlock();
      workpile.consumerCV.condSignal();
    }
  }
  catch (IOException e) {              // Log failure, then ignore it.
    try {client.socket.close();} catch (IOException ioe) {}
    System.out.println("Server[" + selfName +
                    "]\tException during processing." + e);
    InterruptibleThread.exit();
  }
}


}


//                ServerProducerConsumer/Request.java
```

Code Example 17–3 *Producer/Consumer Socket Program (cont.)*

```java
import java.io.*;
import java.net.*;
import Extensions.*;


public class Request {
  Client             client;
  byte[]             bytes;
  Thread             self;
  String             string = "";
  int                count;
  static final int   MessageLength = 70;
  static int         total = 0;



public String toString() {
  int                i = string.indexOf(0);   // Find end-of-string.

  if (i<1) i=1;
  return("<Request: " + client + " " + self.getName() + " '"
        + string.substring(0, i) + "'>");
}



public Request(Client s, byte[] b) {
  client = s;
  bytes = b;
  self = Thread.currentThread();
  string = new String(b, 0);

  synchronized (this.getClass()) {count = ++total;}
  if (Server.DEBUG)
    System.out.println("Server[" + self.getName()
                                 + "]\tCreated: " + this);
  if (((count % 1000) == 0) && Server.DEBUG)
    System.out.println("Server[" + self.getName() + "]\tCreated: "
                     + count + " requests.");
}



public void process() {
  Thread                             self =  Thread.currentThread();
```

Code Example 17–3   *Producer/Consumer Socket Program (cont.)*

383

```
  try {
    byte reply[] = new byte[MessageLength];
    String s = new String(bytes, 0);
    s = "[Server " + self.getName() + "] Reply: " + count + " to: " + s;
    s.getBytes(0, MessageLength-1, reply, 0);
    InterruptibleThread.sleep(Server.delay);
    client.os.write(reply);
    client.decrementOutstandingRequests();

    if ((count % 1000) == 0)
      System.out.println("Server[" + self.getName()
                           + "]\tProcessed: " + count + " requests.");

    if (Server.DEBUG)
      System.out.println("Server[" + self.getName()
                              + "]\tProcessed: " + this);
  }
  catch (IOException e) {                  // Log failure, then ignore it.
    try {client.socket.close();} catch (IOException ioe) {}
    System.out.println("Server[" + self.getName() +
                    "]\tException during processing." + e);
  }
}


}


//              ServerProducerConsumer/Workpile.java

/*
  A Workpile is a container for a list of Requests and the synchronization
  variables that protect its internals. The synchronization and management
  of the list is EXTERNAL to the class because I want to illustrate its
  use in the producer/consumer code (and to make this program as similar
  as possible to the C version).

  The Workpile is constructed on top of a List (see Extensions). It could
  equally well be implemented by subclassing Vector; unfortunately, Vector
  is HORRIBLY inefficient for lists.

*/


import java.io.*;
import Extensions.*;
```

Code Example 17–3 *Producer/Consumer Socket Program (cont.)*

```
public class Workpile {
  List          list = List.nil;
  int           length = 0;
  static int    max = 10;
  Mutex         mutex = new Mutex();
  ConditionVar  producerCV = new ConditionVar();
  ConditionVar  consumerCV = new ConditionVar();
  boolean       stop = false;



public Workpile(int i) {
  max = i;
}



public void add(Request request) {
  list = list.cons(request);
  length++;
}



public Request remove() {
  Request request = (Request) list.first;

  list = list.next;
  length--;
  return(request);
}



public boolean empty() {
  return(length == 0);
}



public boolean full() {
  return(length == max);
}

}
```

Code Example 17–3   *Producer/Consumer Socket Program (cont.)*

Now a little problem we've glossed over. You may have noticed that our program has no way to tell if it has sent out all the
pending replies before the "End" request comes across. It is possible that the client program takes care of this, though ours doesn't.
Obviously, this must be done to have a properly running program.
Lots of techniques are possible, none of which are uniquely outstanding. We made a couple of minor additions to the server which
allow it to keep track of the number of outstanding requests per client. These are the methods incrementOutstandingRe-
quests(), decrementOutstandingRequests(), and
waitForOutstandingRequests(). When the client sends
the "End" message, we will not close the socket until the number
of outstanding requests has dropped to zero.

Making a Native Call to
pthread_setconcurrency()

Here we simply show the basic interface for making a native call to
set the concurrency level to 10. Code Example 17–4 uses the Solaris
UI threads function thr_setconcurrency(), which will run
on all post-Solaris 2.1 systems [pthread_setconcurrency()
is part of UNIX98 and not implemented until Solaris 7].

```
/*              NativeThreads.c  */

#include <thread.h>
#include <unistd.h>
#include <jni.h>

JNIEXPORT void
   JNICALL Java_Test_NativeTSetconc(JNIEnv *env, jclass obj) {
  thr_setconcurrency(10);
}


/*              Test.java          */

public class Test {
  static native void NativeTSetconc();
```

Code Example 17–4 *Setting the Concurrency Level in Solaris
(TimeDiskSetConc.java)*

```
static {System.loadLibrary("NativeThreads");


public static void main(String argv[]) {

  ...
 NativeTSetconc();
  ...
    }
}
```

Code Example 17–4 *Setting the Concurrency Level in Solaris (TimeDiskSetConc.java) (cont.)*

Actual Implementation of POSIX Synchronization

In Code Example 17–5 we have the actual implementations of explicit POSIX-style mutexes and condition variables. Take note of how `InterruptedException` is handled.

```
//              Extensions/Mutex.java

/*
  Pthreads style mutexes.  Not recursive.
  */


package Extensions;

import java.io.*;


public class Mutex {
  Thread                owner = null;


public String toString() {
  String name;

  if (owner == null)
```

Code Example 17–5 *Correct Implementation of Mutexes and Condition Variables*

```
    name = "null";
  else
    name = owner.getName();

  return ("<" + super.toString() + "owner:" + name +">");
}



  // Note that if we are interrupted, we will simply resend that
  // interrupt to ourselves AFTER we've locked the mutex.  The caller
  // code will have to deal with the interrupt.
public synchronized void lock() {
  boolean               interrupted = false;

  while (owner != null) {
    try {wait();}
    catch (InterruptedException ie) {interrupted=true;}
  }
  owner = Thread.currentThread();
  if (interrupted) Thread.currentThread().interrupt();
}


public synchronized void unlock() {
  if (!owner.equals(Thread.currentThread()))
    throw new IllegalMonitorStateException("Not owner");

  owner = null;
  notify();
}

}

//               Extensions/ConditionVar.java

/*
  A Pthreads style condition variable.

  Note that if you use these, you must handle InterruptedException
  carefully. condWait() will return as if from a spurious wakeup
  if interrupted. If your code allows interrupts to be sent, you
  MUST look at InterruptedException inside the while() loop:

  while (!condition) {
```

Code Example 17–5 *Correct Implementation of Mutexes and Condition Variables (cont.)*

```
      condWait(m);
      if (Thread.interrupted()) {throw something/do something!}
      }

*/



package Extensions;

import java.io.*;

public class ConditionVar {


public void condWait(Mutex mutex) {
  boolean        interrupted = false;


  while (true) {
    try {
      synchronized (this) {
        mutex.unlock();
        wait();
        break;
      }
    }
    catch (InterruptedException ie) {interrupted=true;}
  }

    mutex.lock();
    if (interrupted) Thread.currentThread().interrupt();
}



public void condWait(Mutex mutex, long timeout) {
  boolean        interrupted = false;


  while (true) {
    try {
      synchronized (this) {
        mutex.unlock();
```

Code Example 17–5 *Correct Implementation of Mutexes and Condition Variables (cont.)*

```
        wait(timeout);
        break;
      }
    }
    catch (InterruptedException ie) {interrupted=true;}
  }

    mutex.lock();
    if (interrupted) Thread.currentThread().interrupt();
}



public synchronized void condSignal() {
  notify();
}

public synchronized void condBroadcast() {
  notifyAll();
}

}
```

Code Example 17–5   *Correct Implementation of Mutexes and
Condition Variables (cont.)*

A Robust, Interruptible Server

Our next program (Code Example 17–6) is a variation of our old
friend the producer/consumer version of a network server. In this
version of it, we show how we can use InterruptedException to shut down the server on demand as we did in our
StopQueue example. The main distinction between this program
and StopQueue is that this version will not only interrupt the
threads waiting on sockets, but it will also handle any of the
checked exceptions no matter what the client code is doing.

Note that we do close the socket as soon as we get the InterruptedException because it may not be in a recoverable state.

```
//              ServerInterruptible/Server.java

/*
  A simple server program.  It sets up a TCP port for the client
```

Code Example 17–6   *A Robust Server*

program to connect to. Then it accepts connections, spawning a
new producer thread for each. [Java has no "select()" function.]

It starts up nConsumers consumer threads to pull requests off the
list and process them, sending a reply string back to the client.

Any IO failures are handled by printing out an error message, closing
the socket in question, then ignoring it. Check out the location of
the exception handlers and which methods throw exceptions. This is
carefully designed and *should* be fully robust.

This version is really just a producer/consumer program that happens
to run across a socket.

Unlike the StopQueueSolution, which has the consumer threads exit at
stop time (that was done for the illustration of synchronization), this
program simply stops accepting new requests, closing the socket as soon
as the final reply has been issued. The Client program is sent an "End"
message then, and left to its own devices to deal with the fact that the
socket has been closed.

This program uses InterruptedIOException, hence MUST be compiled under
Java 2.
*/


```java
import java.io.*;
import java.net.*;
import Extensions.*;



public class Server {
  ServerSocket        serverSocket;           // reading from  port
  static int          port = 6500;
  static int          delay = 10;             // Sleep time / Request (ms)
  static int          spin = 10;              // CPU-spin time (us)
  static boolean      DEBUG = false;
  static int          nConsumers = 10;
  static int          MAX_LENGTH = 10;        // Max length of Workpile
  static int          MAX_OPEN = 1000;        // Max open file descriptors
  static int          outstandingClients = 0;
  static Workpile     workpile;
  static Thread[]     consumers;
```

Code Example 17–6   *A Robust Server (cont.)*

```
static Thread[]         producers;
static int              nProducers=0;            // # active clients
static int              stopperTimeout = 10;     // 10s
static int              killerTimeout = 120;     // 2min
static boolean          KILL = false;
static Thread           acceptor;                // Thread doing accept()


public static void main(String[] args) {
  Server                server = new Server();

  if (args.length > 0) port  =            Integer.parseInt(args[0]);
  if (args.length > 1) delay =            Integer.parseInt(args[1]);
  if (args.length > 2) spin =             Integer.parseInt(args[2]);
  if (args.length > 3) nConsumers =       Integer.parseInt(args[3]);
  if (args.length > 4) stopperTimeout = Integer.parseInt(args[4]);
  if (args.length > 5) killerTimeout =  Integer.parseInt(args[5]);
  if (System.getProperty("DEBUG") != null) DEBUG = true;
  if (System.getProperty("KILL") != null) KILL = true;

  System.out.println("Server(port: " + port + " delay: " + delay
                  + "ms spin: " + spin + "us nConsumers: "
                  + nConsumers + " stopperTimeout " + stopperTimeout
                  + "s killerTimeout " + killerTimeout + "s)");
  server.runServer();
}



public void runServer() { // Executes in main thread
  Socket                socket;

  if (KILL) new Thread(new Killer(120)).start();
  acceptor = Thread.currentThread();
  consumers = new Thread[nConsumers];
  producers = new Thread[MAX_OPEN];
  workpile = new Workpile(MAX_LENGTH);
  for (int i = 0; i < nConsumers; i++) {
    consumers[i] = new Thread(new Consumer(workpile));
    consumers[i].start();
  }

  for (int i = 0; i < 3; i++) {            // Main start/stop loop
    try {
```

Code Example 17–6   *A Robust Server (cont.)*

```
    serverSocket = new ServerSocket(port);
    System.out.println("\n=========================================");
    System.out.println("Server now listening on port " + port);

    nProducers=0;
    new Thread(new Stopper(workpile, stopperTimeout)).start();
    for (int j=0; true; j++) {          // New client loop
      try {
        socket = serverSocket.accept();
        Client client = new Client(socket);
        synchronized (this) {waitIfTooManyClients();}
        Thread t = new Thread(new Producer(this, client));
        t.start();
        producers[j]=t;
        nProducers=j+1;
        System.out.println("Server[" + t.getName()
                           + "]\tStarted new client: " + client);
      }
      catch (SocketException ie) {
        synchronized (workpile) {
          System.out.println("Acceptor " + ie);
          Thread.interrupted();  //SocketException does NOT clear flag!
          if (workpile.stop) break;    // stop better be true!
          System.out.println("Impossible bug! Stop must be true.");
          System.exit(-1);
        }
      }
    }                                    // End of new client loop
    serverSocket.close();
    waitForOutstandingClients();
    System.out.println("Server shutdown complete.");
    InterruptibleThread.sleep(2000);   // "Feels" better to delay here.
    workpile.stop=false;
  }
  catch (IOException e) {     // Log failure, then die.
    System.out.println("Exiting on " + e);
    System.exit(-1);
  }
}                                       // End of start/stop loop
System.out.println("Exiting normally.");
System.exit(-1);
}
```

Code Example 17–6   *A Robust Server (cont.)*

```
public Server() {
}


public synchronized void incrementOutstandingClients() {
  outstandingClients++;
}


public synchronized void decrementOutstandingClients() {
  outstandingClients--;
  if ((outstandingClients == 0) || (outstandingClients == MAX_OPEN-1))
    notifyAll();                    // In case someday there's more than 1.
}


public synchronized void waitForOutstandingClients() {
  boolean                       interrupted=false;

  while (outstandingClients != 0) {
    try {wait();}
    catch (InterruptedException e) {interrupted = true;}
  }
  if (interrupted) Thread.currentThread().interrupt();
}


public void waitIfTooManyClients() { // NOT synchronized!
  boolean                       interrupted=false;

  while (outstandingClients == MAX_OPEN) {
    try {wait();}
    catch (InterruptedException e) {interrupted = true;}
  }
  if (interrupted) Thread.currentThread().interrupt();
}
}
```

Code Example 17–6   *A Robust Server (cont.)*

```java
//                 ServerInterruptible/Client.java

import java.io.*;
import java.net.*;


public class Client {
public int              outstandingRequests = 0;
public Socket           socket;
public InputStream      is;
public OutputStream     os;
public int              delay = 10;
public int              count = 0;
public static int       total = 0;
public int              MessageLength = 70;




public String toString() {
  return("<Client: " + count + ">");
}



public Client(Socket s) throws IOException {
  try {
    socket = s;
    is = socket.getInputStream();
    os = socket.getOutputStream();
    synchronized (getClass()) {
      total++;
      count = total;
    }
  }
  catch (IOException ie) {       // Included for illustration/debugging
    System.out.println(ie + " in new Client()");
    throw ie;
  }
}
```

Code Example 17–6   *A Robust Server (cont.)*

```java
public Request read() throws InterruptedIOException, IOException {
  byte[] b = new byte[MessageLength];

  try {
    int n = is.read(b);
    if (n != MessageLength)
      throw new IOException(this + " read too few characters " + n);
    incrementOutstandingRequests();
    return new Request(this, b);
  }
  catch (IOException ie) {        // Included for illustration/debugging
    System.out.println(ie + " in client.read()");
    throw ie;
  }
}



// Methods something like these might be useful...   :-)

public synchronized void incrementOutstandingRequests() {
  outstandingRequests++;
}


public synchronized void decrementOutstandingRequests() {
  outstandingRequests--;
  if (outstandingRequests == 0)
    notifyAll();                     // In case someday there's more than 1.
}


public synchronized void waitForOutstandingRequests() {
  boolean interrupted=false;

  while (outstandingRequests != 0) {
    try {wait();}
    catch (InterruptedException e) {interrupted = true;}
  }
  if (interrupted) Thread.currentThread().interrupt();
}

}
```

Code Example 17–6 *A Robust Server (cont.)*

```
//                    ServerInterruptible/Consumer.java

import java.io.*;
import Extensions.*;



public class Consumer implements Runnable {
  Workpile                workpile;



public Consumer(Workpile w) {
  workpile = w;
}



public void run() {
  Request               request;
  String                selfName = Thread.currentThread().getName();

  while (true) {
    try {
      synchronized (workpile) {
        while (workpile.empty()) {workpile.wait();}
        request = workpile.remove();
        workpile.notifyAll();
      }
      request.process();
    }
    catch (InterruptedException ie) {    // Never called.
      System.out.println(ie + " in consumer.run() " + selfName);
    }
  }
}


}



//                    ServerInterruptible/Producer.java

import java.io.*;
```

Code Example 17–6 *A Robust Server (cont.)*

```
import Extensions.*;

public class Producer implements Runnable {
public Workpile         workpile;
public Client           client;
public Server           server;
public static String    END =
"End                                                         ";
public final int        MessageLength = 70;
public byte[]           END_BYTES = new byte[MessageLength];


public Producer(Server s, Client c) {
  server = s;
  workpile = server.workpile;
  client = c;
  END.getBytes(0, MessageLength-1, END_BYTES, 0);
}



public void run() {
  String                 selfName = Thread.currentThread().getName();

  server.incrementOutstandingClients();
  for (int i = 0; true; i++) {
    try {
      Request request = client.read();
      if (request.string.startsWith("End")) {
        client.decrementOutstandingRequests();
        client.waitForOutstandingRequests();

        // Send "End" right back to client.  We're done!
        client.os.write(END_BYTES);
        client.socket.close();
        System.out.println("Server[" + selfName
                                     + "]\tCompleted processing.");
        break;
      }

      synchronized (workpile) {
        while (workpile.full() && !workpile.stop) {workpile.wait();}
        workpile.add(request);
        workpile.notifyAll();
```

Code Example 17–6 *A Robust Server (cont.)*

```
      if (workpile.stop) break;
    }
  }
  catch (InterruptedException e) {
    System.out.println(e + " in producer.run() for " + client);
    synchronized (workpile) {if (workpile.stop) break;}
    System.out.println("Impossible bug. Stop must be true!");
  }

  catch (InterruptedIOException e) {
    System.out.println(e + " in producer.run() for " + client);
    synchronized (workpile) {if (workpile.stop) break;}
    System.out.println("Impossible bug. Stop must be true!");
  }
  catch (IOException e) {               // Log failure, then ignore it.
    System.out.println(e + "in producer.run().");
    break;
  }
}

client.waitForOutstandingRequests();
try {
  client.os.write(END_BYTES);
  client.socket.close();
}
catch (IOException ioe) {}

server.decrementOutstandingClients();
System.out.println("Server[" + selfName
                        + "] exiting from producer.run().");
InterruptibleThread.exit();
}


}


//              ServerInterruptible/Request.java

import java.io.*;
import java.net.*;
import Extensions.*;


public class Request {
 Client                  client;
```

Code Example 17–6 *A Robust Server (cont.)*

```
byte[]                  bytes;
Thread                  self;
String                  string = "";
int                     count;
static final int        MessageLength = 70;
static int              total = 0;


public String toString() {
  int                   i = string.indexOf(0);  // Find end-of-string.

  if (i<1) i=1;
  return("<Request: " + client + " " + self.getName() + " '"
         + string.substring(0, i) + "'>");
}



public Request(Client s, byte[] b) {
  client = s;
  bytes = b;
  self = Thread.currentThread();
  string = new String(b, 0);

  synchronized (this.getClass()) {count = ++total;}

  if (Server.DEBUG)
    System.out.println("Server[" + self.getName()
                                 + "]\tCreated: " + this);
  if (((count % 1000) == 0) && Server.DEBUG)
    System.out.println("Server[" + self.getName() + "]\tCreated: "
                       + count + " requests.");
}




public void process() {
  Thread                self =  Thread.currentThread();

  try {
    byte reply[] = new byte[MessageLength];
    String s = new String(bytes, 0);
    s = "[Server " + self.getName() + "] Reply: " + count + " to: " + s;
```

Code Example 17–6 *A Robust Server (cont.)*

```
    s.getBytes(0, MessageLength-1, reply, 0);
    InterruptibleThread.sleep(Server.delay);
    client.os.write(reply);
    client.decrementOutstandingRequests();

    if ((count % 1000) == 0)
      System.out.println("Server[" + self.getName()
                      + "]\tProcessed: " + count + " requests.");
    if (Server.DEBUG)
      System.out.println("Server[" + self.getName()
                              + "]\tProcessed: " + this);
  }
  catch (InterruptedIOException e) {      // Log failure, then ignore it.
    System.out.println(e + " in request.process().");
  }
  // A consumer *may* still be working on requests for a client that
  // has been closed! (Shouldn't happen.)
  catch (IOException e) {                 // Log failure, then ignore it.
    System.out.println(e + " in request.process().");
  }
}


}


//              ServerInterruptible/Stopper.java

import java.io.*;
import Extensions.*;

public class Stopper implements Runnable {
  Workpile                    workpile;
  int                         delay;



public Stopper(Workpile w, int d) {
  workpile = w;
  delay = d;
}



public void run() {
```

Code Example 17–6   *A Robust Server (cont.)*

```
  InterruptibleThread.sleep(delay*1000);
  System.out.println("Stopping...");
  synchronized (workpile) {
    workpile.stop = true;
    workpile.notifyAll();
  }
  //   for (int i=0; i < Server.nConsumers; i++)
  //       Server.consumers[i].interrupt();
  for (int i = 0; i < Server.nProducers; i++)
    Server.producers[i].interrupt();
  Server.acceptor.interrupt();
}


}


//              ServerInterruptible/Workpile.java

/*
  A Workpile is a container for a list of Requests and the synchronization
  variables that protect its internals. The synchronization and management
  of the list is EXTERNAL to the class because I want to illustrate its
  use in the producer/consumer code  (and to make this program as similar
  as possible to the C version).

  The Workpile is constructed on top of a List (see Extensions). It could
  equally well be implemented by subclassing Vector; unfortunately Vector
  is HORRIBLY inefficient for lists.
*/


import java.io.*;
import Extensions.*;

public class Workpile {
  List          list = List.nil;
  int           length = 0;
  static int    max = 10;
  boolean       stop = false;



public Workpile(int i) {
  max = i;
}
```

Code Example 17–6 *A Robust Server (cont.)*

```
public void add(Request request) {
  list = list.cons(request);
  length++;
}



public Request remove() {
  Request         request = (Request) list.first;

  list = list.next;
  length--;
  return(request);
}



public boolean empty() {
  return(length == 0);
}



public boolean full() {
  return(length == max);
}

}
```

Code Example 17–6   *A Robust Server (cont.)*

Disk Performance with Java

Our final program (Code Example 17–7) is a simple test of disk performance with multiple threads. Because disk controllers can overlap incoming requests from the CPU, having lots of outstanding requests is a good thing and yields a performance improvement upward of twofold. This program demonstrates that fact and the value of making native call to `thr_setconcurrency()` on Solaris platforms. A nearly identical program in C yields slightly (about 25%) better results due to the expense of Java making calls into the native `read()` system call.

```
//              TimeDisk/Test.java

/*

  This program runs a set of read() calls against one large file.
  It runs with one or more threads so you can see the performance
  effect of MT.  Each read() gets one byte from a random location.
  You can run it for a number of iterations and get mean and SD.

  Make sure that there are links in /tmp pointing to wherever you
  can find room.

  lrwxrwxrwx   1 bil other ... time_disk0.tmp -> /disk2/6/temp_disk_test
  ln -s /disk2/6/temp_disk_test /tmp/time_disk0.tmp

  The file must be much larger than physical memory.  10x would be great,
  but 2x will do.  Expect "performance" to improve as the mbufs get
  loaded.  For a file 2x Physical, initial 100/s will improve to 200/s
  (as 50% of the file will become cached).  To populate the cache, you
  can run this program for awhile.

  runtime    = (Physical Memory / PAGE_SIZE)   / READS_PER_SECOND
  eg:
  160seconds = (128MB           / (8KB/PAGE))  / 100


  NB: This only runs under Java 2.
  CF: Same program in C: time_disk.c

*/


import java.io.*;
import java.util.*;
import Extensions.*;


public class Test implements Runnable {
  static int          MAX_FILE_SIZE=1024*1024*1024;
  static int          PAGE_SIZE=8192;
  static int          MAX_PAGES=(MAX_FILE_SIZE/PAGE_SIZE);
  static int          MAX_THREADS=512;
  static int          MAX_DENSITY=100;
```

Code Example 17-7 *Measuring Disk Access Throughput*

```
static int              MAX_READS;
static int[]            hits = new int[MAX_PAGES];
static int[]            density = new int[MAX_DENSITY];
static String           path="/tmp/time_disk0.tmp";
static int              spinTime = 0, runtime=10, nThreads = 1;
static int              iterations=1;
static boolean          setConcurrency=false;
static int[]            nProcessed;
static boolean          DEBUG=false;
static Thread[]         threads;
static boolean          stop=false;

static native void pthread_setconcurrency(int i);
static {System.loadLibrary("PThreadsInterface");}
// System.out.println("Loaded");}

Random                  ran;
int                     me;




public void run() {
  int                   err;
  long                  length;
  byte[]                b = new byte[2];
  RandomAccessFile      fd=null;
  long                  fileOffset;
  Thread                self=Thread.currentThread();

  try {
    fd = new RandomAccessFile(path, "r");
    length = fd.length();

    for (int i = 0; i < MAX_READS; i++) {
      if (stop) break;
      fileOffset =  Math.abs((ran.nextInt() * PAGE_SIZE) % length);
      hits[(int) fileOffset/PAGE_SIZE]++;
      //if (DEBUG)
      // System.out.println(t + " reading at " + fileOffset);

      fd.seek(fileOffset);
      err=fd.read(b, 0, 1);
```

Code Example 17–7 *Measuring Disk Access Throughput (cont.)*

```
      if (err == -1) {throw new IOException();}
      InterruptibleThread.spin(spinTime*1000);
      nProcessed[me]++;

      // It's interesting to see the results of yield() here when
      // using >1 GREEN THREADS.  (The results are what you expect --
      // same performance only spread to all threads.)
      // You would never include this in a "real" program.
      //       Thread.yield();

    }
    stop = true; // If one thread completes MAX_READS, all quit.
                 // This is probably because you're using GREEN THREADS.
  }
  catch (IOException e) {
    System.out.println("Is " + path + " correct? \n" +e);
    System.exit(-1);
  }
}


public static void main(String argv[]) throws Exception {
  int           totalProcessed;
  double[]      rates = new double[MAX_THREADS];
  double        S=0.0, mean, rate_sum=0.0, realtime;
  Thread        t;

  if (argv.length > 0) nThreads = Integer.parseInt(argv[0]);
  if (argv.length > 1) spinTime = Integer.parseInt(argv[1]);
  if (argv.length > 2) runtime = Integer.parseInt(argv[2]);
  if (argv.length > 3) iterations = Integer.parseInt(argv[3]);
  if (argv.length > 4) setConcurrency = (Integer.parseInt(argv[4]) == 1);
  if (System.getProperty("DEBUG") != null) DEBUG = true;
  System.out.println("Test(nThreads: " + nThreads
                  + " spinTime: " + spinTime
                  + "ms runtime: " + runtime
                  + "s iterations " + iterations
                  + " setConcurrency: " + setConcurrency
                  + ")");

  if (spinTime>0) InterruptibleThread.calibrateSpin();

  MAX_READS = 200*runtime;                 // About 2x fastest current disk
  nProcessed=new int[nThreads];
```

Code Example 17–7   *Measuring Disk Access Throughput (cont.)*

```
threads=new Thread[nThreads];
if (setConcurrency) pthread_setconcurrency(nThreads+1);

for (int j=0;j<iterations;j++) {

  for (int i=0;i<MAX_PAGES;i++) hits[i] = 0;
  for (int i=0;i<MAX_DENSITY;i++) density[i]=0;
  for (int i=0;i<nThreads;i++) nProcessed[i]=0;
  totalProcessed=0;

  long start = new Date().getTime();
  for (int i=0;i<nThreads;i++) {
    Random ran = new Random(start+i);
    t = new Thread(new Test(i, ran));
    t.start();
    threads[i] = t;
  }

  start = new Date().getTime();
  InterruptibleThread.sleep(runtime*1000);
  stop = true;
  for (int i=0;i<nThreads;i++) {threads[i].join();}
  long end = new Date().getTime();
  realtime = ((end - start)/1000.0);

  for (int i=0;i<nThreads;i++) {
    if (DEBUG)
      System.out.println("Thread " + i + " processed \t"
                           + nProcessed[i]);
    totalProcessed +=nProcessed[i];
  }

  for (int i=0;i<MAX_PAGES;i++) {
    if (hits[i] < MAX_DENSITY)
      density[hits[i]]++;
    else
      if (DEBUG)
        System.out.println("Page " + i + " got " + hits[i] + " hits!");
  }

  if (DEBUG) {
    System.out.println("nHits \t nPages");
    for (int i=0;i<MAX_DENSITY;i++) {
      if (density[i]>0) System.out.println(i + "\t " + density[i]);
    }
```

Code Example 17–7   *Measuring Disk Access Throughput (cont.)*

```
  }

  if (iterations==1)
    System.out.println("Processed " + totalProcessed + " in " + realtime
                        + "s. Rate\t" + (totalProcessed/realtime) + "/s.");
  rates[j] =  totalProcessed / realtime;
  rate_sum += totalProcessed / realtime;
  stop=false;
  }

  if (iterations>1) {
    mean = rate_sum/iterations;

    for (int i=0; i<iterations; i++) S+=(mean-rates[i])*(mean-rates[i]);
    S = Math.sqrt(S/(iterations-1));
    System.out.println("Mean rate: " + mean
                        + "/sec, Standard Deviation: " + S);
  }
  System.exit(0);
}



public Test(int i, Random r) {
  ran = r;
  me = i;
}

}



/*                TimeDisk/PThreadsInterface.c          */

#include <thread.h>
#include <unistd.h>
#include <jni.h>

JNIEXPORT void JNICALL
  Java_Test_pthread_1setconcurrency(JNIEnv *env, jclass obj, jint i) {
  thr_setconcurrency(i);
}



/*                TimeDisk/compile.csh             */
```

Code Example 17–7 *Measuring Disk Access Throughput (cont.)*

```
# This is a Java2 only-program (for native threads and
# InterruptedIOException).
setenv JAVAHOME /disk2/6/Java/jdk1.2/jdk1.2beta4
setenv JH_INC3 ${JAVAHOME}/include
setenv JH_INC2 ${JAVAHOME}/include/solaris
setenv CLASSPATH .:/export/home/bil/programs/Java/Extensions/classes

# Java's going to get the interface code from .
setenv LD_LIBRARY_PATH ${LD_LIBRARY_PATH}:.

# Tell Java to use native threads.
setenv THREADS_FLAG native

${JAVAHOME}/bin/javac *.java
${JAVAHOME}/bin/javah -stubs Test
${JAVAHOME}/bin/javah -jni Test

cc -G -I${JH_INC3} -I${JH_INC2} PThreadsInterface.c -lthread \
   -o libPThreadsInterface.so
```

Code Example 17–7   *Measuring Disk Access Throughput (cont.)*

Other Programs on the Web

There are a small series of other programs on the Web page that may be of some interest. Each of them has points of interest, but none of them is sufficiently interesting for us to print in its entirety. You may well find the programs helpful in clarifying details about how to write code for specific situations and for how to use the APIs. Several are variations of the programs in previous chapters, and several are simple test programs which illustrate how some of the fancier extension functions work, such as FIFO mutexes, recursive mutexes, mutexes with timeouts.

Summary

Several Java programs were shown, each with a certain point to elucidate. As with all the example programs, translation to POSIX or Win32 is (supposed to be) straightforward and is left as an exercise for the reader.

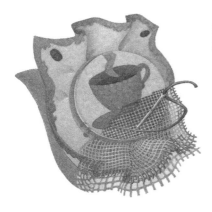

Appendix A

Internet

▼ THREADS NEWSGROUP

▼ CODE EXAMPLES

▼ VENDOR'S THREADS PAGES

▼ THREADS RESEARCH

▼ FREEWARE TOOLS

▼ OTHER POINTERS

▼ THE AUTHORS ON THE NET

Threads Newsgroup

For discussion, questions and answers, and just general debate about threading issues, there is a newsgroup on the Internet (started by Bil). The issues discussed are not confined to any one vendor, implementation, standard, or specification.

comp.programming.threads

There are two FAQs for the newsgroup, the first high-level and general (maintained by Brian), the other very low-level and specific (maintained by Bil):

http://www.serpentine.com/~bos/threads-faq

http://www.LambdaCS.com

Code Examples

All the code examples in this book (and direct counterparts in PThreads) are available via the Web:

http://www.LambdaCS.com

Vendor's Threads Pages

The SunSoft Web page (designed by Marianne, maintained by Dan) includes an FAQ on UI threads, performance data, case studies, and demonstration programs. It also has a lot of pointers to other pages on it.

http://www.sun.com/software/Products/Developer-products/threads/

The IBM threads page includes a short exposition on POSIX threads programming and IBM's implementation:

http://developer.austin.ibm.com/sdp/library/ref/about4.1/df4threa.html

http://www.rs6000.ibm.com/doc_link/en_US/a_doc_lib/aixprggd/genprogc/ thread_quick_ref.htm

DEC's documentation pages include a "Guide to DECthreads":

http://www.unix.digital.com/faqs/publications/base_doc/DOCUMENTATION/HTML/ AA-Q2DPC-TKT1_html/threads_title.html

Or, for something (unfortunately, only slightly) more "wieldy":

http://www.unix.digital.com/faqs/publications/base_doc/DOCUMENTATION/HTML/
    BOOKSHELF.HTM

Threads Research

There is a bibliography of several hundred papers related to threading (created and maintained by Torsten). The papers are largely theoretical, exploring the outer limits of threading and concurrency:

http://liinwww.ira.uka.de/bibliography/Os/threads.html

A good number of people are doing research and development on all sorts of threads-related issues. Here are a few of the major ones.

Doug Lea (the famous author previously mentioned) has written some on-line stuff on Java Threads and has the code for his book there also.

http://gee.cs.oswego.edu/dl

Douglas Schmidt wrote an extensive package to facilitate threading and interprocess communication called "The Adaptive Communication Environment (ACE)."

http://www.cs.wustl.edu/~schmidt/ACE.html

Freeware Tools

Two useful tools are available as unsupported from Sun. TNFview (by Bonnie's group) allows you to look at the exact timing of different events in a program. Proctool (Morgan's brainchild) gives you a view of the high-level operations of processes and LWPs on Solaris.

http://soldc.sun.com/developer/support/driver
    (TNFView)

http://www.sunfreeware.com
    (Proctool)

Other Pointers

You can see the "Single UNIX® Specification" at

http://www.rdg.opengroup.org/unix/online.html

To see all the details on performance measurements, the SPEC homepage is

http://www.specbench.org

For about $140 you can get the actual POSIX threads spec (IEEE 1003.1) from IEEE. It is a *specification*, more intended for implementers than programmers, so it is very likely *not* what you want. But, if you do:

http://www.ieee.org

customer.service@ieee.org

The Authors on the Net

If you would like to contact the authors directly, you can send mail to **Daniel.Berg@sun.com** and **Bil@LambdaCS.COM**. We would like to hear from you about what you liked or disliked about the book, and what we may be able to improve.

Daniel recently left Cyrus Inc. and has returned to Sun as worldwide director of Advanced Internet Consulting Practice.

Bil left Sun and is currently running his own company, Lambda Computer Science, teaching, and consulting on multithreaded programming.

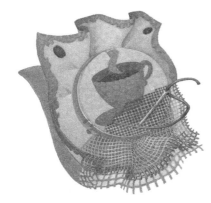

Appendix B

Books

- ▼ THREADS BOOKS
- ▼ RELATED BOOKS

Threads Books

The following are the other books in publication to date. Some of the examples, explanations, figures, etc., in them will be better than those in this text. Some of them will simply explain things better for you. We have read each of them carefully and have our own preferences. All of them are sufficient for their purposes.

Java Threads

Doug Lea, *Concurrent Programming in Java*. Reading, MA: Addison-Wesley, 1997 (240 pages, source on the Web). Describes how to write multithreaded programs in Java, using design patterns. Well written from a computer science point of view, although perhaps overwhelming for the hacker-oriented. Familiarity with design patterns is a necessity.

Scott Oaks and Henry Wong, *Java Threads*. Sebastopol, CA: O'Reilly, 1997 (252 pages, source on the Web). Describes how to write multithreaded programs in Java in a more conventional, programmer-oriented style. Explanations are clear, though often simplistic. The programs illustrate the points well, yet tend to gloss over problem areas in Java.

Stephen J. Hartley, *Concurrent Programming—The Java Programming Language*. Oxford University Press, 1998 (250 pages, source on the Web). Describes how to write multithreaded programs in Java in a more conventional, programmer-oriented style. Somewhat simplistic, intended as an undergraduate text.

POSIX Threads

Steve Kleiman, Devang Shah, and Bart Smaalders, *Programming with Threads*. Upper Saddle River, NJ: SunSoft Press, Feb. 1996 (534 pages, source on the Web). Covers POSIX threads, concentrating on the Solaris implementation. It has a small but adequate introduction, then concentrates on more advanced programming issues. The examples are good because they are realistic and show you what to expect. They are bad because they are very realistic and obscure the main points in the text.

Len Dorfman and Marc J. Neuberger, *Effective Multithreading with OS/2*. New York: McGraw-Hill, Nov. 1995 (280 pages, source on diskette). Gives a brief introduction, then focuses the rest of the discussion on the API and examples. It covers the OS/2 API.

Charles J. Northrup, *Programming with UNIX Threads*. New York: Wiley, Mar. 1996 (400 pages, source via FTP). Covers the UI threads library, focusing on the UNIXware implementation. The presentation is oriented around the API and contains numerous examples.

Thuan Q. Pham and Pankaj K. Garg, *Multithreaded Programming with Windows NT*. Upper Saddle River, NJ: Prentice Hall, Jan. 1996 (220 pages, source on diskette). Focusing on the NT library, this book gives some comparison with other libraries. While it describes concepts and designs well, it lacks many of the practical details and glosses over problems.

Bradford Nichols, Dick Buttlar, and Jacqueline Proulx Farrell, *Pthreads Programming*. Sebastopol, CA: O'Reilly, Nov. 1996 (268 pages, source via FTP). Concentrates on the Digital implementation of POSIX. It gives a good explanation of the concepts but is a little too condensed to do them justice. Includes a major section comparing the final standard to draft 4, DCE.

Scott J. Norton and Mark D. Dipasquale, *ThreadTime*. Upper Saddle River, NJ: HP Professional Books, Dec. 1996 (530 pages, source on diskette). Describes POSIX threads with concentration on the HP-UX implementation. Includes an excellent introduction, computer science descriptions, and standards discussion.

Dave Butenhof, *Programming with POSIX Threads*. Reading, MA: Addison-Wesley, May 1997 (380 pages, source on the Web). Concentrates more on architecture than any specific implementation of POSIX threads. A lucid exposition of concepts and discussion of standards from one of the guys on the committee. Japanese translation available.

Bil Lewis and Daniel J. Berg, *Threads Primer*. Upper Saddle River, NJ: SunSoft Press, Oct. 1995 (320 pages, source on the Web). This is the first edition of the primer, which covers UI threads. It lacks the depth of many of the other books but gives a more extensive explanation of the fundamentals. Japanese translation available.

Bil Lewis and Daniel J. Berg, *Multithreaded Programming with PThreads*. Upper Saddle River, NJ: SunSoft Press, 1998 (380 pages, source on the Web). This is the second edition of the primer, which covers POSIX threads. It has much more depth than the Primer and also gives more extensive explanation of the fundamentals. *Multithreaded Programming with PThreads* is very similar to *Multithreaded Programming with Java Technology,* and the programming examples are directly comparable. Japanese translation available.

Win32 Threads

Jim Beveridge and Robert Wiener, *Multithreading Applications in Win32.* Reading, MA: Addison-Wesley, Jan. 1997 (368 pages, source on diskette). Describes Win32 threads (NT and Win95). Includes some comparison to POSIX. Excellent discussion of the practical aspects of programming Win32. Many insightful comments on both the good parts and the more problematic parts.

Shashi Prasad, *Multithreading Programming Techniques.* New York: McGraw-Hill, Jan. 1997 (410 pages, source on diskette and the Web). Describes and contrasts the multithreading libraries of POSIX, UI, Mach, Win32, and OS/2. Each library has its own chapters and its own code examples. This means that the introduction and presentation of concepts is lighter, but the examples are ported across the various platforms, making this a good reference for porting.

Related Books

Jeffrey Richter, *Advanced Windows NT: The Developer's Guide to the Win32 Application Programming Interface.* Redmond, WA: Microsoft Press, 1994. This book contains about 200 pages that cover the NT threads API and its use. It covers the API well, contains a good amount of code, but has very little on the concepts.

Robert A. Iannucci, Editor, *Multithreaded Computer Architecture: A Summary of the State of the Art.* New York: Kluwer Academic Publishers, 1994. This book is a collection of papers dealing with hardware design considerations for building specialized machines that can support multithreaded programs.

Derrel R. Blain, Kurt R. Delimon, and Jeff English, *Real-World Programming for OS/2 2.1.* Upper Saddle River, NJ: Sams Publishing/Prentice Hall PTR, 1993. This book contains about 50 pages that cover the OS/2 threads API and its use. It covers the API well, contains one nice example, but is very short.

Solaris Multithreaded Programming Guide. Upper Saddle River, NJ: SunSoft Press, 1995. This is the documentation that comes with Solaris 2.4 and contains the UI API. It is also available as part of the Solaris AnswerBook® and on the Web (see *Vendor's Threads Pages* on page 410).

John L. Hennessy and David A. Patterson, *Computer Architecture: A Quantitative Approach,* 2nd ed. San Francisco: Morgan Kaufmann, Inc., 1996 (800 pages). This is the definitive text on computer design—CPU, memory system, and multiprocessors. Not about threads per se, but everything underneath. *Superb* research and exposition!

Daniel E. Lenoski and Wolf-Dietrich Weber, *Scalable Shared-Memory Multiprocessing*. San Francisco: Morgan Kaufmann, 1995 (340 pages). This takes up in great detail what Hennessy and Patterson describe in mere passing detail. It describes the state of SMP research as it led to the Stanford DASH machine, and now the SGI Origin series and HAL Mercury. *Superb* research and exposition!

Jerry R. Jackson and Alan L. McClellan, *Java by Example*. Upper Saddle River, NJ: SunSoft Press, 1997. This is a nice introduction to Java and contains one particular example using threads that we use as the basis for one of our programs (Memory).

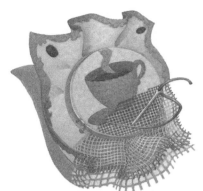

Appendix **C**

Timings

419

The choice of which synchronization variable to use depends partially on its execution speed. This is particularly applicable when choosing between using a mutex lock and a readers/writer lock. The design of programs calling Java functions in tight loops will also depend upon these numbers for optimizations. For the most part, however, all of these times are short enough that they may be ignored.

Because of the dependence of these tests upon several unusual instructions (`ldstub` and `stbar` on SPARC), machines with different cache or bus designs will exhibit nonuniform scaling (meaning that a context switch may be twice as fast on a 20-MHz processor as it is on a 10-MHz processor, but locking a mutex might take the same amount of time). Different releases of Java may also exhibit different timings.

Execution times on other platforms may also differ significantly, but probably in roughly the same ratios (e.g., creating a thread will be a couple of orders of magnitude faster than creating a process). The one obvious exception to this is the semaphore, which should be almost as fast as mutexes on machines with the more complex atomic instructions.

The major conclusions you should draw from these numbers are:

- Synchronized sections are faster than RWlocks.
- Testing for interruption is moderately fast. Disabling it is slower.
- Processes are more expensive than threads.
- TSD is slower than just using instance variables ("fake" TSD).

The programs we ran to get the numbers shown in Table C–1 are available on the Web.

The tests in C are in the PThreads directory, and those in Java are all in the `TimeTests` directory. The Java tests are run by calling

```
%java Test.
```

Mutex Lock/Unlock

Acquire, then release, a POSIX mutex (Java `Mutex`) with no contention.

Table C–1   *Timings of Various Thread-Related Functions on POSIX and Java (μs)*

Function	PThreads	Java 1.1.5	Java 2
Mutex lock/unlock	1.8	30	30
Explicit synchronized		10	3
Implicit synchronized		13	4
Readers/writer lock/unlock	4.5	70	80
Semaphore post/wait	4.3	40	20
object.notify()	n/a	3	3
CV.condSignal()	0.2	30	30
Context switch (unbound threads)	89	430	80
Context switch (bound threads)	42	n/a	n/a
Context switch (processes)	54	n/a	n/a
Cancellation disable/enable	0.6	50	50
Test for deferred cancellation	0.25	7	0.2
Create an unbound thread	330	1500	1500
Create a bound thread	720	n/a	n/a
Create a process	45,000	n/a	n/a
Reference a global variable	0.02	0.2	0.08
Reference thread-specific data	0.59	n/a	65
Reference "fake" TSD	n/a	7	3

Explicit Synchronized

Acquire, then release, a synchronized section with no contention with the object mentioned explicitly: `synchronized(object){}`.

Implicit Synchronized

Call an empty synchronized method with no contention .

Readers/Writer Lock/Unlock

Acquire, then release, a readers/writer lock as a writer with no contention.

Semaphore Post/Wait

Increment an unnamed semaphore, then decrement it. (On machines with `LoadLocked` instructions, in POSIX this operation should take about the same time as a simple mutex lock/unlock.)

notify()

Call `notify()` on an object that has no waiters.

condSignal()

Call `condSignal()` on a condition variable that has no waiters.

Local Context Switch (unbound)

Call `sched_yield()` from each of two unbound threads. (This number is much higher than expected, much slower than seen on an SS10.)
Call `Thread.yield()`.

Local Context Switch (bound)

Call `sched_yield()` from each of two bound threads.

Process Context Switch

Call `sched_yield()` from each of two processes.

Cancellation Disable/Enable

Call `pthread_setcancelstate(DISABLE)` then `ENABLE`.
Call `InterruptibleThread.disable()`, then `InterruptibleThread.enable()`.

Test for Deferred Cancellation

Call `pthread_testcancel()`.
Call `Thread.interrupted()`.

Reference a Global Variable

Load a single word into a register.

Reference Thread-Specific Data

Call `pthread_getspecific()`.
Call `(Integer) tsd.get()`.

Reference "Fake" Thread-Specific Data

Call `(TSDThread) Thread.currentThread().j`.

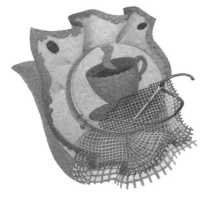

Appendix D

APIs

This appendix contains a very brief description of the Java threads API.

Function Descriptions

In the sample entry below, the method name comes first. Next are the method and argument list (sometimes there'll be two methods shown, should they be very closely related). A short paragraph describing the basic operation follows (it may well leave out some details). Next comes a reference to the most applicable portion of the text. Finally, any comments that seem appropriate are given.

start

```
public void start()
        throws IllegalThreadStateException
```

Calling the `start()` method on an instance of `Thread` will cause the appropriate `run()` method to execute in a new thread.

Reference: Chapter 4.

The Class java.lang.Thread

The class `Thread` defines thread *objects*. When the `start()` method is called, an actual running thread is created which the `Thread` object can control. It is important to distinguish between the object (which is just memory and a set of methods) and the running thread (which executes code). All static thread methods apply to the current thread.

Thread

```
public Thread()
public Thread(String name)
public Thread(Runnable runObj)
public Thread(Runnable runObj, String name)
        throws SecurityException,
        IllegalThreadStateException
```

These create a new thread object.

References: Chapters 4 and 10.

MIN_PRIORITY MAX_PRIORITY NORM_PRIORITY

```
public final static int MIN_PRIORITY = 1;
public final static int MAX_PRIORITY = 10;
public final static int NORM_PRIORITY = 5;
```

These are the minimum, maximum, and default priorities for normal threads.

Reference: Chapter 5.

Comment: You will probably never use these functions.

start

```
public void start()
      throws IllegalThreadStateException
```

Calling the start() method on an instance of Thread will cause the appropriate run() method to execute in a new thread.

Reference: Chapter 4.

run

```
public void run()
```

This is the method you define that actually executes the code you want. The base method simply looks to see if there is a Runnable and calls its run() method.

Reference: Chapter 4.

currentThread

```
public static Thread currentThread()
```

This method returns the current thread object.

Reference: Chapter 4.

join

```
public final void join()
public final void join(long milliseconds)
public final void join(long milliseconds, long nanosec)
    throws InterruptedException
```

This waits for the thread to exit.

Reference: Chapter 4.

Comment: Rarely used.

stop

```
public final stop()
public final stop(Throwable t)
```

This kills the thread asynchronously.

Reference: Chapter 4.

Comment: It is deprecated in Java 2. Don't use it.

sleep

```
public static void sleep(long milliseconds)
public static void sleep(long milliseconds, long nanosec)
    throws InterruptedException
```

This causes the current thread to go to sleep for the specified time. The precision of the wakeup is OS dependent. A typical minimum resolution is 10 ms. (Solaris defaults to 10 ms; root can set it to 1 ms. On Digital UNIX it's a mibisecond, 1/1024 second, 0.9765 ms.)

Reference: Chapter 4.

Comment: Fine for test programs. Probably will never use this in a real program.

destroy

```
public final void destroy()
```

> This causes the thread to exit immediately, running no
> `finally` sections, and releasing no locks. This was
> included in the Java spec to handle the extreme case of
> broken threads that ignore `stop()`. It is virtually impos-
> sible to use correctly and has never been implemented.

> *Reference:*   Chapter 4.

isAlive

```
public final boolean isAlive()
```

> This returns true if the target thread is still alive.

> *Reference:*   Chapter 4.

yield

```
public static void yield()
```

> This causes the current thread to give up its LWP (or CPU)
> to another thread at the same or a higher priority level (if
> any). It is legal for `yield()` to do nothing, so you must not
> rely on it.

> *Reference:*   Chapter 5.

> *Comment:*   You probably will never use this function.

setPriority getPriority

```
public final void setPriority(int newPriority)
     throws SecurityException, IllegalArgumentException
public final int getPriority()
```

> These change (return) the priority level of the thread. The
> priority level must be between MIN_PRIORITY and
> MAX_PRIORITY if the thread group to which this thread
> belongs may set a lower bound than MAX_PRIORITY.

> *Reference:*   Chapter 5.
>
> *Comment:*   You probably will never use these functions.

---

suspend

```
public final void suspend()
```

> This causes the thread to stop running and wait until you call `thread.resume()`. Because suspension is asynchronous, you have no idea what the target thread was doing when you suspended it. For example, it may hold some locks that your other threads need. This makes it virtually impossible to use.

> *Reference:*   Chapter 5.
>
> *Comment:*   It has been deprecated in Java 2.

---

resume

```
public final void resume()
```

> This causes a suspended thread to resume.

> *Reference:*   Chapter 5.
>
> *Comment:*   It has been deprecated in Java 2.

---

interrupt

```
public void interrupt()
```

> This sets the interrupt flag and causes the target thread to throw an `InterruptedException` if it is blocked on (or as soon as it executes) an interruptible method or `InterruptedIOException` if it is blocked on I/O.

> *Reference:*   Chapter 9.

interrupted

```
public static boolean interrupted()
```

> This returns the value of the interrupt flag for the current thread and clears it.

Reference: Chapter 9.

isInterrupted

```
public boolean isInterrupted()
```

> This returns the value of the interrupt flag for the thread.

Reference: Chapter 9.

Comment: You will probably never use this.

getThreadGroup

```
public final ThreadGroup getThreadGroup()
```

> This returns the thread group for this thread object.

Reference: Chapter 10.

checkAccess

```
public void checkAccess() throws SecurityException
```

> If there is a security manager, its checkAccess() method is called with the Thread as an argument.

Reference: Chapter 10.

getName setName

```
public String getName()
public void setName(String name)
            throws SecurityException
```

This gets/sets the print name for the thread.

Reference: Chapter 4.

isDaemon setDaemon

```
public boolean isDaemon()
public void setDaemon(boolean on)
            throws SecurityException,
            IllegalThreadStateException
```

This gets/sets this thread to be a daemon. You cannot change the status of a running thread.

Reference: Chapter 10.

countStackFrames

```
public int countStackFrames()
```

This returns the depth of the stack.

Reference: Chapter 10.

Comments: Deprecated in Java 2. Not well defined in any case.

dumpStack

```
public static void dumpStack()
```

This prints out the stack.

Reference: Chapter 10.

---

activeCount

    public static int activeCount()

> This returns the number of active threads in the current thread's thread group.

Reference: Chapter 10.

Comments: Deprecated in Java 1.1. See `ThreadGroup.allThreadsCount()`.

---

enumerate

    public static final int enumerate(Thread tarray[])

> This fills `tarray` with as many currently active threads as fit, returning that number.

Reference: Chapter 4.

Comment: Deprecated in Java 1.1. See `ThreadGroup.allThreads()`.

The Interface java.lang.Runnable

> This interface provides the building blocks for threads. You implement this interface, define a `run()` method on the class, and pass an instance of it to the thread.

---

run

    public void run()

> This is the method you define that actually executes the code you want.

Reference: Chapter 4.

Comment: This is the only way to start anything.

The Class java.lang.Object

All objects have a lock and wait set associated with them.

synchronized

synchronized

This language keyword causes the current thread to obtain the hidden lock for the object. If the lock is already held by the current thread, it will essentially increment a counter for that lock (it's a recursive lock). If the lock is held by a different thread, this thread will go to sleep waiting for it to become available.

Reference: Chapter 6.

wait

public void wait()
    throws InterruptedException

This causes the current thread to block until it is awakened by either a call to notify(), interruption, or by a spurious wakeup. It will release the synchronization lock for the object as it goes to sleep and reacquire it before returning.

Reference: Chapter 6.

notify notifyAll

public void notify()
public void notifyAll()

These cause (one/all) of the threads that are in a wait() call for this object to wake up and return.

Reference: Chapter 6.

The Class java.lang.ThreadLocal

This class implements thread local storage by defining an object that can hold different values for different threads.

ThreadLocal

```
public ThreadLocal()
```

This creates a new thread local object.

Reference: Chapter 8.

get set

```
public Object get()
public void set(Object o)
```

These functions set/get a thread-local value for this object.

Reference: Chapter 8.

The Class java.lang.ThreadGroup

ThreadGroup

```
public ThreadGroup(String name) throws SecurityException
public ThreadGroup(ThreadGroup parent, String name)
    throws SecurityException, Null Pointer Exception
```

These create a new thread group.

Reference: Chapter 10.

toString

```
public String toString()
```

This returns a printable string.

Reference: Chapter 10.

checkAccess

```
public final void checkAccess() throws SecurityException
```

If there is a security manager, its `checkAccess()` method is called with the `ThreadGroup` as an argument.

Reference: Chapter 10.

getName

```
public final String getName()
```

This returns the name that you gave to the group.

Reference: Chapter 10.

getParent

```
public final ThreadGroup getParent()
```

This returns the parent of this group.

Reference: Chapter 10.

parentOf

```
public final boolean parentOf(ThreadGroup g)
```

This returns true if this is the parent.

Reference: Chapter 10.

stop

```
public final void stop()throws SecurityException
```

This calls `stop()` on every thread and thread group in this group.

Reference: Chapter 10.

Comments: Deprecated in Java 2.

suspend

```
public final void suspend()
            throws SecurityException
```

This calls `suspend()` on every thread and thread group in this group.

Reference: Chapter 10.

Comments: Deprecated in Java 2.

resume

```
public final void resume()
            throws SecurityException
```

This calls `resume()` on every thread and thread group in this group.

Reference: Chapter 10.

Comments: Deprecated in Java 2.

destroy

```
public final void destroy()
            throws SecurityException,
            IllegalThreadStateException
```

This removes the group if it is empty. If the thread group has subgroups, `destroy()` is called on each of those first. Finally, the newly destroyed thread group is removed from its parent.

Reference: Chapter 10.

---

getMaxPriority setMaxPriority

```
public final void getMaxPriority()
public final void setMaxPriority(int newMaxPrio)throws
    SecurityException, IllegalArgumentException
```

This gets/sets the maximum priority allowed for any thread in this group.

Reference: Chapter 10.

---

isDaemon setDaemon

```
public final void isDaemon()
public final void setDaemon(boolean daemon) throws
    SecurityException
```

This gets/sets this group to be a daemon.

Reference: Chapter 10.

---

threadsCount

```
public int threadsCount()
```

This counts the threads in this group.

Reference: Chapter 10.

---

allThreadsCount

```
public int allThreadsCount()
```

This counts the threads in this group and subgroups.

Reference: Chapter 10.

---

groupsCount

```
public int groupsCount()
```

This counts the groups in this group.

Reference: Chapter 10.

allGroupsCount

```
public int allGroupsCount()
```

> This counts the groups in this group and subgroups.

Reference: Chapter 10.

threads

```
public Thread[] threads()
```

> This returns an array of all the threads in this group.

Reference: Chapter 10.

allThreads

```
public Thread[] allThreads()
```

> This returns an array of all the threads in this group and subgroups.

Reference: Chapter 10.

groups

```
public ThreadGroup[] groups()
```

> This returns an array of all the groups in this group.

Reference: Chapter 10.

allGroups

```
public ThreadGroup[] allGroups()
```

> This returns an array of all the groups in this group and subgroups.

Reference: Chapter 10.

---

activeCount

```
public int activeCount()
```

This returns the number of groups in this group.

Reference: Chapter 10.

Comments: Deprecated in Java 1.1. Use
`allThreadsCount()`.

---

activeGroupCount

```
public int activeGroupCount()
```

This returns the number of groups in this group.

Reference: Chapter 10.

Comments: Deprecated in Java 1.1. Use
`allGroupsCount()`.

---

enumerate

```
public int enumerate(ThreadGroup list[])
public final void enumerate(ThreadGroup list[], boolean
     recurse)
```

This is deprecated. Use `allThreads()`.

Reference: Chapter 10.

Comments: Deprecated in Java 1.1. Use `allThreads-`
`Count()` or `threads()`, `allGroups()`, or
`groups()`.

---

list

```
public final void list()
```

This is a debugging utility that prints out a detailed
description of this thread group.

Reference: Chapter 10.

allowThreadSuspension

```
public final boolean allowThreadSuspension(boolean on)
```

> This was never implemented.

uncaughtException

```
public final void uncaughtException(Thread t, Throwable e)
```

> This is called whenever a thread in this group dies via an uncaught exception.

> *Reference:*   Chapter 10.

Helper Classes from Our Extensions Library

The Class Extensions.InterruptibleThread

> This is one of the classes that we defined for this book to provide a consistent interface for dealing with certain problems. Some of those problems are artificial, a product of trying to write uniform example code in both POSIX and Java.

exit

```
public void exit()
```

> This causes the current thread to exit. It is syntactic sugar for `Thread.currentThread().stop()`.

> *Reference:*   Chapter 4.

> *Comment:*   We wrote this method while trying to deal with the absence of such a function and the absence of any advice on this apparent oversight. We have subsequently been convinced that this is the wrong way to do things and that you should always return from the `run()` method (see *Exiting a Thread* on page 49).

```
public void interrupt()
```

> This sets the interrupt flag and causes the target thread to throw an `InterruptedException` if it is blocked on (or as soon as it executes) an interruptible method or `InterruptedIOException` if it is blocked on I/O.

Reference: Chapter 9.

disableInterrupts

```
public void disableInterrupts()
```

> This causes the current thread to set a flag indicating that it is not interruptible. The method `interrupt()` will look at this.

Reference: Chapter 9.

enableInterrupts

```
public void enableInterrupts()
```

> This causes the current thread to set a flag indicating that it is interruptible. The method `interrupt()` will look at this. If the flag indicates a pending interrupt, that interrupt will be reissued at this time.

Reference: Chapter 9.

The Class Extensions.Semaphore

> This is one of our classes. It implements POSIX-style semaphores. It is probably not useful except for demo programs.

semWait

```
public void semWait()
```

> This attempts to decrement the value of the semaphore. If it succeeds, it simply returns. If the value is zero, this will

cause the current thread to go to sleep until another thread increments it.

Reference: Chapter 6.

---

semPost

```
public void semPost()
```

This increments the value of the semaphore, waking up one thread (if any are sleeping).

Reference: Chapter 6.

The Class Extensions.Mutex

This is one of our classes. It implements POSIX-style (non-recursive) mutex locks. Use *only* when synchronized sections won't work, such as chained locking.

---

lock

```
public void lock()
```

This locks the mutex. If the lock is held by a different thread, this thread will go to sleep, waiting for it to become available.

Reference: Chapter 6.

---

unlock

```
public void unlock()
```

This unlocks the mutex, waking up one thread (if any are sleeping).

Reference: Chapter 6.

The Class Extensions.ConditionVar

This is one of our classes. It implements POSIX-style condition variables. Use *only* when synchronized sections and wait/notify won't work.

condWait

```
public void condWait(Mutex m)
```

This causes the current thread to block until it is awakened by either a call to `condSignal()` or by a spurious wakeup (not by interruption). It will release the mutex lock for the object as it goes to sleep, and reacquire it before returning.

Reference: Chapter 6.

condSignal condBroadcast

```
public void condSignal()
public void condBroadcast()
```

These cause (one/all) of the threads that are in a `condWait()` call to wake up and return.

Reference: Chapter 6.

The Class Extensions.RWLock

This is one of our classes. It implements POSIX-style readers/writer locks. RWlocks are useful only in very limited circumstances. Time your program carefully first!

readLock writeLock

```
public void readLock()
public void writeLock()
```

This locks the RWLock in either reader or writer mode. If a read lock is held by a different thread, this thread will be able to get another read lock directly. If a write lock is requested, the current thread must go to sleep, waiting for it to become available.

Reference: Chapter 7.

unlock

```
public void unlock()
```

This unlocks the RWLock (both for readers and for writers). If this is the last reader, it will wake up one writer thread (if any are sleeping). If this is a writer, it will wake up one writer thread (if any are sleeping); otherwise, it will wake up all the sleeping threads with reader requests.

Reference: Chapter 7.

The Class Extensions.Barrier

This is one of our classes. It implements barriers.

Comment: You won't use these very often, but if you're implementing something like a simulation, these might come in useful.

Barrier

```
public Barrier (int i)
```

This creates a barrier object with a count of i.

Reference: Chapter 7.

barrierSet

```
public synchronized void barrierSet(int i)
```

This resets the barrier count to i.

Reference: Chapter 7.

barrierWait

    public synchronized void barrierWait() {

> This causes the calling thread to block until count threads have called barrierWait().

> *Reference:*   Chapter 7.

The Class Extensions.SingleBarrier

> This is one of our classes. It implements barriers with a divided set of waiters and posters.

> *Comment:*   You won't use these very often, perhaps only for example programs.

SingleBarrier

    public SingleBarrier (int i)

> This creates a single-barrier object with a count of i.

> *Reference:*   Chapter 7.

barrierSet

    public synchronized void barrierSet(int i)

> This resets the single barrier count to i.

> *Reference:*   Chapter 7.

barrierWait

    public synchronized void barrierWait() {

> This causes the calling thread to block until barrierPost() has been called count times.

> *Reference:*   Chapter 7.

barrierPost

```
public synchronized void barrierPost() {
```

This increments the counter for how many times `barrierPost()` has been called.

Reference: Chapter 7.

Glossary

API

> The set of function calls in a library, along with their arguments and their semantics. APIs are published so that programmers can always know which interface a vendor supports.

asynchronous signal

> A signal that is sent to a process independently of what the process happens to be doing. An asynchronous signal can arrive at any time whatsoever, with no relation to what the program happens to be doing (*cf.* synchronous signal).

async I/O

> An abbreviation for *asynchronous input/output*—normally, I/O calls block in the kernel while waiting for data to come off a disk, a tape, or some other "slow" device. But async I/O calls are designed not to block. Such calls return immediately, so the user can continue to work. Whenever the data comes off the disk, the process will be sent a signal to let it know the call has completed.

atomic operation

> An operation that is guaranteed to take place "at a single time." No other operation can do anything in the middle of an atomic operation that would change the result.

blocking system call

A system call that blocks in the kernel while it waits for something to happen. Disk reads and reading from a terminal are typically blocking calls.

cache memory

A section of very fast (and expensive) memory that is located very close to the CPU. It is an extra layer in the storage hierarchy and helps "well-behaved" programs run much faster.

CDE

An abbreviation for *common desktop environment*—the specification for the look and feel that the major UNIX vendors have adopted. CDE includes a set of desktop tools.

CDE is the major result of the Cose agreement. It is a set of tools and window toolkits (Motif 1.2.3), along with supporting cross-process communications software (ToolTalk®), which will form the basis of the window offerings of all major UNIX vendors. Each vendor will productize CDE in its own fashion and ultimately maintain separate source bases, doing its own value-add and its own bug fixing.

coarse-grained locking

See fine-grained locking.

context switch

The process of removing one process (or LWP or thread) from a CPU and moving another one on.

critical section

A section of code that must not be interrupted. If it doesn't complete atomically, some data or resource may be left in an inconsistent state.

daemon

A process or a thread that works in the background. The pager is a daemon process in UNIX.

DCE

An abbreviation for *distributed computing environment*—a set of functions deemed sufficient to write network programs. It was settled upon and implemented by the original OSF (Open Software Foundation). DCE is the environment of choice of a number of vendors including DEC and HP, while Sun has stayed with ONC+™. As part of the Cose agreement, all of the vendors will support both DCE and ONC+.

deadlock

A situation in which two things are stuck, each waiting for the other to do something first. More things can be stuck in a ring, waiting for each other, and even one thing could be stuck, waiting for itself.

device driver

A program that controls a physical device. The driver is always run as part of the kernel, with full kernel permissions. Device drivers may be threaded, but they would use the kernel threads library, not the library discussed in this book.

dynamic library

A library of routines that a user program can load into core "dynamically." That is, the library is not linked in as part of the user's executable image but is loaded only when the user program is run.

errno

An integer variable that is defined for all ANSI C programs (PCs running DOS as well as workstations running UNIX). It is the place where the operating system puts the return status for system calls when they return error codes.

external cache

Cache memory that is not physically located on the same chip as the CPU. External cache (a.k.a. "E$") is slower than internal cache (typically, around five cycles versus one) but faster than main memory (upward of 100 cycles, depending upon architecture).

FIFO

An abbreviation for *first in, first out*—a kind of a queue. Contrast to *last in, first out*, which is a stack.

file descriptor

An element in the process structure that describes the state of a file in use by that process. The actual file descriptor is in kernel space, but the user program also has a file descriptor that refers to this kernel structure.

fine-grained locking

The concept of putting lots of locks around tiny fragments of code. It's good because it means that there's less contention for the individual locks. It's bad because it means that the program must spend a lot of time obtaining locks. Coarse-grained locking is the opposite concept and has exactly the opposite qualities.

green threads

This is a threads package that was used during the initial development of Java. It is not a native threads library and cannot take advantage of multiple CPUs, nor can it do concurrent I/O.

internal cache

Cache memory (a.k.a. I$) that is located on the same chip as the CPU and hence is very fast.

interrupt

An external signal that interrupts the CPU. Typically, when an external device wants to get the CPU's attention, it asserts a voltage level on one of the CPU pins. This causes the CPU to stop what it's doing and run an interrupt handler.

Java also has an `interrupt()` method that interrupts a thread.

interrupt handler

A section of code in the kernel that is called when an interrupt comes in. Different interrupts will run different handlers.

kernel mode

A mode of operation for a CPU in which all instructions are allowed (*cf.* user mode).

kernel space

The portion of memory that the kernel uses for itself. User programs cannot access it (*cf.* user space).

kernel stack

A stack in kernel space that the kernel uses when running system calls on behalf of a user program. All LWPs must have a kernel stack.

kernel threads

Threads that are used to write the operating system ("the kernel"). The various kernel threads libraries may be similar to the user threads library (e.g., Solaris) or may be totally different (e.g., Digital UNIX).

LADDIS

A standardized set of calls used to benchmark NFS performance. It was created by and is monitored by SPEC.

library

A collection of routines that many different programs may wish to use. Similar routines are grouped together into a single file and called a library.

library call

      One of the routines in a library.

LWP

      An abbreviation for *lightweight process*—a kernel schedulable entity.

memory management unit

      See MMU.

memory-mapped file

      A file that has been "mapped" into core. This is just like loading the file into core, except that any changes will be written back to the file itself. Because of this, that area of memory does not need any "backing store" for paging. It is also much faster than doing reads and writes because the kernel does not need to copy the kernel buffer.

MMU

      An abbreviation for *memory management unit*—the part of the computer that figures out which physical page of memory corresponds to which virtual page and takes care of keeping everything straight.

Motif

      A description of what windows should look like, how mouse buttons work, etc. Motif is the GUI that is the basis for CDE. The word *Motif* is also used as the name of the libraries that implement the Motif look and feel.

multitasking OS

      An operating system that can run one process for awhile, then switch to another one, return to the first, etc. UNIX, VMS, MVS, TOPS, etc., are all multitasking systems. DOS and Microsoft® Windows™ are single-tasking operating systems. (Although MS-Windows™ can have more than one program active on the desktop, it does not do any kind of preemptive context switching between them.)

NFS

      An abbreviation for *network file system*—a kernel program that makes it possible to access files across the network without the user ever knowing that the network was involved.

page fault

The process of bringing in a page from disk when it is not memory resident. When a program accesses a word in virtual memory, the MMU must translate that virtual address into a physical one. If that block of memory is currently out on disk, the MMU must load that page in.

page table

A table used by the MMU to show which virtual pages map to which physical pages.

POSIX

An acronym for *portable operating system interface.* This refers to a set of committees in the IEEE that are concerned with creating an API that can be common to all UNIX systems. There is a committee in POSIX that is concerned with creating a standard for writing multithreaded programs.

preemption

The act of forcing a thread to stop running.

preemptive scheduling

Scheduling that uses preemption. Time slicing is preemptive, but preemption does not imply time slicing.

process

A running program and all the states associated with it.

process structure

A kernel structure that describes all the relevant aspects of a process.

program counter

A register in the CPU that defines which instruction will be executed next.

race condition

A situation in which the outcome of a program depends upon the luck of the draw—which thread happens to run first.

realtime

Anything that is timed by a wall clock. Typically, this is used by external devices that require servicing within some period of time, such as raster printers and aircraft autopilots. Realtime does not mean any particular amount of time but is almost always used to refer to sub-100-ms (and often sub-1-ms) response time.

reentrant

A function is reentrant when it is possible for it to be called at the same time by more than one thread. This implies that any global state be protected by mutexes. Note that this term is not used uniformly and is sometimes used to mean either recursive or signal-safe. These three issues are orthogonal.

shared memory

Memory that is shared by more than one process. Any process may write into this memory, and the others will see the change.

SIGLWP

A signal that is implemented in Solaris and used to preempt a thread.

signal

A mechanism that UNIX systems use to allow a process to be notified of some event, typically asynchronous and external. It is a software analog to hardware interrupts.

signal mask

A mask that tells the kernel (or threads library) which signals will be accepted and which must be put onto a "pending" queue.

SIGSEGV

A signal that is generated by UNIX systems when a user program attempts to access an address that it has not mapped into its address space.

SIGWAITING

A signal that is implemented in Solaris and used to tell a threaded process that it should consider creating a new LWP.

SPEC

An organization that creates benchmark programs and monitors their use.

store buffer

A buffer in a CPU that caches writes to main memory, allowing the CPU to run without waiting for main memory. It is a special case of cache memory.

SVR4

An abbreviation for *System Five, Release 4*—the merger of several different flavors of UNIX that was done by Sun and AT&T. SPEC 1170 merges SVR4, POSIX, and BSD—the main UNIX "flavors"— to specify a common base for all future UNIX implementations.

synchronous signal

A signal that is sent to a process "synchronously." This means that it is the direct result of something that process did, such as dividing by zero. Should a program do a divide-by-zero, the CPU will immediately trap into a kernel routine, which in turn will send a signal to the process (*cf.* asynchronous signal).

system call

A function that sets up its arguments, then traps into the kernel in order to have the kernel do something for it. This is the only means a user program has for communication with the kernel.

time-sliced scheduling

An algorithm that allocates a set amount of time for a process (or LWP or thread) to run before it is preempted from the CPU and another one is given time to run.

trap

An instruction that causes the CPU to stop what it is doing and jump to a special routine in the kernel (*cf.* system call).

user mode

An operating mode for a CPU in which certain instructions are not allowed. A user program runs in user mode (*cf.* kernel mode).

user space

That area of memory devoted to user programs. The kernel sets up this space but generally never looks inside (*cf.* kernel space).

virtual memory

The memory space that a program thinks it is using. It is mapped into physical memory by the MMU. Virtual memory allows a program to behave as if it had 100 Mbytes, even though the system has only 32 Mbytes.

XView

A library of routines that draws and operates Openlook GUI components on a screen. It is based on the SunView™ library of the mid-1980s and has been superseded by CDE Motif.

Index

Professional Technical Reference
Tomorrow's Solutions for Today's Professionals.

Keep Up-to-Date with
PH PTR Online!

We strive to stay on the cutting-edge of what's happening in professional computer science and engineering. Here's a bit of what you'll find when you stop by **www.phptr.com**:

@ **Special interest areas** offering our latest books, book series, software, features of the month, related links and other useful information to help you get the job done.

Deals, deals, deals! Come to our promotions section for the latest bargains offered to you exclusively from our retailers.

$ **Need to find a bookstore?** Chances are, there's a bookseller near you that carries a broad selection of PTR titles. Locate a Magnet bookstore near you at www.phptr.com.

! **What's New at PH PTR?** We don't just publish books for the professional community, we're a part of it. Check out our convention schedule, join an author chat, get the latest reviews and press releases on topics of interest to you.

✉ **Subscribe Today!** **Join PH PTR's monthly email newsletter!**

Want to be kept up-to-date on your area of interest? Choose a targeted category on our website, and we'll keep you informed of the latest PH PTR products, author events, reviews and conferences in your interest area.

Visit our mailroom to subscribe today! **http://www.phptr.com/mail_lists**